EXAM ESSENTIALS PRACTICE TESTS

Cambridge English: First (FCE)

2

Helen Chilton
Helen Tiliouine

NATIONAL GEOGRAPHIC LEARNING | CENGAGE Learning

Australia • Brazil • Japan • Korea • Mexico • Singapore • Spain • United Kingdom • United States

ngl.cengage.com/eltexampreparation

PASSWORD examessentialsfirs!F3#2

Exam Essentials Practice Tests 2
Cambridge English: First (FCE) (with key)
Helen Chilton and Helen Tiliouine

Publisher: Gavin McLean

Publishing Consultant: Karen Spiller

Editorial Project Manager: Stephanie Parker

Development Editor: Helen Holwill

Strategic Marketing Manager: Charlotte Ellis

Project Editor: Tom Relf

Manufacturing Buyer: Eyvett Davis

Cover design: Oliver Hutton

Compositor: Cenveo® Publisher Services

National Geographic Liaison: Wesley Della Volla

Audio: Martin Williamson, Prolingua
  Productions

DVD-ROM: Tom, Dick and Debbie Ltd

Contributing writer: Elaine Hodgson
  (video materials)

© 2015 National Geographic Learning, as part of Cengage Learning

ISBN: 978-1-285-74502-2

National Geographic Learning
Cheriton House, North Way, Andover, Hampshire, SP10 5BE
United Kingdom

Cengage Learning is a leading provider of customized learning solutions with office locations around the globe, including Singapore, the United Kingdom, Australia, Mexico, Brazil and Japan. Locate your local office at:
international.cengage.com/region

Cengage Learning products are represented in Canada by Nelson Education, Ltd.

Visit National Geographic Learning online at **ngl.cengage.com**

Visit our corporate website at **www.cengage.com**

Photos
The publisher would like to thank the following sources for permission to reproduce their copyright protected photographs:

159 b (Shutterstock), 159 t (ambrozinio/Alamy), 160 t (By Ian Miles-Flashpoint Pictures/Alamy), 160 b (Getty Images), 162 b (Getty Images), 162 t (Alamy), 163 b (Alamy), 163 t (Shutterstock), 165 t (Alamy), 165 b (Getty Images), 166 b (Alamy), 166 t (Eric Nathan/Alamy), 168 t (Juice Images/Alamy), 168 b (2013 Hiroyuki Ito/Getty Images), 169 t (Getty Images), 169 b (Colin Underhill/Alamy), 171 t (Alamy), 171 b (PHOVOIR/Alamy), 172 b (Alamy), 172 t (Catchlight Visual Services/Alamy), 174 b (2012 AFP/Getty Images), 174 t (Alamy), 175 t (Image Source/Getty Images), 175 b (Assembly/Getty Images), 177 b (Alamy), 177 t (Getty Images), 178 t (Alamy), 178 b (Alamy), 180 b (Alamy), 180 t (Judith Haeusler/Getty Images), 181 t (Alamy), 181 b (Alamy)

Text
The publishers would like to thank the following for permission to use copyright material:

Page 12: Adapted from 'Lucy Cooke, Digital Storyteller/Zoologist', http://www.nationalgeographic.com/explorers/bios/lucy-cooke/. Page 32: Adapted from 'A Journey To The Hottest Place On Earth: Dallol Ethiopia' by Colleen Kinder (RSS feed), 31.5.12, Content © 2013 AOL Inc. Used with permission. Page 34: Adapted from 'Stop Food Cravings Through Imaginary Eating?' by Christine Dell'Amore, http://news.nationalgeographic.com/news/2010/12/101209-chocolate-obesity-science-mind-diet-weight-loss-eat-food/, 9.12.10. Page 52: Adapted from 'How I got hooked on open-water swimming' by Joanna Ruck, theguardian.com, 19.6.13, Copyright Guardian News & Media Ltd 2013. Page 54: Adapted from 'Prehistoric cave art in the Dordogne' by Robin McKie, The Observer, 26.5.13, Copyright Guardian News & Media Ltd 2013. Page 57: Adapted from 'Traveling like a travel writer' by Robert Reid, http://intelligenttravel.nationalgeographic.com/2013/06/13/traveling-like-a-travel-writer/, 13.6.13. Page 70: Adapted from 'Bright Nights, big problems' by Paul Bogard, http://news.nationalgeographic.com/news/2013/07/130720-night-dark-light-pollution-science-stars/, 19.7.13. Page 72: Adapted from 'Chimps can be team players, selfless helpers, studies show' by Maryann Mott, http://news.nationalgeographic.co.uk/news/2006/03/0302_060302_chimps.html, 2.3.06. Page 88: Adapted from 'Procrastination: Not now – I'm busy' by Harriet Walker, The Independent, 14.2.12, Copyright The Independent. Page 90: Adapted from 'Don't just run – get running and blogging!' by Laura Fountain, theguardian.com, 12.6.13, Copyright Guardian News & Media Ltd 2013. Page 106: Adapted from 'Fear Factor: Success and Risk in Extreme Sports' by Brian Handwerk, http://news.nationalgeographic.com/news/2004/07/0709_040709_sciencerisk_2.html, 9.7.04. Page 108: Adapted from 'The world's fastest bird?' by Ker Than, http://news.nationalgeographic.com/news/2011/06/110606-fastest-birds-flight-animals-migration-science/, 6.6.11. Page 124: Adapted from 'Mary McCartney on photography: I've always been drawn to strong women' by Tim Lewis, theguardian.com, 10.3.13, Copyright Guardian News & Media Ltd 2013. Page 126: Adapted from 'Build your own bike with the Bamboo Bicycle Club' by Will Coldwell, The Independent, 20.3.13, Copyright The Independent. Page 142: Adapted from 'The Family Challenge: Drums' by Jill Tunstall, The Guardian, 20.9.08, Copyright Guardian News & Media Ltd 2008. Page 144: Adapted from 'Blind Olympic athletes show the universal nature of body language' by Ed Yong, National Geographic, 13 August 2008, with permission from the author. Page 147: Adapted from 'Artist Fiona Rae loves to show off in paint' by Fiona Rae, The Observer, 20.9.09, Copyright Guardian News & Media Ltd 2008.

Although every effort has been made to contact copyright holders before publication, this has not always been possible. If notified, the publisher will undertake to rectify any errors or omissions at the earliest opportunity. Note that the sample answer sheets in the Practice tests are not the updated official answer sheets provided by Cambridge as these were not available at the time of publication.

Printed in China by RR Donnelley
Print Number: 04   Print Year: 2017

Contents

CAMBRIDGE ENGLISH: First (FCE)

Paper 1: READING AND USE OF ENGLISH (1 hour 15 minutes)

Part	Task type and focus	Number of questions	Task format
1	**Multiple-choice cloze** Task focus: vocabulary	8	A multiple-choice cloze text with eight gaps, followed by eight four-option questions.
2	**Open cloze** Task focus: grammar and some vocabulary	8	A modified cloze text with eight gaps which you must fill with the appropriate word.
3	**Word formation** Task focus: vocabulary	8	A text with eight gaps. You are asked to complete the text by making an appropriate word from the word prompt you are given for each gap.
4	**Key word transformations** Task focus: grammar and vocabulary	6	This task consists of six discrete key word transformations. You are asked to complete a sentence which means the same as the given sentence using the key word.
5	**Multiple choice** Task focus: reading for detailed understanding of a text, gist, opinion, attitude, tone, purpose, main idea, meaning from context, implication, text organisation features	6	You answer six four-option multiple-choice questions on a text.
6	**Gapped text** Task focus: reading to understand how a text is structured	6	Six sentences have been removed and placed in jumbled order after a text. You decide from where in the text the sentences have been removed.
7	**Multiple matching** Task focus: reading for specific information in a text, detail, opinion, attitude	10	You match ten questions with different texts or different sections of a text.

Paper 2: WRITING (1 hour 20 minutes)

Part	Task type and focus	Number of questions	Task format
1	**Question 1** Essay	Part 1 is compulsory. 140–190 words	You must write an essay based on a given title and accompanying ideas, including one of your own.
2	**(FIRST candidates)** **Questions 2–4** may include an article, an email/a letter, a report, a review.	You choose one task from a choice of three. 140–190 words	You must carry out a writing task, using the appropriate style and format.
2	**(FIRST FOR SCHOOLS candidates)** **Questions 2–4** may include an article, an email/a letter, a review, a story. **Question 5** is based on the set book. It may be an essay.	You choose one task from a choice of four. 140–190 words	You must carry out a writing task, using the appropriate style and format.

Paper 3: LISTENING (40 minutes approximately)

Part	Task type and focus	Number of questions	Task format
1	**Multiple choice** Task focus: understanding gist, detail, function, purpose, feeling, attitude, opinion, genre, agreement, etc.	8	A series of short unrelated extracts of approximately 30 seconds each, from monologues or exchanges between interacting speakers. There is one three-option question for each extract.
2	**Sentence completion** Task focus: detail, specific information, stated opinion	10	A monologue of 3–4 minutes. The task consists of ten gapped sentences.
3	**Multiple matching** Task focus: understanding gist, detail, function, purpose, feeling, attitude, opinion, genre, agreement, etc.	5	A series of short related extracts, of approximately 30 seconds each, from monologues. The five questions require selection of the correct option from a list of eight.
4	**Multiple choice** Task focus: understanding attitude and opinion, main idea, specific information and gist	7	A text between two speakers of 3–4 minutes. There are seven three-option questions.

Paper 4: SPEAKING (14 minutes approximately)

Part	Task format	Input	Functions
1 **Interview** 2 mins	The interlocutor asks each candidate to say a little about themselves.	Verbal questions	You must be able to • give personal information. • talk about present circumstances / past experiences. • talk about future plans.
2 **Individual long turn** 4 mins	Each candidate talks about a pair of photographs for 1 minute, followed by a 30-second response from the second candidate.	Visual stimuli, with verbal and written instructions	You must be able to • give information. • express your opinions. • relate photos to yourself and your own experience.
3 **Two-way collaborative task** 4 mins	The interlocutor asks candidates to carry out a task based on written prompts.	A written question with written stimuli and verbal instructions	You must be able to • exchange information and opinions. • express and justify opinions. • agree, disagree or partly agree. • suggest and speculate.
4 **Discussion** 4 mins	The interlocutor asks candidates general opinion questions related to the topic covered in Part 3.	Verbal prompts	You must be able to • exchange information and opinions. • express and justify opinions. • agree, disagree or partly agree.

Exam Essentials Practice Tests is a new series of materials published by National Geographic Learning for students preparing for the following major EFL/ESL examinations: Cambridge English: First (FCE), Cambridge English: Advanced (CAE), and Cambridge English: IELTS (International English Language Testing System). The series is characterised by the close attention each component pays to developing a detailed knowledge of the skills and strategies needed for success in each paper or part of the exams.

Cambridge English: First (FCE) Practice Tests helps learners become aware of the exam requirements for Cambridge English: First (FCE), offers details about the format and language in the exam, and helps learners develop exam skills necessary for success. The book also offers extensive practice in all parts of the exam, using the actual test format.

Taking the exam

Cambridge English: First is one of a series of five Cambridge English exams corresponding to different levels of the Common European Framework of Reference for Languages (CEFR):

• Cambridge English: Key (KET) CEFR Level A2

• Cambridge English: Preliminary (PET) CEFR Level B1

• Cambridge English: First (FCE) CEFR Level B2

• Cambridge English: Advanced (CAE) CEFR Level C1

• Cambridge English: Proficiency (CPE) CEFR Level C2

Cambridge English: First is widely recognised in commerce and industry, and by universities and similar educational institutions, as proof that the holder of this qualification can do office work or take a course of study in English.

The exam can be taken on many dates during a year, and can be taken on paper or on a computer. It consists of four Papers:

Paper 1, Reading and Use of English (1 hour 15 minutes)

Seven parts: four Use of English tasks including cloze tests, word formation and key word transformations focusing on vocabulary and grammar, followed by three reading comprehension tasks. The reading tasks consist of a long text followed by multiple-choice questions, a gapped text with whole sentences removed and a multiple-matching task. The focus in the reading tasks is on understanding gist, main points, detail, attitude, implication, purpose, opinion and text structure as well as deducing the meaning of words and phrases from context.

Paper 2, Writing (1 hour 20 minutes)

Two parts, each requiring you to produce a piece of writing. In Part 1, candidates of both Cambridge English: First and Cambridge English: First for Schools have to write a compulsory essay in Part 1.

In Part 2, 'Cambridge English: First' candidates choose one task from a choice of three questions. These may be an informal letter or email, a formal letter or email, an article, a report, or a review written for a given purpose and target reader.

In Part 2, 'Cambridge English: First for Schools' candidates choose one task from a choice of four questions. These may be an informal letter or email, an article, a review, a story, or a question on a set text written for a given purpose and target reader.

Paper 3, Listening (40 minutes approximately)

Four parts, consisting of recorded texts and comprehension questions. Tasks include multiple choice, sentence completion and multiple matching. The focus is on understanding gist, meaning, main points or specific information, detail, purpose, function, feeling, attitude, opinion, genre and agreement.

Paper 4, Speaking (14 minutes approximately)

Four parts, involving two candidates and two examiners (one examiner asks the questions and the other listens). The Speaking Paper focuses on the candidates' ability to use general interactional and social language, organise a larger unit of discourse (comparing, describing, expressing opinions), sustain an interaction, exchange ideas, express and justify opinions, etc.

Preparing for the exam

In preparing for the four papers, the following points should be taken into account:

Reading and Use of English: To prepare for the **Use of English** (Parts 1, 2, 3 and 4), as well as getting general practice in grammar and vocabulary, you should practise the precise skills necessary for the tasks here: how to use a word or phrase in context, how words with similar meanings are used in different collocations, accuracy with common structures, phrasal verbs and lexical phrases, and the different methods of word formation.

To prepare for the **Reading** (Parts 5, 6 and 7) you need to be familiar with a range of reading materials, such as newspaper articles, advertisements, brochures, guides, manuals and correspondence, as well as with different approaches to reading. It is important be aware that different strategies can be used for different parts of the Reading

Paper. For example, reading to find specific information is the best strategy in Part 7, where candidates have to find out where a certain piece of information is located.

Writing: You must be able to write an essay for Part 1 and an article, email/a letter, essay, report, review, or story for Part 2 (see above for the difference between the Paper 2 content of Cambridge English: First and Cambridge English: First for Schools exams), so practice of these types of writing is essential. You should practise covering all the points provided in the input and your writing must display organisation and coherence, clear layout, appropriate register, control and accuracy of language.

Listening: Practice with pre-listening tasks (focusing on developing an expectation of what might be said) is essential here, as is thorough familiarity with a wide variety of spoken English in terms of discourse types and genres. Listening for different purposes should also be exercised: to get the gist or to find specific information.

Speaking: You need practice in using spoken English effectively, which includes mastery of conversational skills (such as turn taking and the appropriate way to participate in a discussion), providing full but natural answers to questions, requesting clarification and speaking clearly and audibly at all times.

Further information can be obtained from the following website: www.cambridgeenglish.org.

Practice Tests: contents

Cambridge English: First (FCE) in the *Exam Essentials Practice Tests* series prepares candidates for the Cambridge English: First examination by providing **eight full practice tests,** accurately following the latest exam specifications.

There are **two guided tests** at the beginning, which feature **essential tips** to practise exam strategy. These essential tips offer guidance and general strategies for approaching each task. Other tips offer advice relevant to specific questions in the guided tests. These two comprehensive guided tests will help students prepare for each paper in the ways described in the previous section, while the following **six tests (without guidance)** will offer students thorough practice up to and beyond the level of the exam.

The DVD-ROM accompanying the book includes the **audio materials** for Paper 3 (Listening), which have been recorded so as to accurately reflect the audio element of the actual exam. (Please see the DVD-ROM Introduction for more information about the content of this component.)

A **writing bank** includes sample answers for the tasks in Paper 2 (Writing), writing tips in the form of **notes**, and **useful phrases** and **expressions** for the different task types.

Varied **visual materials** for Paper 4 (Speaking) have also

been included, while a **language bank** supplies useful phrases and expressions for use in the Speaking Paper when discussing the visual and written stimuli.

There is also a **glossary** at the end of each test, explaining vocabulary from Paper 1 that is likely to be unfamiliar to students.

Clear and straightforward design simplifies use of the book. **Exam overview** tables ensure that key information is readily accessible, while a specially designed menu makes it easy to navigate through the different papers and parts of each practice test.

You will find sample exam answer sheets on pages 156–158 which you can photocopy and use to note down your answers. These will give you practice in using the answer sheets provided in the real exam.

For more practice, there is also an additional book of tests for this exam: *Exam Essentials Practice tests 1, Cambridge English: First (FCE).*

Practice Tests: principles

In writing this book, three guiding principles have been observed:

Firstly, that it should be useful for teachers, and for students whether sitting the Cambridge English: First exam for the first time, or re-sitting the exam, and whether working alone or in a class. Students approaching the exam for the first time would be best advised to work through the book linearly, developing their skills and confidence; those re-sitting the exam can consult the overview tables to concentrate on particular areas for targeted revision. The **without key** edition can be used by students working in a class, while the **with key** edition provides a detailed **answer key** and all the **audio scripts**, ensuring that students working alone can benefit from active support while attempting these tests.

The second principle is that the questions should accurately reflect the whole range of questions found in the Cambridge English: First exam. Thus students obtain guidance concerning the general content and the best way of approaching the tasks from the questions themselves. Seeing the questions in this light – as instructions to the candidate from the examiner, rather than intimidating challenges – also helps students feel less daunted by the whole experience of sitting a major exam like this.

The third principle is that the texts used in the practice tests should not only be fully representative of those used in the exam but also varied and interesting. Everyone finds it easier to learn a skill if the subject matter is relevant to his or her lifestyle and interests. In choosing, editing and creating the texts here, we have done our utmost to ensure that the experience of working with this book is as stimulating and rewarding as possible.

PAPER 1	Reading and ▶	Part 1
	Use of English	Part 2
PAPER 2	Writing	Part 3
		Part 4
PAPER 3	Listening	Part 5
PAPER 4	Speaking	Part 6
		Part 7

For questions **1–8**, read the text below and decide which answer (**A**, **B**, **C** or **D**) best fits each gap. There is an example at the beginning (**0**).

Mark your answers **on the separate answer sheet**.

Example:

0 **A** whole   **B** complete   **C** full   **D** entire

| 0 | A | B | C | D |

Essential tips

▶ Read the title and quickly skim through the text to find out what it is about, ignoring the gaps.

▶ For each question, you need to decide which of the four options fits best in the gap.

▶ The options are often four words that are similar in meaning, but only one is correct in that particular sentence.

▶ The answer may be part of an expression, a fixed phrase, a phrasal verb or a collocation (two or more words that are frequently used together by native speakers, so they sound natural together).

▶ Look carefully at the words before and after each gap. There may be a preposition, verb form or article which means that only one option can be correct.

▶ Try saying the sentence to yourself in your head, and see if the option you have chosen sounds right.

Question 1: All these words can have a similar meaning, but only one collocates with 'sound'.

Question 4: All these verbs could be used to show that the volunteers said something about themselves, but only one can be followed by 'as'.

Question 6: Water can do all these things, but only one of these words collocates with 'tap'.

Question 8: Which word, followed by the preposition 'to', means 'cause to exist' or 'have as a result'?

How well do you sleep?

Do you need (**0**) .... silence to sleep well at night? While some people can sleep through a great deal of noise, others are woken up by the (**1**) .... sound. It appears that as we sleep, our brains produce rapid pulses, or waves, called 'sleep spindles'. Research has (**2**) .... that our ability to sleep soundly may (**3**) .... on the number of sleep spindles we produce.

Scientists conducted a three-day study on 12 volunteers, all of whom (**4**) .... themselves as good sleepers. On the first night, the scientists (**5**) .... the volunteers sleep in silence. On the following nights, however, they were subjected to various noises, ranging from the sound of a (**6**) .... tap to jet engine roars.

Measurements of brain activity showed that the participants who reacted least to the noise were the ones who produced more sleep spindles, (**7**) .... on the quiet night. It is hoped that this discovery will (**8**) .... to new ways to help people who have difficulty sleeping.

1	**A** lightest	**B** finest	**C** slightest	**D** weakest
2	**A** exposed	**B** revealed	**C** displayed	**D** uncovered
3	**A** depend	**B** involve	**C** rest	**D** base
4	**A** assured	**B** declared	**C** claimed	**D** described
5	**A** permitted	**B** agreed	**C** let	**D** allowed
6	**A** pouring	**B** running	**C** streaming	**D** flowing
7	**A** even	**B** precisely	**C** still	**D** exactly
8	**A** head	**B** take	**C** guide	**D** lead

PAPER 1 Reading and ▸
        Use of English
PAPER 2 Writing
PAPER 3 Listening
PAPER 4 Speaking

Part 1
Part 2
Part 3
Part 4
Part 5
Part 6
Part 7

For questions **9–16**, read the text below and think of the word which best fits each gap. Use only **one** word in each gap. There is an example at the beginning (**0**).

Write your answers **IN CAPITAL LETTERS on the separate answer sheet.**

Example: | 0 | A | S | | | | | | | | | | | | | | | | | | | | | | |

Europe's giant sand dune

On the Atlantic coast of France, about 60 km from the city of Bordeaux, there is a giant sand dune known (**0**) …….. 'La Dune du Pilat'. Around 110 m high, 3 km long and 500 m wide, it is (**9**) …….. famous that it receives about a million visitors a year. It is not (**10**) …….. the largest sand dune in Europe, but is also moving away from the coast (**11**) …….. an average rate of nearly 5 m a year. Over (**12**) …….. last 57 years, it has travelled 280 m inland. This is as a result (**13**) …….. winds from the Atlantic blowing sand off the side facing the sea onto the side facing the land. Any roads, trees and houses that lie in its path (**14**) …….. slowly being covered in sand. People (**15**) …….. climb the dune are rewarded by stunning views of the coast, the forest and the Pyrenees mountains. And they can choose (**16**) …….. walk, run or roll back down!

Essential tips

▸ First read through the text quickly, ignoring the gaps, to see what it is about.

▸ Look at each gap and work out what kind of word is needed. It could be an auxiliary verb, pronoun, article, preposition, etc.

▸ You can only put one word in each gap.

▸ Always put a word in the gap – the correct answer is never a blank.

▸ You must not use part of a contracted form to complete the gap. For example, if the key is *are* and it comes after *you* in the text, write *are*, not *'re*.

▸ Read through the text when you have finished to see if your answers sound right.

Question 10: '*not _____ …. , but also …*' is a common way of linking two ideas. What is the missing word in this structure?
Question 14: What form of the verb 'cover' is used here? Is it active or passive?
Question 15: What kind of pronoun is needed here to refer to *people*?

PAPER 1	Reading and ▶	Part 1
	Use of English	Part 2
		Part 3
PAPER 2	Writing	Part 4
		Part 5
PAPER 3	Listening	Part 6
PAPER 4	Speaking	Part 7

For questions **17–24**, read the text below. Use the word given in capitals at the end of some of the lines to form a word that fits the gap **in the same line**. There is an example at the beginning (**0**).

Write your answers **IN CAPITAL LETTERS on the separate answer sheet**.

Example: | 0 | U | N | F | O | R | T | U | N | A | T | E | | | | | | | | |

Essential tips

▶ Read the title first. This gives you an idea of what the text is about.

▶ Read the whole text quickly to get a general understanding. Ignore the gaps at this point.

▶ Now decide whether the word you need to fill each gap is a noun, adjective, verb, etc.

▶ Look at the context of the gapped sentences text around each gap carefully. The word you need may be positive or negative, or a past or present form of a verb, for example.

▶ Remember that you may need to make more than one change to the prompt word.

▶ You may need to add a prefix or suffix, or change the middle of the word to create the form you need (for example, HIGH → HEIGHT).

▶ Check the spelling of each new word carefully.

Question 17: Look at the word given. The word is followed by a verb, so in this case you need a noun. Could you add a suffix to make a noun that means 'when there is no light at night'?

Question 21: This word follows the verb *promote* which is a transitive verb, so it must be a noun. How can you make a noun from *relax*? You need to add a suffix to form this noun.

Question 23: You need to make two changes to the prompt word. The first change makes a new verb which means to transfer data to a website. The second change is related to the tense. What tense do you need to put the verb into?

Listening to birdsong makes you happy!

For people (**0**) .... enough to live in countries with long, cold   **FORTUNE**

winters, when (**17**) .... sets in early and poor weather conditions   **DARK**

discourage outdoor (**18**) .... , it's easy to feel a little sad.   **ACTIVE**

(**19**) .... hoping to help people feel better in the depths of winter   **SCIENCE**

have come up with an interesting philosophy, linking human

mood and birdsong. Even birds which haven't migrated to warmer

climates during winter sing less, making it difficult to hear their

(**20**) .... chirping at this time of year. Scientists believe birdsong   **ENERGY**

conjures up images of summer days and being outside, which

promotes (**21**) ....   **RELAX**

With this in mind, they have made (**22**) .... of various birds   **RECORD**

singing their most cheerful melodies and have (**23**) .... them   **LOAD**

to a website where you can tune in whenever you feel in need of

a boost to your mood. Just five minutes of listening to birdsong

provides a sense of well-being during what can be a (**24**) ....   **DEPRESS**

time of year.

Essential tips

▶ Read the first sentence carefully and think about its meaning.

▶ Then look at the word given and the second sentence. The words before and after the gap will help you to decide which structure you need to complete the sentence (reported speech, passive voice, etc.).

▶ You must use between two and five words only to complete the gap. Remember that contractions (*they're*, *hasn't*, etc.) count as two words.

▶ Do not change the word given in any way.

▶ Make sure that the second sentence is as close as possible in meaning to the first sentence. Don't miss out any important information (but don't add unnecessary information either).

▶ Check that all the words are spelled correctly.

Question 25: Who is Vikki talking to? What is the reminder?

Question 27: Which tense is used with the expression 'I wish' to express regret?

Question 30: Which phrase do you know that means the same as 'to be able to do something well'? Which form of the verb follows this phrase?

For questions **25–30**, complete the second sentence so that it has a similar meaning to the first sentence, using the word given. **Do not change the word given**. You must use between **two** and **five** words, including the word given. Here is an example (**0**).

Example:

0 I've never seen a film as boring as this one.

SUCH

I've never seen .... as this one.

The gap can be filled by the words 'such a boring film', so you write:

Example: | 0 | SUCH A BORING FILM |

Write **only** the missing words **IN CAPITAL LETTERS on the separate answer sheet**.

___

25 'Don't forget to buy some printer paper,' Vikki told me.

REMINDED

Vikki .... some printer paper.

26 I found it difficult to choose a university course.

DIFFICULTY

I .... a university course.

27 Peter regretted leaving his wallet at home.

WISH

'I .... my wallet at home,' said Peter.

28 I'm sure it wasn't Jenny you saw – she's off sick.

HAVE

It .... Jenny you saw – she's off sick.

29 I'll only call you if there are any problems.

UNLESS

I .... there are any problems.

30 Zeke gives effective presentations.

GOOD

Zeke .... giving presentations.

PAPER 1   Reading and ▸
          Use of English

PAPER 2   Writing

PAPER 3   Listening

PAPER 4   Speaking

Part 1
Part 2
Part 3
Part 4
Part 5
Part 6
Part 7

You are going to read an article about a zoologist called Lucy Cooke. For questions **31–36**, choose the answer (**A**, **B**, **C** or **D**) which you think fits best according to the text.

Mark your answers **on the separate answer sheet**.

Animal defender

Zoologist Lucy Cooke draws attention to some of the world's least attractive animals.

Which species pulls at your heartstrings – a panda or a toad? A lion or a dung beetle? When it comes to emotional attachment, research funding, global popularity and conservation support, the fluffier your fur and the bigger your eyes, the better your chances – unless zoologist Lucy Cooke has a vote. She's on a one-woman mission to show the world why some of the most unlovable animals are actually the most interesting and deserving of our attention, study and protection.

Cooke's popular blogs, online videos, films and TV programmes bring her characteristic sense of humour and unusual storytelling style to a serious message: If we only care for the best known and best loved species, other enormously important parts of the web of life could vanish forever. With her unconventional attitude, she's taking advantage of the power of the internet to reach a new audience that more traditional wildlife programmes have yet to tap.

'My goal is to persuade the unconvinced,' says Cooke. 'A lot of conservation messages are difficult to hear; they make people feel guilty. I think humour is the sugar coating that helps people swallow the pill. If you manage to make someone laugh while you tell them something important, they'll stick around and listen to more.'

Cooke worries about what she calls 'the tyranny of the cute'. 'There are so many television shows about koala bears and kittens,' she observes. 'All the attention seems focused on a handful of charismatic "celebrity" animals. Even scientists get less funding for animals that aren't sweet and cuddly. In fact, large mammal species appear in 500 times as many articles in scientific journals as threatened amphibians.' She adds: 'Weird, freaky creatures fascinate me because they tell an amazing evolutionary story. I'm interested in all of nature, not just the shiny, fluffy bits.'

Amphibians – animals like frogs that live both on land and in water – top Cooke's list. 'Over a third of amphibians are going extinct; it's the worst extinction crisis since the dinosaurs were wiped off the planet. Yet I couldn't convince anyone to commission a film about it. That motivated me to start my Amphibian Avenger blog.' The widely read blog showcases creatures that rarely attract the spotlight. 'Frogs are such a fascinating miracle of evolution that I could study them forever.'

line 27 Amphibians also occupy a crucial spot in the middle of the food chain. 'If you remove them, everything else goes haywire,' she notes. 'When amphibians go extinct, birds and snakes that eat them also disappear. Since amphibians breathe through their delicate skin, they are very vulnerable to pollution, climate change, and disease. That makes them fantastic barometers of the health of ecosystems. If amphibians aren't doing well, chances are their overall environment is sick.'

One of Cooke's most popular online videos is about sloths – extremely slow-moving mammals that live in trees. Cooke would like to help elevate the status of sloths, animals that she insists are unfairly laughed at and misunderstood. 'They've always had a reputation for being lazy and stupid.' In fact, 'slothfulness' is the key to the animal's success. A slow metabolism allows the sloth's liver to process poisonous substances found in the leaves it eats. Moving slowly also keeps it hidden from predators. 'My video showed the world how interesting they are,' Cooke says.

The wobbly-nosed proboscis monkey, dung beetles, bats and more get their moment in the sun thanks to Cooke. 'It's about telling their stories in a way that engages a wider audience. I want people to share my sense of wonder, amazement and love for these creatures. Once you understand why they're ugly or odd, I hope you'll appreciate and want to save them as much as I do.'

- ▶ Read the instructions, the title and the byline (in italics under the title) to see what the text is about.

- ▶ Read through the text quickly to get a general idea of the content. Don't worry if you don't understand every single word – you should still be able to answer the questions.

- ▶ The questions always come in the same order as the relevant information in the text. The first part of the question (the stem) usually tells you where and what to look for in the text.

- ▶ Read the stem carefully and look at the text to see if you can find the answer. Underline the relevant part or parts of the text.

- ▶ Now look at the options and decide which one corresponds to the parts of the text that you have underlined.

- ▶ Sometimes you have to look at the options first and then look for information that supports one of them in the text. Underline that information and check that it means the same as the option you have chosen.

Question 31: The stem tells you that the information you need is in the second paragraph. Read that paragraph carefully to see what you can find out about Lucy Cooke. Look at the options. Which option is supported by information in the text? Underline this information.

Question 33: This question asks you to identify the *main* point of the paragraph. Bear in mind that more than one of the options may be a true statement, but is it the *main* point of the paragraph?

Question 34: Look at the stem. You need to answer the following question: 'Why did Cooke start her Amphibian Avenger blog?' Find the answer in the text and underline it. Now look at the options. Does one of them correspond to what you have underlined?

31 What are we told about Cooke in the second paragraph?

    A She hopes to make more conventional nature documentaries in the future.
    B She is communicating her ideas to people who have not heard them before.
    C Her approach is more suited to the internet than to other media.
    D Her manner shows a lack of concern about the problems she mentions.

32 According to Cooke, what is many people's attitude to nature conservation?

    A They are embarrassed at their lack of knowledge of the subject.
    B They are reluctant to think about the subject.
    C They find it hard to take the subject seriously.
    D They are tired of hearing so much about it.

33 What is Cooke's main point in the fourth paragraph?

    A It is a mistake to limit the types of species that are studied carefully.
    B Too much research is being done into animals that are endangered.
    C Scientists are wasting public money on unnecessary animal studies.
    D Television programmes rarely concentrate on larger species.

34 Cooke says she started her Amphibian Avenger blog because

    A she wanted to raise funds to make a film.
    B she felt inspired to start a search for a new species.
    C she realised she would have to inform people herself.
    D she knew she would always have something interesting to write about.

35 What does 'goes haywire' in line 27 mean?

    A tends to do better
    B carries on as it always has
    C finds ways of coping
    D stops working as it should

36 Cooke's video about sloths is an example of

    A why she believes it is more important to save some animals rather than others.
    B how other scientists have been unwilling to tell people about their work.
    C how she is trying to change people's minds.
    D why some animals deserve their reputation.

For the Glossary see page 27 ▶

PAPER 1	Reading and Use of English ▶	Part 1
		Part 2
PAPER 2	Writing	Part 3
		Part 4
PAPER 3	Listening	Part 5
PAPER 4	Speaking	**Part 6**
		Part 7

You are going to read an article about someone whose home was used in the making of a film. Six sentences have been removed from the article. Choose from the sentences **A–G** the one which fits each gap (37–42). There is one extra sentence which you do not need to use.

Mark your answers **on the separate answer sheet**.

My home, their film set

What's it like to have a film production crew take over your house?

Graphic designer Jessica Fleischmann lives and works in an arty, clapboard house in a hilly neighbourhood of Los Angeles, in the US. Two years ago, there was a knock on Fleischmann's door. It was a man from a Hollywood film studio. He told Fleischmann he was a location scout – someone who looks for suitable places for films to be made in. Her house looked perfect for a film he was working on – would she be interested in renting it out for a few weeks?

The money he offered was decent, but there was one more thing. They'd dig up her garden, which she'd nurtured for years, and replace it with weeds. **37** 'I was a little hesitant and asked people I knew in the film industry what they thought,' says Fleischmann. 'People said: "If you need the money, do it – but be prepared to have things broken."'

The location scout, Charles Fagin, had been driving around Fleischmann's neighbourhood for days looking at houses. 'I knew as soon as I saw her backyard that this was the house,' he says. **38**

Fagin gave her a copy of the script and explained the terms. They'd paint some rooms, but they'd repaint them after the shoot, and anything they drilled into, they'd fix. **39** Preparation on the house began a month before the film shoot. The crew painted the living room a blue-toned shade of grey. They brought in a larger sofa and drilled holes in the ceiling to rig up the lights. This actually worked to Fleischmann's advantage. 'It meant they had to repaint it, and it needed to be painted anyway,' she says.

For the film shoot, which took place over four days, Fleischmann agreed to be out of her house, opting to stay with relatives. **40** 'It's important to be there,' she says, 'otherwise, they might destroy your house. It's not that they're bad people, but their main interest is in getting the right shot.'

Fortunately for Fleischmann, the shoot went well. Yes, a few items were lost, and a grubby handprint or two was left on a wall. And the scenic painters' attempt at repainting her living room before they left were so poor she ended up painting it again herself. **41** The blue-grey walls helped her decide on a more neutral shade of grey, and after seeing her place so minimally accessorised, she realised she didn't need so many trinkets.

What was it like seeing her home on the big screen? 'When I saw the film for the first time, I was mostly watching the house. They used a lot of my artwork, and even left some personal cards and drawings up,' Fleischmann says. **42** 'I don't think I'd do it again. If you're attached to your home, like me, it's a big disruption. But if they make it worth your while financially, I'd say go ahead.'

A   And very importantly, her garden would also be replanted and returned to its previous state as far as possible.

B   That was a bit annoying, as she hadn't expected to have to do it, but overall, she says, it was a good experience.

C   This was to reflect the character in the movie, and would be temporary, of course.

D   She had hoped to be able to find out more about those beforehand.

E   But she visited every day, not only to access her studio but also on the recommendation of friends in the industry.

F   She felt like a proud parent, particularly as one review said something about the locations being characters that contributed to the movie.

G   Of the 50 being considered, Fleischmann's was selected.

Essential tips

- ▶ Read the main text from which the sentences have been removed to see what the text is about.

- ▶ Read the text carefully before and after each gap. Can you guess what the missing information might be?

- ▶ Look at the gapped sentences. Are there any linking words that connect ideas in the text and ideas in the gaps?

- ▶ Look for words or phrases that refer to what has gone before or what comes after them.

Question 38: The sentences before the gap are about the location scout finding the right house after looking at a lot of houses. Is there a sentence option about something being chosen from a number of others?

Question 39: The sentence before the gap is about what the film company promised to do to make sure the house was returned to a good state after the shoot. Are there any sentence options about another thing that they would put right?

Question 41: Before the gap, we are told about things that were problems for Fleischmann. After the gap, we are told about some things which were improvements. Which sentence option refers to the problem mentioned just before the gap, but also leads to the positive ideas after the gap?

For the Glossary see page 27 ▶

PAPER 1 Reading and ▶
Use of English

PAPER 2 Writing
PAPER 3 Listening
PAPER 4 Speaking

Part 1
Part 2
Part 3
Part 4
Part 5
Part 6
Part 7

You are going to read an article in which four people talk about their first day at work. For questions **43–52**, choose from the people (**A–D**). The people may be chosen more than once.

Mark your answers **on the separate answer sheet**.

Which person

achieved more than she had hoped to?	43
tried to appear busier than she really was?	44
imagined how she would personalise her workspace?	45
found it difficult to remember all her colleagues' names?	46
was surprised at how unprepared her colleagues were for her arrival?	47
discovered her working hours could be longer than she had expected?	48
felt too embarrassed to ask for assistance?	49
was relieved to see a familiar face?	50
realised how much she still had to learn?	51
regretted ignoring some advice she had been given?	52

Essential tips

▶ Read the instructions, the title and the byline to see what the texts are about.

▶ Read the texts quickly to get a general idea of what they say.

▶ Look at the questions carefully. Underline the key words in each question.

▶ Read the first text carefully and underline information that corresponds to each question. Sometimes you will find a paraphrase of the information (different words meaning the same thing) rather than the key words themselves.

▶ Now follow the same procedure with each of the remaining three texts.

Question 43: This person did more on their first day than she thought she would. Who describes how she hadn't expected to do much, but was actually proud of what she had achieved by the end of the day?

Question 49: This person wanted some assistance from other people, but felt too embarrassed to ask them. What is another word for 'assistance'? Which text refers to someone needing it, but being worried about other people's reaction if she said so?

Question 51: This person says she realised she still had a lot to learn. Can you find a paraphrase of this in one of the texts?

For the Glossary see page 27 ▶

My first day at work

Four young people remember their first day in a new job.

A Sheila

My first day at work was alright, really. When I walked into the office the first person I saw was the person who'd interviewed me. She didn't make much of an effort to put me at my ease. I just sat down where she told me to and got on with it. They gave me a load of data to input, so I had plenty to do straight away, which was a relief. I wasn't familiar with the computer system, but I thought if I told anyone I needed help with it, they might just laugh at me. Now I know how kind everyone actually is, I know it would have been fine if I had. I decided I'd bring in some pictures and a plant for my desk, just to make it feel more mine. I could see that's what the others had done. I've been there for two years now, and I've made some good friends and learnt an awful lot.

B Judy

On my first day, everyone in my new team seemed to know all about me, which I hadn't expected. They all introduced themselves and were very friendly, but I immediately got everyone muddled up, because I felt pretty nervous. I thought my course had prepared me for the work, but in fact it was soon clear to me that there were huge gaps in my knowledge. I was asked to write a press release and then left on my own for ages. I didn't do it particularly well, mainly because I did it quite quickly. I didn't want to look as if I had nothing to do, though, so I typed it out three times. It was a bit disappointing, because I'd thought I'd get so much more done. Now I often wish I had a bit more time like I did on that first day – I never seem to stop!

C Marion

The first thing I did was learn what everybody was called – not too hard as I'm good at that sort of thing. It was a nice surprise to be greeted by someone I was at school with – it turned out we'd be working together. That was great as I'd been a little worried about not knowing anyone there at all. She showed me where everything was and it was a thrill to have my very own desk and even a locker with my name on! I was a little taken aback when she told me most people went home fairly late and I'd have to do the same if I wanted to be considered for promotion in the future. I should have realised that, I suppose, because my friends had warned me that might be the case. I didn't mind, though – I knew I was very lucky to be there.

D Valerie

I remember being quite nervous, and when I got there, nobody seemed to know who I was or what I should be doing. That was a little odd, I thought, but my boss turned out to be very friendly and soon made me feel at ease. I was very smartly dressed and everyone else was fairly casual – I wished I'd listened to a friend who'd worked there the previous summer and had told me not to wear a suit. I'd imagined I might not actually do much, but I was asked to look for some photographs of animals to go with an article my boss was writing. I found several suitable ones, and went home at the end of a long day feeling pretty pleased with myself! I've learnt a lot since then but I'll always remember that first day!

PAPER 1 Reading and
            Use of English

PAPER 2 Writing ▶ | Part 1 |
                          | Part 2 |

PAPER 3 Listening

PAPER 4 Speaking

You **must** answer this question. Write your answer in **140–190** words in an appropriate style.

1   In your English class you have been talking about the internet. Now your English teacher has asked you to write an essay.

Write your essay using **all** the notes and give reasons for your point of view.

Essential tips

Part 1

▶ Read the question and the notes carefully to see exactly what you are being asked to write about.

▶ Think about what your own idea will be. For example, it could be learning how to cook, or about the history of art, or how to make friends – anything that people can learn.

▶ Start your essay with an **introduction** and state your opinion. Do you agree or disagree with the statement? Or do you think it is true in some cases but not in others?

▶ In the **body of the essay**, address the three points in the notes. Remember to include your own idea, which must be a separate point and not the conclusion of the essay. Say what you think, and why you think it.

▶ Organise your ideas clearly in paragraphs, and use linking words and expressions appropriately.

▶ Use the **final paragraph** to summarise your opinion.

▶ Use neutral or semi-formal language. It is important that your style is the same throughout the essay.

▶ Check the length of your essay, your grammar, spelling and punctuation.

> Some people say that using the internet is the best way of learning things.
>
> Do you agree?
>
> **Notes**
> Write about:
>
> 1. learning a language
> 2. playing a musical instrument
> 3. .... (your own idea)

PAPER 1 Reading and
        Use of English
PAPER 2 Writing ▶ Part 1
PAPER 3 Listening   Part 2
PAPER 4 Speaking

Write an answer to **one** of the questions 2–5 in this part. Write your answer in **140–190** words in an appropriate style.

2   This is part of an email you have received from your English-speaking friend, Dan.

> **From:** Dan
> **Subject:** Getting fit
>
> Hi
>
> I'm feeling a bit unfit at the moment and would like to do some sport or exercise to improve my physical condition. I haven't done any exercise for about a year because I've been too busy. What advice can you give me? Is there anything I shouldn't do?
>
> Thanks,
>
> Dan

Write your **email**.

3   You see this announcement on an international English-language website.

> **Articles wanted – A great place to live!**
>
> Tell us about a place you think is great to live in. It could be where you already live, or somewhere else. Why do you think it is such a good place to live in? Is there anything that would make it even better?
>
> The best articles will be posted on the website.

Write your **article**.

Essential tips

Part 2

▸ Read all the questions, and decide which one to answer. Do you have some ideas and vocabulary that mean you can answer one of the questions particularly well?

▸ Underline the key words and phrases in the instructions. These tell you what to include in your writing.

▸ Think about who you are writing to, or for. This will affect whether you use informal or more formal language.

▸ Make sure your ideas are clearly organised, and use appropriate linking words and expressions.

Question 2

Read the email carefully. How many questions do you have to answer? Here, there are two. Make sure you answer them both.

In an email to a friend, use neutral or informal language. Remember, however, that this is an exam, so you should write in grammatically correct sentences and use correct spelling. Don't use abbreviations you might use when texting, for example.

Use language for giving advice: *Why don't you ...? How about ...? Have you thought about ...?*

Start your email by greeting your friend. You could say you are happy to give him some advice. You could end the email by wishing him luck with getting fit. Use a closing formula, e.g. *Best wishes* or *Write soon* at the end.

Question 3

Decide which place you are going to write about. There are three things to do here: give some information about the place you choose, and address the two questions. Make sure you answer both the questions. If you think the place is absolutely perfect, say you think it can't be improved.

Your audience is international, so the style should be neutral or semi-formal. Think of a short title (here, the name of the place would be enough). Organise your ideas clearly.

Remember that you are writing a website article, so try to keep your tone engaging and friendly, without being too informal.

Continued on next page ▶

PAPER 1 Reading and
Use of English
PAPER 2 Writing ▶
Part 1
Part 2
PAPER 3 Listening
PAPER 4 Speaking

Essential tips

Question 4

Read the question carefully. Make sure your report covers all three of the points.

Organise your ideas clearly. How many paragraphs will you need? Think of appropriate headings for each paragraph.

In the final paragraph, summarise your suggestions.

Question 5

(*for FIRST FOR SCHOOLS candidates only*)

Only answer this question if you have read the set text. Your answer must clearly relate to the story and give details which show you have read the book.

Think about the different characters in the text. Which one do you personally admire the most? It doesn't have to be the main character.

4 Your English teacher has asked you to write a report on things your college could do to become more environmentally friendly. You should suggest what changes could be made **and** say how they would help the environment. Can you do anything yourself to help?

Write your **report**.

5 (*for FIRST FOR SCHOOLS candidates only*)

Answer the following question based on the set text you have read.

Your English class has had a discussion about the different characters in the book. Now your English teacher has given you this essay for homework.

Which character in the book do you admire the most, and why?

Write your **essay**.

PAPER 1   Reading and
          Use of English

PAPER 2   Writing

PAPER 3   Listening   ▶   Part 1
                                 Part 2
PAPER 4   Speaking   Part 3
                                 Part 4

🎧 **Track 1**

You will hear people talking in eight different situations. For questions **1–8**, choose the best answer (**A**, **B** or **C**).

1 You hear a student talking to her tutor about studying history at university.
What does the student say about studying history?
A It will provide her with some valuable skills.
B It is necessary for the career she has chosen.
C It wasn't her first choice of subject.

2 You hear a man talking about poetry.
What is he doing?
A describing differences between poetry and other literature
B persuading people to get involved in writing poetry
C explaining why a popular belief about poetry is incorrect

3 You hear a young woman talking about having studied abroad.
What does she say about it?
A It helped her get a job in the field she wanted.
B It wasn't an easy thing to have done.
C It gave interviewers an incorrect impression of her.

4 You hear two students talking about a lecture on choosing colours for websites.
What do they agree about?
A how important it is to keep a consistent image
B how useful it is to adapt websites for different countries
C how interesting it is to study the use of colour on websites

5 You hear a tutor discussing a student's work with him.
What is the purpose of their conversation?
A to discuss the student's ideas for an essay he's working on
B to check the student understands the point of some feedback
C to help the student think of ways to improve his work

6 You hear a woman talking about a hobby she has taken up.
What does she think about it?
A It isn't worth the effort required.
B It's harder than she expected it to be.
C The teacher's instructions aren't always clear.

7 You hear two friends discussing a film adaptation of a book they have read.
The students agree that the film adaptation
A was unnecessarily different from the book.
B failed to get the point of the story across.
C must have been disappointing for the book's author.

8 You hear a student talking about giving a presentation to his class.
How did he feel about it at first?
A determined to prepare as well as he could
B unwilling to use techniques people had suggested
C convinced he wouldn't be able to do it well

Essential tips

▶ Read the context sentence carefully. This tells you something about what you are going to hear. Remember you may hear a monologue (one speaker) or a dialogue (two speakers).

▶ Read the question and the options and underline any key words in the time you are given before you listen to the recordings.

▶ In the recording, you may hear ideas from all of the options, but only one option answers the question correctly.

▶ The words you hear may not be the same as the words in the options. Listen for the general meaning of the text rather than the exact phrases of the options.

▶ Don't worry if you aren't sure about the answer the first time you listen. You will hear each recording twice.

Question 2: The answer does not always come from a single phrase or sentence. In this case you need to listen for the main message of the whole text to know what the speaker is doing.

Question 4: Elements of all three of the options are mentioned in the recording. However, the question asks what *both* students think. Only one option is correct.

Question 8: This question focuses on the feelings of the speaker. Look at the question carefully. Which part of the process are we interested to know his feelings about?

PAPER 1 Reading and
          Use of English

PAPER 2 Writing

PAPER 3 Listening

PAPER 4 Speaking

> Part 1
> **Part 2**
> Part 3
> Part 4

🎧 **Track 2**

You will hear a weather forecaster called Laura Armstrong talking about her work. For questions **9–18**, complete the sentences with a word or short phrase.

Laura Armstrong: weather forecaster

Laura currently works as a weather forecaster at a

(**9**) .... station.

Laura refers to what forecasters call weather (**10**) ....

before she makes a forecast each day.

Part of Laura's job on 'big weather days' is to provide

(**11**) .... and maintain website information.

Laura's interest in the weather grew from a fear of

(**12**) .... when she was younger.

Laura says the most important skill in weather forecasting is deciding

what (**13**) .... mean.

Laura initially did a (**14**) .... course, unlike many other

weather forecasters.

Laura says forecasters are often criticised for not being

(**15**) .... enough in their predictions.

Laura is interested in discovering more about (**16**) ....

later in her career.

Laura says it is possible to gain work experience in the

(**17**) .... section of a weather organisation.

Laura has given weather forecasts at important sports events, like a

(**18**) .... competition last year.

Essential tips

▶ Read the title on the question paper. This gives you some information about what you are going to listen to.

▶ Read the questions (the gapped sentences) carefully in the time you are given before you listen to the recording. Think about what kind of word might go in each gap, for example, a noun or a verb.

▶ The questions are in the same order as you will hear the information in the text.

▶ Remember that the wording of the questions will not be exactly the same as the words you hear on the recording.

▶ You should only complete the gaps with words you hear in the recording. You should not change the form of the word you hear.

Question 10: The word you need forms part of a compound noun (a noun which is made up of two or more words). What is the first word of the compound noun? You need to listen for a reference to something that forecasters have a specific name for.

Question 12: What is another way to say you have a fear of something? Listen for words or phrases that have the same meaning in the recording.

Question 14: The sentence mentions a course, so you need to listen for what subject Laura studied.

Question 18: Sports events are mentioned in the sentence, so what kind of word do you think is needed to complete the gap?

🎧 **Track 3**

You will hear five short extracts in which people are talking about the benefits of volunteering. For questions **19–23**, choose from the list (**A–H**) what each speaker says. Use the letters only once. There are three extra letters which you do not need to use.

A I developed leadership skills.

B I discovered a natural talent.

Speaker 1 ☐ **19**

C It made me feel part of the wider community.

Speaker 2 ☐ **20**

D It opened up a new career opportunity for me.

Speaker 3 ☐ **21**

E It increased my confidence.

Speaker 4 ☐ **22**

F It motivated me to improve my own life.

Speaker 5 ☐ **23**

G I made great friends for life.

H I understood the importance of teamwork for the first time.

Essential tips

▸ Read the instructions carefully and underline the key words. This information tells you what you need to listen for in order to decide which answer is correct for each speaker, so it is very important to read this.

▸ Read the options carefully. Remember that the words you hear are unlikely to be exactly the same as the words in the options.

▸ The options are not necessarily in the order that you will hear them mentioned in the recording.

▸ Parts of the different options may be mentioned more than once in the recordings. Remember that only one option is correct for each question.

▸ In order to decide which option is correct, remember to refer back to the instruction given at the beginning. For example, if you are asked what benefit each speaker gained from volunteering, you should make sure that you answer this question for each speaker.

▸ Remember that you do not need to use all of the options.

Speaker 1: This person is talking about a skill they have and how that skill has helped them in some way. How has their skill helped them?

Speaker 3: This person is talking about something they realised as they volunteered. What was this?

Speaker 5: This person made a change to their life after volunteering. What change did they make?

PAPER 1 Reading and
            Use of English

PAPER 2 Writing

PAPER 3 Listening ►

PAPER 4 Speaking

Part 1
Part 2
Part 3
Part 4

🎧 **Track 4**

You will hear part of an interview with a language expert called Rod Chambers, who is talking about languages which are at risk of disappearing. For questions **24–30**, choose the best answer (**A**, **B** or **C**).

24 How did Rod become interested in saving endangered languages?
    A   He studied endangered languages during his time at university.
    B   He met a group of people whose language was endangered.
    C   He saw the effects of the issue on his own family.

25 When talking about why languages become extinct, Rod says that
    A   parents tend not to consider the language choices they make.
    B   people recognise the need to be able to communicate widely.
    C   some schools refuse to continue teaching minority languages.

26 What does Rod say about the ways in which languages can be saved?
    A   Some of the ideas are less helpful than others.
    B   Promoting a minority language is easier than people think.
    C   The methods won't be successful without public support.

27 When talking about the importance of keeping languages alive, Rod says that
    A   languages can be compared to living creatures.
    B   there are more important global issues to deal with.
    C   the matter of culture loss isn't taken seriously enough.

28 What does Rod say about working on his current project?
    A   He likes listening to people's life stories.
    B   He prefers to focus on examples of natural speech.
    C   He doesn't enjoy examining grammatical forms.

29 Rod says that data collected as part of language-saving projects can
    A   inform youngsters about their own family history.
    B   be used in teacher training courses.
    C   help a language come back into use.

30 What does Rod say listeners can do to help save languages?
    A   Encourage native speakers to use their language more.
    B   Attend foreign language classes in their local area.
    C   Approach experts for help on recording languages.

Essential tips

▶ Read the questions and options carefully in the time you are given before you listen to the recording and underline any key words.

▶ The order of the questions is the same as the order in which you will hear the information.

▶ Remember that the words in the questions and options may not be exactly the same as you hear on the recording.

▶ Alternatively, you may hear some of the words and phrases from an option in the recording, but this does not necessarily mean that the option is correct.

▶ Don't worry if you aren't sure about your answers straightaway. You will hear the recording twice.

Question 24: For this question, you will hear elements from all three of the options mentioned in the recording. Remember you need to listen out for what it was that made him interested in the issue.

Question 27: Before you listen to the recording, you may have an idea of what the correct option may be. Listen carefully, because the correct answer may be different to what you expected.

Question 30: Rod mentions lots of different people in the final part of the recording. Who do you need to listen for information about?

┌─────────────┐
│ **Part 1** │
│ **Part 2** │
│ Part 3   │
│ Part 4   │
└─────────────┘

Part 1 (2 minutes)

The examiner (interlocutor) will ask each of you to speak briefly in turn and to give personal information about yourselves. You can expect a variety of questions, such as:

How do you like spending your free time? (Why?)
Who do you enjoy spending your free time with? (Why?)
What did you do when you last had some free time?
Which free-time activities would you like to try? (Why?)

Part 2 (4 minutes)

You will each be asked to talk for a minute without interruption. You will each be given two different photographs in turn to talk about. After your partner has finished speaking, you will be asked a brief question connected with your partner's photographs.

1 Mealtimes

Look at the two photographs on page 159 which show people eating meals in different places at home.

Candidate A, compare these photographs, and say why you think the people enjoy eating their meals in these different places at home.

Candidate B, where do you prefer to eat your meals at home?

2 Families

Look at the two photographs on page 160 which show families doing different activities together.

Candidate B, compare these photographs, and say why the families might be doing these different activities together.

Candidate A, which activity would you prefer to do with your family?

Essential tips

Part 1

▶ The examiner will ask you questions about you and your life. Make sure you are ready to answer questions about where you live, about your home, family and interests, for example.

▶ Don't prepare a speech for this section – you need to sound as natural as possible.

▶ Make sure you answer the questions fully, but don't talk for longer than necessary.

▶ Listen carefully to what the examiner has asked you and answer only this question.

Part 2

▶ In Part 2, you have to compare the two photographs you are shown. When you compare the photographs, you should say what is similar about them and what is different about them.

▶ Listen very carefully to the question the examiner asks you. This is what you should talk about when you are comparing the photographs.

▶ Remember that there is no right or wrong answer. The examiner is interested in your ability to express your own opinion.

▶ You have to speak for one full minute. Time yourself speaking for a minute before the test, so that you know how this feels.

▶ You will also have to comment briefly on your partner's photographs. Listen carefully to the examiner's question as it will probably be slightly different to the question your partner was asked. You need to speak for about 30 seconds.

▶ Remember that this part of the exam is not a discussion, so don't interrupt while your partner is speaking. Listen carefully to what your partner says and then answer the question the examiner asks you.

Part 3 (4 minutes)

You will be asked to discuss something together without interruption by the examiner. You will have a page of ideas and a question to help you.

Healthy activities

Imagine your teacher has asked you to give a talk to your class about different ways of staying healthy. Turn to page 161 which shows some ways in which people can stay healthy. Talk to each other about how each activity helps people to stay healthy. Then decide which **two** of the activities you would include in your talk.

Part 4 (4 minutes)

The examiner will encourage you to develop the topic of your discussion in Part 3 by asking questions, such as:

What other things can you do to help you stay healthy?
What are the most enjoyable ways to stay healthy? (Why?)
Do you think it's easy or difficult to lead a healthy lifestyle? (Why?)
Do you think it's expensive to follow a healthy lifestyle? (Why?)
How important is it for schools to educate young people about being healthy?
How does learning to be healthy at a young age help people later in life?

Essential tips

Part 3

▶ Listen carefully to the question you are asked. The question will also appear on the prompts page to remind you what to talk about. You are given some time to look at the question and the ideas before you start talking.

▶ Make sure that you work with your partner. Discuss the question and ideas and decide together on an answer.

▶ Both you and your partner should take an equal part in the discussion. Make sure you give your partner a chance to speak.

▶ Before the exam, learn and practise phrases for giving your opinion, asking for your partner's opinion, and agreeing/disagreeing, for example *In my opinion ... , What do you think?, I'm not sure I agree with you.*

▶ Remember that you don't have to agree with your partner's opinions, but you should reach a decision together.

Part 4

▶ Listen carefully to the questions the examiner asks you. Remember that the questions will be related to the topic you discussed in Part 3, but you do not need to refer to the prompts again.

▶ This part of the exam is also a discussion. Don't interrupt when your partner is speaking, but make sure you give your own opinion, too.

▶ You don't have to agree with what your partner says, but you need to react to what he or she says and be able to give reasons for your opinion.

▸▸ **PART 5**

pull at your heartstrings (phr) make you feel sympathy

dung beetle (n) an insect with a smooth hard back that feeds on the waste (dung) of a large animal such as an elephant or a cow

mission (n) an important assignment or task

blog (n) regular comment article written online

vanish (v) to disappear completely

tap (v) to make use of or benefit from

tyranny (n) large amount of negative power

a handful (phr) a small number of something

charismatic (adj) very charming

cuddly (adj) soft and pleasant to hold

journal (n) a magazine containing articles related to a particular subject or profession

freaky (adj) very strange and a little frightening

crisis (n) very bad situation

showcase (v) to publicly focus on the good qualities of something

crucial (adj) very important

vulnerable (adj) easily affected by

elevate (v) to raise

metabolism (n) the chemical processes in a living organism that keep it alive

engage (v) to attract and keep someone's interest

▸▸ **PART 6**

arty (adj) artistic

clapboard (n) overlapping wooden planks used to cover the outside of a building

hilly (adj) an area with lots of hills

decent (adj) quite good

nurture (v) to take care of

terms (n) the conditions of an agreement or contract

shoot (n) a session of filming / a photograph or film scene

drill (v) to make a small hole with a handheld (often electric) machine

rig up (phr) put up and fix

opt (v) to choose

grubby (adj) dirty

minimally accessorised (phr) decorated in a simple way

trinket (n) a small decoration that is often not very valuable

disruption (n) disturbance or interruption

make something worth your while (phr) to make something benefit you

▸▸ **PART 7**

put someone at his / her ease (phr) to make someone feel comfortable

input (v) to enter into a computer system

muddle up (v) to confuse or put in the wrong order

gaps in my knowledge (phr) things I didn't know

press release (n) an official statement or report that an organisation gives to journalists, for example about a recent event or a new product

greet (v) to say hello to

thrill (n) excitement

locker (n) a personal cupboard with a lock on it

taken aback (phr) surprised

promotion (n) a move to a more senior position within a company

Essential tips

▶ Reading the title of the text will give you a good idea about its topic. You can then start to think about the kind of vocabulary that you might see in the text.

▶ After you have read the text quickly to gain a general understanding of the topic, read it again and try to predict the word that might go in each gap.

▶ The words in the options are often similar in meaning to each other. Make sure you read the gapped sentence carefully in order to choose the right option for the context.

▶ Don't just read the gapped sentences or the words directly in front or after each gap: reading the whole text will help you to understand its meaning and choose the correct options.

▶ The four options are always the same part of speech (noun, verb, adjective, etc.) and in the same form (plural, past simple tense, etc.).

▶ If you aren't sure whether an answer is correct, continue with the rest of the task and come back to check it at the end.

Question 3: The word you need explains more about what the computer program is doing. It's analysing messages to find out how happy people are. Which word reflects this kind of evaluation?

Question 5: The word you need is a synonym of *holiday*.

Question 8: The word you need completes a set phrase. If you don't recognise the phrase at first, read it aloud to see which word sounds right and make a guess. It's better to make a guess than leave the question unanswered.

For questions **1–8**, read the text below and decide which answer (**A**, **B**, **C** or **D**) best fits each gap. There is an example at the beginning (**0**).

Mark your answers **on the separate answer sheet**.

Example:

0 **A** study   **B** action   **C** discovery   **D** review

0	**A**	B	C	D

Can computers measure happiness?

In a fascinating (**0**) .... , researchers asked volunteers to rate words in the English language from one to nine on a 'scale of happiness'. Words associated with feeling good (**1**) .... scored highly: 'laughter', for example, received a score of 8.5 on the scale, whereas words connected with sadness didn't score well at all.

Using this (**2**) .... , the researchers developed a computer program which analysed millions of messages posted by users of social networking sites, (**3**) .... their happiness according to the words they used in their on-screen messages. They found that happiness (**4**) .... to reach a high point during weekends, and drop again when people returned to work after a (**5**) .... They also discovered that, on an (**6**) .... day, people feel happier in the morning and less so as the day wears on.

Whether the results are an accurate evaluation of how happy people are (**7**) .... unclear. Can a computer program really understand the message (**8**) .... the words? Probably not.

1	**A** absolutely	**B** predictably	**C** probably	**D** automatically
2	**A** document	**B** proof	**C** information	**D** fact
3	**A** assessing	**B** advising	**C** inspecting	**D** choosing
4	**A** aimed	**B** went	**C** moved	**D** tended
5	**A** break	**B** gap	**C** stop	**D** pause
6	**A** original	**B** average	**C** obvious	**D** alternate
7	**A** maintains	**B** keeps	**C** remains	**D** goes
8	**A** underneath	**B** below	**C** over	**D** behind

PAPER 1	Reading and ▶	Part 1
	Use of English	Part 2
PAPER 2	Writing	Part 3
		Part 4
PAPER 3	Listening	Part 5
PAPER 4	Speaking	Part 6
		Part 7

For questions **9–16**, read the text below and think of the word which best fits each gap. Use only **one** word in each gap. There is an example at the beginning (**0**).

Write your answers **IN CAPITAL LETTERS on the separate answer sheet.**

Example: | 0 | I | N | S | T | E | A | D | | | | | | | | | | | |

What astronauts eat

Eating and drinking in space is a tricky business. Let go of a piece of bread and (**0**) …….. of falling to the floor, it floats around. Drinks don't stay put in conventional cups, but hang about (**9**) …….. the air.

It's taken decades (**10**) …….. scientists to develop tasty food that astronauts can easily consume in space. Much of this is freeze-dried; a process by (**11**) …….. the food is cooked, frozen, and then it (**12**) …….. all its water sucked out. Freeze-dried food lasts for a long time and doesn't need to be refrigerated, making (**13**) …….. ideal for space travel. When astronauts get hungry, they simply rehydrate the food with water from a special dispenser and wait for 20 to 30 minutes until it's ready. The food containers can then be attached to trays with fasteners to secure (**14**) …….. . Salt and pepper can (**15**) …….. added to foods as liquids, too, as powders can have (**16**) …….. negative impact on spacecraft equipment.

Essential tips

▶ Read the title of the text first. This will give you an idea of what the text is about.

▶ Then read the whole text to gain a general understanding of the topic before you read it again more carefully.

▶ Look at each gap and read the sentence it is in. Quite often the first word you think of will be correct, because you have seen it used in a similar context. However, remember to read carefully in order to make sure it's right.

▶ If you think a verb is needed, think about the tense of the sentence before you decide which form of the verb you need. If you need a noun or pronoun, think about whether it should be singular or plural.

▶ Don't worry if you aren't sure about an answer at first. Read the whole text through again at the end and check that it makes sense.

Question 2: Which tense does this sentence begin with? Does *decades* refer to a period of time or a point in time?

Question 5: What is being referred to in this sentence? You can only write one word in the gap, so *freeze-dried food* won't fit. Which word can you use instead to refer to an object?

Question 8: This word comes before a noun. We usually use an article before a noun. Do we need the definite (*the*) or indefinite (*a/an*) article here?

For questions **17–24**, read the text below. Use the word given in capitals at the end of some of the lines to form a word that fits the gap **in the same line**. There is an example at the beginning (**0**).

Write your answers **IN CAPITAL LETTERS on the separate answer sheet.**

Example: | 0 | S U R R O U N D I N G | | | | | | |

Gentoo penguins

Gentoo penguins live on the Antarctic peninsula and many of the
(**0**) .... islands. They have brightly coloured orange beaks and **SURROUND**
feet, and grow to a (**17**) .... of around 75 cm. They are very **HIGH**
(**18**) .... birds, and are very fast underwater **ACT**
(**19**) .... They spend the whole day hunting close to the shore, **SWIM**
though they sometimes swim as far away as 26 km from land.
They can also dive to (**20**) .... of 200 m. **DEEP**

Gentoo penguins are very good parents, and the male and female
of each pair work together to build a (**21**) .... nest out of stones, **CIRCLE**
grass, feathers and soft plants. Then the parents take it in turns
to sit on the eggs for more than a month. In the future, however,
there is a real danger that gentoo penguins may (**22**) .... from **APPEAR**
our planet. Apart from (**23**) .... predators like leopard seals and **NATURE**
orcas, these beautiful little creatures are also threatened by
(**24**) .... on some of the islands where they live. **POLLUTE**

Essential tips

▸ Read the title and text.

▸ Decide what kind of word could fill each gap, e.g. a verb, adjective, adverb, etc.

▸ Remember that you always have to change the word at the end of the sentence. The correct answer will never be the same word left unchanged.

▸ Look at the text around each gap and decide whether the word you need to fill each gap is positive or negative (for example USEFUL or USELESS, POSSIBLE or IMPOSSIBLE). Decide if you need to change the word given at the end of the line by adding a prefix, or a suffix, or both.

▸ If the missing word is a noun, decide whether it should be singular or plural.

▸ Check your spelling carefully. You may need to remove an 'e' at the end of the word given, for example, before adding a suffix (e.g. VALUE → VALUABLE).

Question 19: The birds swim, so you need a noun meaning a person or animal who swims. Do you need a singular or a plural noun? What is the spelling rule for a consonant preceded by a single vowel when you make the word longer?

Question 21: What adjective can you form from the word *circle*?

Question 24: What suffix added to *pollute* forms a noun? What spelling change do you have to make to *pollute* before adding the suffix?

PAPER 1 Reading and ▶
          Use of English

PAPER 2 Writing

PAPER 3 Listening

PAPER 4 Speaking

Part 1
Part 2
Part 3
Part 4
Part 5
Part 6
Part 7

For questions **25–30**, complete the second sentence so that it has a similar meaning to the first sentence, using the word given. **Do not change the word given.** You must use between **two** and **five** words, including the word given. Here is an example (**0**).

Example:

0 I've never seen a film as boring as this one.

SUCH

I've never seen .... as this one.

The gap can be filled by the words 'such a boring film', so you write:

Example: | 0 | SUCH A BORING FILM

Write **only** the missing words **IN CAPITAL LETTERS on the separate answer sheet.**

---

25 Mario managed to solve the maths problem without any help.

SUCCEEDED

Mario .... the maths problem without any help.

26 I'll set up the new equipment provided you carry it into the building.

AS

I'll set up the new equipment .... you carry it into the building.

27 Laura finished the project on time despite all the delays.

SO

Laura finished the project on time even .... many delays.

28 John's friends had to leave without him because he only got to the station after the train had left.

TURN

John .... until after the train had left, so his friends had to leave without him.

29 Take a coat because it might get cold later.

CASE

Take a coat .... cold later.

30 The children can't eat sweets just before dinner.

ALLOWED

The children .... sweets just before dinner.

Essential tips

▶ After reading the first sentence carefully, look at the beginning of the next sentence and the given word.

▶ Think of a structure, phrasal verb or expression suggested by the given word and by the word or words before the gap. Sometimes the given word has to be followed by a gerund, an infinitive, or a particular preposition.

▶ You can use contractions, but you must use the word given without changing or contracting it. Remember that contractions count as two words.

▶ After writing the missing words in the gap, check that the whole sentence makes sense and means the same as the first sentence.

▶ Check your spelling and the number of words you have used carefully.

Question 25: The given word is *succeeded*. What preposition should you use after it? What form of the verb is used after a preposition? Are there any spelling rules that can help you spell the second verb correctly?

Question 27: Which word can you use after *even* to form an expression that means the same as *despite*? In the first sentence *all* is used for emphasis. Can you use *so* in the second sentence to emphasise the number of delays?

Question 28: Which phrasal verb means 'to arrive'? Should you use an affirmative or negative form of the verb before *until* in the second sentence?

PAPER 1	Reading and Use of English ▶	Part 1
		Part 2
PAPER 2	Writing	Part 3
		Part 4
PAPER 3	Listening	**Part 5**
PAPER 4	Speaking	Part 6
		Part 7

You are going to read an article about a traveller called Colleen Kinder, who has visited the hottest place in the world. For questions **31–36**, choose the answer (**A**, **B**, **C** or **D**) which you think fits best according to the text.

Mark your answers **on the separate answer sheet**.

A journey to the hottest place on earth

Colleen Kinder travels with her father to the Danakil desert in Africa.

No one travels alone to the hottest place on earth. You need, for starters, a driver and a Jeep stocked with water and four days of non-perishable food. There are no places to lodge or dine in this desert, so you'll need space for beds and someone who knows how to cook. And finally, because a journey like this costs many thousands of dollars, you'll need some fellow travelers to split the bill – the sort of people who like to fry themselves on vacation.

My father is the easiest recruit. Dad, who naps best roasting in the afternoon sun, is a lover of extreme heat. He's also an extreme traveler, drawn to the fringes of places, all the countries where no one vacations. From my father, I've inherited both tendencies: I'm known for getting bright pink sunburns, and also for stalking the edges of maps. The Danakil desert lies on the fringes of several countries, which claim a sliver of this sweltering, low-lying desert, named the cruelest place on earth. I don't have to mention this to my father – not the endless salt flats, lakes the bright color of mouthwash, or camels by the thousands. When Dad starts calling this desert 'the frying pan', I know he's in.

line 16   We enlist three more people and in Mekele, the starting place for our voyage, we merge with four others. We fill five Jeeps and have nothing in common but a love of travel, and a willingness to sweat for it. The Jeeps plunge down mountains for hours. The heat, of course, is brutal. I remind myself this is just a warm-up. The real heat won't strike until we reach the sizzling edge of the frying pan, an uninhabited region, roughly 130 meters below sea level, called Dallol, which holds the record for the highest average annual temperature: 94 degrees.

As we continue, sand gives way to salt, and soon we're in a landscape of white crystals glinting in the fresh morning light. The ground is miraculously flat. Our driver, who has been battling fine sand, cannot resist the urge to go for it. We surge ahead of the other cars in what looks like a Jeep race across some frozen lake. Suddenly, in the pure white expanse, a huge brown mound appears. We're ordered by our guides to find a full liter of bottled water, and to bring it with us up the lumpy brown mountain.

At the summit, I find my travel mates standing in a kind of silent daydream. Astonished, they crouch down beside pale green toadstools – mineral formations whose glossy tabletops are smooth as marble. The hottest place on earth is an assault of color: yellow and deep rust, pea green and purple. Some of the formations look like coral reefs, others like egg shells, air-blown from the hot breath of the earth below. Everyone wanders off alone, crunching over the earth, heads down, staring at the ground and shaking their heads.

I know the ground is hot – you can even hear water boiling underground. Everywhere we step, things break and splinter. Just when I work up the nerve to step with force, the purple ground collapses beneath my foot. The sneaker I pull back out is covered in bright yellow stuff. You start to think: we really shouldn't *be* here. This desert wasn't built to handle a human intrusion, and the human body certainly wasn't built to handle this desert.

Back in the Jeeps, blazing towards the white horizon, I look down at my sneakers. The fluorescent yellow stuff has faded into neutral dirt, like that was all just some fever dream up there, a place we made right up.

- Once you're sure you understand the question, you need to locate the right information in the text. The information may be in a single sentence, in the whole paragraph, or it may be a question about the whole text.

- Remember that you may not find exactly the same words in the text that are in the options. Think carefully about the meaning of the text.

- Look out for line numbers given in the questions. These refer to a word or phrase in the text. You will find the line number referenced in the correct part of the text so you don't need to count the lines to find it.

Question 33: Find the line reference and the specific phrase in the text. Sometimes what's being referred to may come after the phrase, but sometimes it comes before. Read the whole paragraph to identify where the correct information is.

Question 34: The text mentions *white crystals, fine sand*, a *frozen lake*, a *huge brown mound* and a *lumpy brown mountain*. These are similar to the ideas in the options, but only one of them is being compared to the landscape in the text. What language of comparison does the writer use?

Question 35: There is plenty of description about the surroundings in which the travellers find themselves, but what does the writer say the travellers are doing? Imagine how people who behave like this might be feeling.

31 What point does the writer make in the first paragraph?

A Planning for a trip in the desert is straightforward.
B High temperatures can cause problems for travellers.
C Travelling individually in the desert is unwise.
D The expense of desert travel puts many people off.

32 What does the writer say about her father in the second paragraph?

A He's passed on his love of travelling in remote places to his daughter.
B He misses having company when he goes to unusual places.
C He prefers to research places for himself than listen to others.
D He likes to plan every detail of a journey by studying maps.

33 What do the words 'remind myself this is just a warm-up' refer to in line 16?

A that the writer is still getting to know the people she is travelling with
B that the real challenge of the journey is still ahead of them
C that they have a long way to go before they reach their destination
D that the drivers are still learning how to find their way in the mountains

34 What does the writer compare the landscape to in paragraph four?

A a beach
B mud
C ice
D dust

35 What does the writer suggest about her fellow travellers in paragraph five?

A They find it difficult to look at the brightness of the colours.
B They are disappointed by some of the things they see.
C Their surroundings are impossible to make sense of.
D They are unable to take their eyes off the scene in front of them.

36 How does the writer feel as she is walking around on her own?

A shocked by the fact that the ground is so soft
B afraid that she might never find her way out of the place
C worried that she is going to hurt herself
D uncertain about whether she is doing the right thing

For the Glossary see page 47 ▶

PAPER 1	Reading and Use of English	▶	Part 1
			Part 2
PAPER 2	Writing		Part 3
			Part 4
PAPER 3	Listening		Part 5
PAPER 4	Speaking		**Part 6**
			Part 7

You are going to read an article about how we can stop eating foods that are bad for us. Six sentences have been removed from the article. Choose from the sentences **A–G** the one which fits each gap (**37–42**). There is one extra sentence which you do not need to use.

Mark your answers **on the separate answer sheet**.

Can we stop food cravings through imaginary eating?

A study says that imaginary chewing and swallowing can reduce our desire to eat the wrong kind of foods.

Are you fighting an urge to reach for some chocolate right now? Then, let it melt in your mind, not in your mouth. According to recent research, imagining eating a specific food reduces your interest in that food, so you eat less of it.

This reaction to repeated exposure to food – being less interested in something because you've experienced it too much – is called habituation and it's well known to occur while eating. **37** [ ]

But the new research is the first to show that habituation can occur solely via the power of the mind. ' **38** [ ] This research suggests that may not be the best strategy,' said study leader Carey Morewedge, a psychologist at Carnegie Mellon University in Pittsburgh.

'If you just think about the food itself – how it tastes, smells, and looks – that will increase your appetite,' he continued. 'This research suggests that it might be better, actually, to force yourself to repeatedly think about tasting, swallowing and chewing the food you want in order to reduce your cravings. What's more, the technique only works with the specific food you've imagined,' he added. **39** [ ]

Morewedge and his colleagues conducted five experiments, all of which revealed that people who repeatedly imagined eating bread or cream would eat less of that food than people who pictured themselves eating the food fewer times, eating a different food, or not eating at all. In one experiment, for instance, 51 subjects were divided into three groups. One group was asked to imagine inserting 30 coins into a laundry washing machine and then eating three chocolates. **40** [ ] Another group was asked to imagine inserting three coins into a laundry machine and then eating 30 chocolates. Lastly, a control group imagined just inserting 33 coins into the machine – with no chocolates.

All participants then ate freely from bowls containing the same amount of chocolate each. **41** [ ] The results showed that the group that had imagined eating 30 chocolates each ate fewer of the chocolates than both the control group and the group that imagined eating three chocolates.

The study is part of a new area of research looking into the triggers that make us eat more than we actually need, Morewedge noted. **42** [ ] Recent research suggests that psychological factors, such as habituation or the size of a plate, also influence how much a person eats. The new study, Morewedge said, may lead to new behavioural techniques for people looking to eat more healthily, or exert control over other habits.

A A lot of people who want to stop eating certain foods that they know are bad for them try to avoid thinking about the foods they really want.

B When they said they had finished, these were taken away and weighed.

C A tenth bite, for example, is desired less than the first bite, according to the study authors.

D Indeed, this is what most of us think when faced with foods we really like, but think we shouldn't eat.

E For instance, visualising yourself eating chocolate wouldn't prevent you from eating lots of cheese.

F Physical, digestive cues – that full stomach feeling – are only part of what tells us that we've finished a meal.

G This requires the same motor skills as eating small chocolates from a packet, the study says.

Essential tips

> Read the title and the byline (in italics under the title). These will give you a good idea of what the text is about and help you to understand the context of what you're about to read.

> Don't worry about any words that you don't understand. Focus on understanding the general meaning of the text.

> Remember that the missing information may be linked to an idea that comes earlier in the same paragraph, or in the next paragraph.

> Often, the text develops and 'tells a story'. Think about the sequence of events described. This will help you to decide which is the correct answer.

Question 39: The whole paragraph focuses on imagining eating certain foods. Are there any options which include a synonym for *imagining*? What about vocabulary for items of food?

Question 40: In the sentence before the gap, an experiment is being explained, where the participants are doing something. Think carefully about what they're doing and try to picture the action. Are there any options that have a link with this action?

Question 42: This paragraph contains information about 'triggers' (things that make us start thinking about something). After the gap, we learn about psychological triggers. What other kind of triggers are there?

For the Glossary see page 47 ▶

PAPER 1	Reading and Use of English	▶	Part 1
			Part 2
PAPER 2	Writing		Part 3
			Part 4
PAPER 3	Listening		Part 5
			Part 6
PAPER 4	Speaking		**Part 7**

You are going to read an article about surfing. For question **43–52**, choose from the sections (**A–D**). The sections may be chosen more than once.

Mark your answers **on the separate answer sheet**.

___

Which section mentions the writer's

uncertainty about what he ought to be doing?   **43** ☐

amazement at the skill of the surfers?   **44** ☐

awareness of how eager his instructor is to share his knowledge? **45** ☐

surprise at the way the surfers behave at a certain point? **46** ☐

negative comparison of himself with an experienced surfer? **47** ☐

excitement at the opportunity to try out an activity?   **48** ☐

concern about his ability to remember unfamiliar information? **49** ☐

recognition of a widely-accepted rule amongst surfers?   **50** ☐

reason for being involved in an activity?   **51** ☐

observation of surfers practising a particular move?   **52** ☐

Essential tips

▶ The text you read may be made up of several separate accounts, or may be one continuous text that is divided into paragraphs or sections. You should approach the task in the same way, whichever kind of text you read.

▶ Spend time reading the options very carefully, so that you understand their meaning.

▶ Make sure you focus on the idea expressed in the option and find where this is mentioned in the text.

▶ Don't be misled by vocabulary items. You may see a word in an option and the same or similar word in the text. This may not be where the answer is in the text, so make sure you read carefully.

Question 43: The relevant part of the text shows that the writer doesn't know what he should be doing at a certain point. How could someone find out what they are supposed to be doing?

Question 45: The relevant part of the text refers to the writer's instructor. What is a synonym of 'eager'? How can a person demonstrate eagerness? Perhaps by speaking or behaving in a particular way? Look for examples of the instructor's behaviour in the text.

Question 48: The relevant part of the text shows the writer's excitement as he is about to try surfing. What synonyms for 'excitement' are there in the text? In which part of the text are you likely to find this information?

For the Glossary see page 47 ▶

Surfing

Journalist Dean Jones learns how to surf with champion Danny Waite.

A In a bid to produce an article for the sports magazine I work on, I'm learning to surf, and that's how I find myself standing on a rocky headland with 19-year-old surf champion, Danny Waite.

'There's no denying the ocean is a powerful force of nature,' says Danny thoughtfully, as we stand overlooking Blacksands Bay in one of the country's prime surfing spots. 'You've got to respect it, but if you follow a few basic rules, there's little to fear.' That's easy for him to say, having spent his youth with a surfboard glued to his feet, while I haven't even pulled on a wetsuit before.

'First, you need to stand and observe the surf for a while,' he tells me from our vantage point above the bay. I stare blankly, then ask what it is I'm meant to be looking out for. 'The waves,' he says. 'How they're breaking, what the patterns are as they approach the beach.' It all sounds rather technical to me.

B That's only the start of it. Warming to his role of teacher, Danny launches into an enthusiastic account of things I've never heard of: 'surf plans', 'rip currents' and 'wave sets'. There's no stopping him as I desperately will my already-overwhelmed brain to hold on to this vital information.

Once a surfer has figured out how he's going to enter the waves, Danny informs me, he paddles out on his board, lying flat against it, and using his hands to 'swim' through the water, before leaping to his feet and riding the wave.

I watch surfers limbering up in preparation, stretching and jumping from their stomachs to their feet on their boards. Then they're off, racing to the sea and heading towards what seem to me to be pretty fearsome breakers – huge waves rolling and crashing towards the shore.

C The surfers paddle out on their boards until they reach an area beyond the breaking waves where the water's calmer. I notice that they don't immediately jump into action but sit around on their boards with their legs dangling into the water. Rather than looking in the direction the waves are travelling – as I would have expected – they appear to be looking out to sea.

'They're watching the waves come in,' explains Danny, 'to decide where the best place is to take off from.' When the decision's been made, the surfers paddle their way from the waiting zone to what's known as the line-up. 'Surfers must know their place,' Danny continues. 'The surfer positioned closest to the breaking wave gets to ride it.' 'Dropping in', or attempting to ride a wave before it's your turn, is, I become aware, to be avoided at all costs.

D Eventually a surfer will find himself first in line, and that's where the real fun starts. Surfing is all about timing; being ready to catch the wave at just the right moment. Having observed the waves in the waiting zone, a surfer should have a good idea of where the wave will break and when to get to his feet.

The surfers I can see today are advanced and pop up to a standing position on their boards with ease. I watch in awe as they ride the waves, expertly zigzagging their way towards the beach, harnessing the power of the rushing water. It's thrilling to watch and, though I'm not sure of how I'll perform myself, I'm full of inspiration.

'Ready to give it a go?' asks Danny. I nod readily, and we head towards the beach.

You **must** answer this question. Write your answer in **140–190** words in an appropriate style.

1   In your English class you have been talking about activities that people do in their free time. Now your English teacher has asked you to write an essay.

Write your essay using **all** the notes and give reasons for your point of view.

'Everyone should take part in a free-time
activity with other people.'

Do you agree?

Notes
Write about:

1. meeting different people
2. learning / improving skills
3. .... (your own idea)

Essential tips

Part 1

▶ Plan your essay before you start writing. Think about what **your own idea** will be. For example, it could be keeping fit, or being part of a community.

▶ Remember, you won't have time to write a full draft of your essay in the exam, so make a few notes only when you are planning your answer.

▶ Your essay will need an **introduction**, a **main body** and a **conclusion**. Decide what you will say in each paragraph.

▶ Decide approximately how many words you will use in each section (but don't spend too much time counting them!). The main body will need the highest number of words.

▶ When you have finished writing your essay, check your grammar, spelling and punctuation carefully.

▶ If you need to cross anything out or add anything during the checking process, make sure you do this neatly, so that the examiner can read your handwriting easily.

PAPER 1 Reading and
         Use of English

PAPER 2 Writing   ▶   Part 1
                              Part 2
PAPER 3 Listening

PAPER 4 Speaking

Write an answer to **one** of the questions **2–5** in this part. Write your answer in **140–190** words in an appropriate style.

2   You see this announcement in an English-language magazine.

> **Articles wanted – Using your imagination**
>
> Is it important to have a good imagination? How can having lots of ideas help us in life? When might it be less important to have a good imagination? Write us an article answering these questions.
>
> The best articles will be printed in next month's magazine.

Write your **article**.

3   You see this notice on an English-language website called Games.

> **Reviews wanted – A computer game you can learn from**
>
> Have you played a computer game recently which you learned from in some way? Write us a review of the game. You should include a description of the game, what you learned from playing the game, **and** say whether you would recommend the game to other people your age.
>
> We'll post the best reviews on the website next month.

Write your **review**.

Essential tips

Part 2

▶ Remember you must only do **one** of the tasks in Part 2.

▶ Some of the tasks in Part 2 include questions which you should answer. You must answer **all** of the questions that you are asked and make sure that the information you include is relevant.

▶ You don't have to write about true events or opinions. You can use your imagination to come up with information that helps you to answer the question.

▶ Don't forget to spend a few minutes at the beginning planning your work, and a few minutes at the end checking it.

▶ *For FIRST FOR SCHOOLS candidates only:* If you have read the set text and want to answer question 5, make sure you **only** write about **the book the question refers to** and **no other**. You **must not** answer question 5 if you have not read the book it refers to.

Question 2

Read the task carefully. There are three questions which you have to answer here. Make sure your article answers each question, but don't repeat yourself.

The article doesn't mention the word 'opinion' but you are being asked to express your own ideas. There are no right or wrong answers to the questions.

Articles need a short **introduction** and **conclusion**, just like essays. The introduction should make the reader want to read the article, and the conclusion should leave them thinking about what you have said.

Question 3

You have to write a review for an English language website, so make sure you use a neutral style. Organise your ideas into paragraphs.

How many things do you have to write about? In your **introduction**, write about the game. Then explain what you have to do, any characters that might be in the game, and where the game is set, for example.

For the **second point** you have to say what you learned from playing the game. What kinds of things can you learn from paying a game? Do you learn facts, or can you learn any physical skills, too?

The **final point** you have to talk about is whether or not you would recommend the game to other people of your age. Don't forget to say why (or why not).

Continued on next page ▶

PAPER 1 Reading and
         Use of English

PAPER 2 Writing ▶   Part 1
                      Part 2
PAPER 3 Listening

PAPER 4 Speaking

4   (*for FIRST candidates only*)

Your English teacher has asked you to write a report about an event that has taken place in your town. Describe the event in your report and say whether it brought people of different ages together. Was there anything about the event that could have been better?

Write your **report**.

(*for FIRST FOR SCHOOLS candidates only*)

You have seen this announcement in an international magazine.

Stories wanted

We are looking for stories to publish in our international magazine. Your story must begin with this sentence:

Stephanie walked into the room and everyone turned to look at her.

Your story must include:
- a lost letter
- a celebration

We'll publish the best stories in the magazine!

Write your **story**.

5   (*for FIRST FOR SCHOOLS candidates only*)

Answer the following question based on the set text you have read.

Your English class has had a discussion about the main topic of the book you have read. Now your English teacher has given you this essay for homework.

What is the main topic of the book you have read? Describe the central idea that runs through the book and explain what you have learned about it.

Write your **essay**.

Essential tips

Question 4

(*for FIRST candidates only*)

How many points do you have to address in your report? Make sure you address each point in a separate section.

Use **headings** to help you organise your report, and put the points into a logical order. For example, Reports usually end with recommendations/suggestions.

Think about who you are writing the report for. Who might read the report?.

Question 4

(*for FIRST FOR SCHOOLS candidates only*)

Who is Stephanie? Who are the people who turn to look at her and where are they? What did the letter say? Who wrote the letter and who did they send it to? What kind of celebration took place and why?

You **must** include the two elements (a letter AND a celebration) in your story.

Remember that your story must follow on from the prompt sentence. Make sure your story develops logically and uses appropriate narrative tenses to make it interesting.

Question 5

(*for FIRST FOR SCHOOLS candidates only*)

Only answer this question if you have read the set text. Your answer must clearly relate to the story and give details which show you have read the book.

Think about the main idea or theme presented in the book. What kind of book is it? Who is it written for?

Explain the main theme of the book. Think about what you already knew about the theme before you read the book. What was new to you?

Essential tips

▶ Always read the question through carefully at the beginning, so you get an idea of what you are about to hear.

▶ If you hear a word from one of the options, this does not necessarily mean that the option is correct – to know whether or not it is correct, you need to understand the meaning of what is being said.

▶ Sometimes you are asked about what the two speakers agree about. One speaker may say something that seems to make an option correct, but if the other person disagrees with them, then the option is incorrect.

▶ The speakers will have accents from a range of English-speaking countries (the UK, the US, Australia, etc.) but the accents will not be very strong.

Question 3: The options are all language functions. The speaker's words tell you what the function is, but she doesn't use the words *express concern*, *regret* or *criticise*.

Question 5: The speaker says something about the plot, the characters and the setting, but only one of the options reflects something he says.

Question 6: This question asks about the speaker's feelings when she got home after an event she talks about. There is reference to what she expected before she went, but her feelings on her return provide the key.

🎧 **Track 5**

You will hear people talking in eight different situations. For questions **1–8**, choose the best answer (**A**, **B** or **C**).

1 You hear two people talking about their new boss.
   What do they agree about?
   A She didn't seem very confident at first.
   B She doesn't appear to enjoy her work.
   C She probably won't be easy to work for.

2 You hear a young man talking about his sports studies course.
   What does he say about it?
   A The teaching is better than he'd expected.
   B Some of the students should have chosen a different course.
   C It will qualify him to teach a wide variety of sports.

3 You hear a woman talking about a trip to the theatre.
   What is she doing?
   A expressing concern for someone on the trip
   B regretting having gone on the trip
   C criticising the way somebody behaved on the trip

4 You hear a lecturer discussing a scientific experiment with a student.
   What is the lecturer's purpose?
   A to show the student how to interpret the results
   B to help the student make sure the results are accurate
   C to explain to the student why the results were wrong

5 You hear a man talking about a novel he has read.
   What does he think about it?
   A the plot is not predictable
   B the characters are interesting
   C the setting is unusual

6 You hear a student talking about a geography trip.
   How did she feel about it when she got home?
   A Relieved that she'd been able to take part in all the activities.
   B Pleased to have got to know so many people on her course.
   C Disappointed because she'd learned less than she'd hoped to.

7 You hear two friends talking in an art gallery.
   What does the woman say about the exhibition?
   A It will probably be a success with the public.
   B It is similar to other ones she has seen recently.
   C It has a surprisingly large number of paintings in it.

8 You hear a student talking about learning a new language.
   What does he say about it?
   A He is finding it quite easy.
   B He knows it will be useful.
   C He thinks it should be compulsory.

PAPER 1 Reading and Use of English

PAPER 2 Writing

PAPER 3 Listening ▶

PAPER 4 Speaking

Part 1
Part 2
Part 3
Part 4

Essential tips

▶ Use the time before the recording starts to read the sentences carefully.

▶ Think about what sort of information might go into the gap.

▶ As you listen to the recording, listen carefully so you know when the information you need is coming up.

▶ If you miss the answer or are not sure what exactly was said, you have a second chance when you hear the recording again.

▶ Always write down an answer. There are no negative marks if you get the answer wrong.

Question 9: The word you need describes a specific type of music magazine, which the speaker says is aimed at industry insiders.

Question 11: Listen for the type of work unpaid interns may have to do. The type of work they don't often have to do is mentioned too, to distract you.

Question 15: The speaker says that all experience is useful and mentions two kinds of knowledge. What kind of knowledge does volunteering show you have?

Question 18: What professionals are mentioned by name apart from lawyers?

🎧 **Track 6**

You will hear a man called Jim Green talking about how to get into the music industry. For questions **9–18**, complete the sentences with a word or short phrase.

Getting into the music industry

Jim recommends looking at (9) .... magazines to learn more about the music industry.

Jim stresses the importance of having a (10) .... CV.

Jim points out that many unpaid internships involve doing (11) .... work.

Jim says he himself started out working as what is called a '(12) .... '.

Jim advises people not to (13) .... themselves when applying for internships.

Jim volunteered at music (14) .... before he got his first job.

According to Jim, having volunteering experience shows that a person has gained (15) .... knowledge.

Jim also recommends attending (16) .... , networking events and specialist talks.

Jim mentions some events where people can talk to music industry professionals in jobs ranging from (17) .... to producing music digitally.

Jim points out that people also work as (18) .... and lawyers in the music industry.

PAPER 1 Reading and
Use of English

PAPER 2 Writing

PAPER 3 Listening ▶

PAPER 4 Speaking

Part 1
Part 2
Part 3
Part 4

 Track 7

You will hear five short extracts in which people are talking about listening to music. For questions **19–23**, choose from the list (**A–H**) what each speaker says about listening to music. Use the letters only once. There are three extra letters which you do not need to use.

A It helps me to focus at work.

B It brings back memories.

Speaker 1	19

C It is a good way to relax.

Speaker 2	20

D It provides me with inspiration.

Speaker 3	21

E It is a requirement of my job.

Speaker 4	22

F It makes me feel more energetic.

Speaker 5	23

G It makes time seem to pass more quickly.

H It is something I can sit and enjoy with other people.

Essential tips

▶ When you've read the instructions carefully and underlined the key words, read through the options to get an idea of what each speaker will be talking about.

▶ As you listen to the speakers, you will probably hear words and ideas from a number of different options, but only one option will correctly reflect what each speaker says.

▶ Three of the options are extra options and are incorrect for all of the speakers.

▶ An option will never be correct for more than one speaker: if option C is the correct option for Speaker 2, then option C will not be correct for any other speaker.

Option A: Which speaker describes how they use music to help them concentrate when they are at work?

Option E: Which speaker mentions the job they do? Do they also say that doing this job means you have to listen to music?

Option G: Although several speakers use the word *time*, does one of them say that time seems to go faster when they are listening to music, or that it seems to go slower when they aren't?

PAPER 1 Reading and Use of English

PAPER 2 Writing

PAPER 3 Listening ▶ Part 1 / Part 2 / Part 3 / **Part 4**

PAPER 4 Speaking

🎧 **Track 8**

You will hear an interview with a biology student called Gail Koch, who is spending a year in the rainforest working as a field scientist. For questions **24–30**, choose the best answer (**A**, **B** or **C**).

24 What does Gail say about being a field scientist?
   A She sometimes fears she will never be a proper one.
   B Being so keen compensates for what she does not know.
   C It can be difficult to do a job that is rarely understood.

25 What does Gail enjoy about her life in the rainforest?
   A the early evenings
   B the varied wildlife
   C the pleasant climate

26 Gail's research involves
   A finding out about lizards from local guides.
   B more excitement than other field researchers experience.
   C moving carefully through the rainforest.

27 What does Gail find most inspiring about her work?
   A the chance of winning an academic prize
   B the opportunity to contribute to scientific knowledge
   C the hope that she will make a discovery before others do

28 According to Gail, working as a field scientist is
   A a popular career choice.
   B well paid after people have qualified.
   C good preparation for work in other scientific areas.

29 What does Gail say about her time at the research station?
   A She has developed her ability to analyse statistics.
   B It has improved her chances of doing another course.
   C She has learned how to complete each of her projects on time.

30 What disadvantage of being at the research station does Gail mention?
   A She sometimes feels she has too much work to get through.
   B She has spent a lot of time trying to make herself more comfortable.
   C She may not be keeping up to date with new developments.

Essential tips

▶ Read the question stem very carefully before you listen to the recording: this is the information you will be listening for.

▶ The stem can be a question, or the first part of a sentence which can be completed correctly by one of the options. All the options will complete the sentence grammatically correctly – it is the correct **information** that you need to listen for.

▶ The interviewer asks questions that may be similar to the questions in the stem. Choose the correct option as you listen to the interviewee's reply.

▶ Some of the options may say the opposite of what you hear in the recording, and some of them may say something on a similar topic, but not what the speaker says in the recording.

Question 25: Gail mentions all these things, but which one does she say she enjoys?

Question 27: One of these options is a paraphrase of what Gail says (expressing the same thing but using different words).

Question 28: The correct option is a paraphrase of what Gail says. One incorrect option is the opposite of what she says. The other incorrect option is about a topic Gail mentions, but not a paraphrase of what she says about it.

Part 1 (2 minutes)

The examiner (interlocutor) will ask each of you to speak briefly in turn and to give personal information about yourselves. You can expect a variety of questions, such as:

What do you usually do in the evenings? (Why?)
What did you do last weekend? (Did you enjoy it? Why?)
What are your plans for next weekend?

Part 2 (4 minutes)

You will each be asked to talk for a minute without interruption. You will each be given two different photographs in turn to talk about. After your partner has finished speaking, you will be asked a brief question connected with your partner's photographs.

1 Holidays

Look at the two photographs on page 162 which show people on holiday in different places.

Candidate A, compare these photographs, and say why you think the people have chosen to do these different holiday activities.

Candidate B, which of these holidays would you prefer?

2 Being in a crowd or being alone

Look at the two photographs on page 163 which show people in different situations.

Candidate B, compare these photographs, and say what the people might like about being where they are.

Candidate A, do you like busy places? (Why? / Why not?)

Essential tips

Part 1

▶ There are always two examiners in the speaking test. One of them (the interlocutor) will speak to you and manage the test. The other examiner (the assessor) will listen to you and mark your language ability in detail. The interlocutor will also give you a mark.

▶ The examiner will ask you questions about you and your life. Be prepared to answer questions about your daily life, plans for the future, or things you have done in the past.

▶ If you give a short answer, that's fine, but expect the examiner to ask more questions like 'Why?' or 'What was that like?' to encourage you to answer more fully.

Part 2

▶ Look at the pictures and focus on the question the examiner asks you.

▶ You may need to describe what you can see in the picture, but only if it is relevant to the question you are asked.

▶ If you don't know the exact word in English for something you can see in the picture, use other words to describe what you see. For example, *I'm not sure what this is called in English, but it's used for …* The examiner will give you credit for being able to deal with unknown vocabulary.

▶ The examiner may interrupt you after you have been speaking for about a minute. This is not because you have done something wrong or because the examiner is being rude, but because you have spoken for long enough for the examiners to assess your language ability in this part of the test.

PAPER 1 Reading and
            Use of English

PAPER 2 Writing

PAPER 3 Listening

PAPER 4 Speaking ▶
                    Part 1
                    Part 2
                    Part 3
                    Part 4

Part 3 (4 minutes)

You will be asked to discuss something together without interruption by the examiner. You will have a page of ideas and a question to help you.

Different jobs

Turn to the prompts on page 164 which show different jobs. Talk to each other about the advantages and disadvantages of doing these different jobs. Then decide which **two** of the jobs you would like to do and say why.

Part 4 (4 minutes)

The examiner will encourage you to develop the topic of your discussion in Part 3 by asking questions, such as:

What do people think about when they are choosing a career? (Why?)

What sort of jobs are popular with people your age in your country? (Why?)

Do you think it's a good idea for people to have a part-time job while they are still at school or at college? (Why / Why not?)

Who should people ask for advice about careers? (Why?)

Is it a good idea for young people to be able to spend time watching people doing different jobs before deciding what to do as a career? (Why / Why not?)

Essential tips

Part 3

▶ You will usually take the speaking test with one other student, but sometimes candidates are examined in a group of three. Extra time is given for groups of three.

▶ Make sure you give your partner the chance to speak too. You can use a question such as, *What do you think?* or *Do you agree?* after you have given your own opinion.

▶ You may not reach a decision before the interlocutor stops you and moves on to Part 4. This doesn't matter and will not affect your mark, but the aim of your conversation should be to make a decision together.

Part 4

▶ Listen carefully to the examiner's questions. If you don't understand any of the questions, ask the examiner to repeat themselves or explain further.

▶ Listen carefully to what your partner says and respond to their comments. If you don't agree with him or her, make sure you say why before moving on to give your own opinion.

▶ The interlocutor may ask several questions, but if you and your partner have plenty to say in response to the first question or two, they may not need to ask you any further questions.

▶ Remember that it is your language that is being tested, not your opinions.

PAPER 1 Reading and Use of English

▸▸ **PART 5**

stock with (v) to equip or fill with

non-perishable (adj) that will not go bad quickly

recruit (n) a new member

be drawn to (v) to be attracted to

fringe (n) edge

inherit (v) to receive a characteristic from

tendency (n) a likelihood to do a particular thing

stalk (v) to follow

sweltering (adj) extremely hot

enlist (v) to ask someone to help or take part

merge (v) to come together with

plunge (v) to move down very quickly

brutal (adj) cruel, extreme

sizzling (adj) very hot

uninhabited (adj) a place that is uninhabited has no people living there

give way to (phr v) to be replaced by

glint (v) to shine with quick flashes of light

miraculously (adv) amazingly

urge (n) an impulse or instinct

surge (v) to move forward quickly

expanse (n) a large area of land, water or sky

mound (n) a small hill

lumpy (adj) uneven, not smooth

summit (n) the top

crouch (v) to move your body close to the ground by bending your knees

glossy (adj) shiny

marble (n) a hard rock, often used in building

assault (n) an attack

coral reef (n) a hard structure under the sea that is formed by a community of coral plants

crunch (v) to make a noise like something being crushed

splinter (v) to break into tiny sharp pieces

work up the nerve (phr) to find courage

intrusion (n) the act of being somewhere that you should not be, where you are not welcome

blaze (v) to move very quickly

horizon (n) the point where the earth appears to meet the sky

fluorescent (adj) very bright

neutral (adj) without bright or strong colour

▸▸ **PART 6**

exposure (n) being in a situation where you can experience something

solely (adv) just, simply

strategy (n) a plan or method for achieving something

insert (v) to put into (e.g. a coin into a machine)

trigger (n) an event or prompt that sets off another event

exert control over (phr) to make an effort to have control

visualise (v) to imagine

motor skills (n) the ability to perform movements using muscles

▸▸ **PART 7**

bid (n) an attempt

headland (n) a point of land sticks out into the sea

prime (adj) best

vantage point (n) a position which gives a good view

break (v) if a wave breaks, it reaches its highest point and begins to fall

warm to (v) to become enthusiastic about

be overwhelmed (v) to be presented with a very large amount of something to the point where you feel you cannot cope

paddle (v) to move through the water using the hands

leap (v) to jump

limber up (phr v) to do gentle exercises that make your muscles warm

breaker (n) a large wave

dangle (v) to hang loosely

pop up (v) to jump up

awe (n) respect

zigzag (v) to move from side to side, changing direction suddenly

harness (v) to gain control of

nod (v) to move the head up and down as if to say 'yes'

For questions **1–8**, read the text below and decide which answer (**A, B, C** or **D**) best fits each gap. There is an example at the beginning (**0**).

Mark your answers **on the separate answer sheet**.

Example:

0   **A**   shape   **B**   place   **C**   form   **D**   part

0	A	B	C	D
	⌣	**▬**	⌣	⌣

Precious metals

What is known as the 'California Gold Rush' took (**0**) …….. in the US in the middle of the 19th century. Miners searched for gold, silver and copper in the (**1**) …….. of becoming rich. As they dug, they (**2**) …….. piles of unwanted dirt and rocks. The miners who worked there so long ago would have been amazed to know that over 150 years later, these waste products are in (**3**) …….. demand. Geologists have analysed samples and discovered that some of them contain valuable minerals, called rare earth elements, which are used in the production of (**4**) …….. electronic devices.

Rare earth elements are not actually very rare, but they are (**5**) …….. to mine. This is mainly because they (**6**) …….. naturally in very small quantities and are difficult to (**7**) …….. from other elements surrounding them. In (**8**) …….. , the precious minerals are relatively easy to extract from the 19th century mines' unwanted waste products.

1	**A** luck	**B** hope	**C** chance	**D** wish
2	**A** raised	**B** built	**C** created	**D** developed
3	**A** great	**B** large	**C** grand	**D** big
4	**A** frequent	**B** wanted	**C** popular	**D** daily
5	**A** uneasy	**B** stubborn	**C** clumsy	**D** awkward
6	**A** occur	**B** happen	**C** arise	**D** reveal
7	**A** divide	**B** separate	**C** undo	**D** disconnect
8	**A** conflict	**B** difference	**C** opposition	**D** contrast

PAPER 1	Reading and ▶	Part 1
	Use of English	Part 2
PAPER 2	Writing	Part 3
		Part 4
PAPER 3	Listening	Part 5
PAPER 4	Speaking	Part 6
		Part 7

For questions **9–16**, read the text below and think of the word which best fits each gap. Use only **one** word in each gap. There is an example at the beginning (**0**).

Write your answers **IN CAPITAL LETTERS on the separate answer sheet**.

Example: | 0 | T | H | A | T | | | | | | | | | | | | | | | | | |

Vanilla

Vanilla is the seed pod of an orchid flower (**0**) .... grows close to the equator. Another name for vanilla is 'black flower', because the pod and beans turn black shortly after (**9**) .... picked. Vanilla is used (**10**) .... over the world as a flavouring in food, drinks and medicines, as (**11**) .... as in many perfumes.

The first people to use vanilla were probably the Totonac Indians in Mexico, and it was taken to Europe in 1520. Only very few people (**12**) .... afford it, however, until in 1841 a 12-year-old boy called Edmond Albius discovered that (**13**) .... was possible to transfer pollen from flower to flower by hand. After that, growers (**14**) .... longer had to rely on bees and other animals to do this, and vanilla was grown (**15**) .... far larger quantities. A number of different countries now export it, and Mexico, (**16**) .... the vanilla orchid originated, produces only a small percentage of the harvest these days.

PAPER 1	Reading and Use of English ▶	Part 1
		Part 2
PAPER 2	Writing	Part 3
		Part 4
PAPER 3	Listening	Part 5
PAPER 4	Speaking	Part 6
		Part 7

For questions **17–24**, read the text below. Use the word given in capitals at the end of some of the lines to form a word that fits the gap **in the same line**. There is an example at the beginning (**0**).

Write your answers **IN CAPITAL LETTERS on the separate answer sheet.**

Example: | 0 | D | A | N | G | E | R | O | U | S | | | | | | | | |

The truth about wolves

Wolves are considered one of the world's most (**0**) …….. animals.   **DANGER**

However, it is extremely (**17**) ………….. for them to ever attack   **USUAL**

humans and even then they only do so when they are (**18**) …….. .   **THREAT**

These highly intelligent creatures are, in fact as afraid of us as we

are of them.

The largest of the dog family, wolves share (**19**) …….. with their –   **SIMILAR**

often domesticated – cousins. Frequently misrepresented in

stories as evil creatures that howl at the moon, wolves really use

this call to communicate their (**20**) …….. to other members of   **LOCATE**

their pack. Far from the (**21**) …….. the traditional image suggests,   **MAD**

wolves raise their heads to howl simply because this is how the

sound is (**22**) …….. produced.   **PHYSICAL**

Just like dogs, wolves also use warning barks, indicate dominance

through a low growl and (**23**) …….. whimper when they want to   **SOFT**

make a friendly (**24**) …….. . Wolf handlers have been known to say   **GREET**

they feel safer with wolves than people!

For questions **25–30**, complete the second sentence so that it has a similar meaning to the first sentence, using the word given. **Do not change the word given.** You must use between **two** and **five** words, including the word given. Here is an example (**0**).

Example:

0   I've never seen a film as boring as this one.

SUCH

I've never seen .... as this one.

The gap can be filled by the words 'such a boring film', so you write:

Example: | 0 | | SUCH A BORING FILM |

Write **only** the missing words **IN CAPITAL LETTERS on the separate answer sheet**.

___

25   I don't want to go to my piano lesson today.

FEEL

I don't .... to my piano lesson today.

26   His boss said to Jan that he must do the work quickly.

TOLD

Jan did the work quickly because his boss had .... so.

27   I only went out because I was sure you had your keys.

HAD

I wouldn't have gone out .... you didn't have your keys.

28   Xavier can't wait to start university.

FORWARD

Xavier's really .... university.

29   'Don't leave the computer on,' my boss told me.

ASKED

My boss .... leave the computer on.

30   I think it's going to rain.

IF

It .... it's going to rain.

PAPER 1	Reading and ▶	Part 1
	Use of English	Part 2
PAPER 2	Writing	Part 3
		Part 4
PAPER 3	Listening	**Part 5**
PAPER 4	Speaking	Part 6
		Part 7

You are going to read an article by reporter Joanna Ruck about a swimming event in a lake in the north of England. For questions **31–36**, choose the answer (**A**, **B**, **C** or **D**) which you think fits best according to the text.

Mark your answers **on the separate answer sheet**.

Open water swimming

Reporter Joanna Ruck recently attempted her first long-distance swim in a large lake.

I had only swum in open water a few times, and always in calm reservoirs or gentle lakes, so I wasn't quite prepared for how imposing and rough Lake Windermere, in the north of England, appeared on a cold grey day. But I, along with 10,000 others, was about to brave the lake to complete the challenge of the Great North Swim.

I'd arrived on a train packed with people descending on Windermere, and the hotel was buzzing with talk about what distances they were doing, and everyone was swapping techniques and advice. I headed to the lake just as the 5 km race was finishing, the longest distance over the weekend. A swimmer who had just completed this race told me the water felt colder than the 15.6°C it had been measured at, and that the water was a bit rough. But if 10,000 other people weren't put off, I wouldn't be either.

My training had involved a few sessions in a local reservoir, but had mainly been in a pool where seeing where you're going is fairly straightforward. It's very different in rough water. My new wetsuit had only
line 12   arrived two days before the swim so I'd popped to my local open-air swimming pool to give it a quick try out. I'd managed to do the mile (1.61 km) there in 29 ½ minutes – but how would I fare in open water?

Most of the people taking part were doing a one-mile race. 26 races were planned over the whole weekend. There seemed to be a mix of open-water enthusiasts alongside complete novices – which, according to the organisers, is precisely the aim of the swims, to get as many people as possible completing their own challenge. The oldest woman competing was 77, taking part in the two-mile race alongside a man who last year had swum in every one-mile race.

I had opted for the third one-mile race of the day. This gave me time to watch the impressive performance from the elites, who have their own races before everyone else gets going, and the start of the masses. A former Olympic swimmer emerged from his mile event, completing it in 22 minutes 29 seconds, and I asked his advice for my race. He told me: 'You'll be fine, it's all about focusing on where you're going and
line 23   staying calm.' Easy for him to say.

There were just over 200 people in my race. We were all taken through an acclimatisation area, a children's paddling pool-sized part of the lake where we plunged in to feel how cold the water was. 'Not too bad' was the verdict! We took off with a flurry of splashes and headed out towards the middle of the lake. We'd been warned that the first 100 m would be really rough, but that it would feel much calmer after that. Somewhere near the 750 m mark I was still waiting for the calm; it felt more like swimming in the sea than a lake. I felt battered by the water. I tried to focus on my breathing and technique, and just keep going. Then, as I approached the 400 m-to-go mark my lower right leg cramped painfully. I recalled overhearing people in the hotel the night before talking about how they keep swimming through cramp, so I tried.

It didn't work, so now instead of just my lower calf cramping the entire leg went into spasm. I didn't want to stop, so flexed my foot and just kicked with the left leg: fine until a friendly steward in a kayak pointed out that I'd drifted off course. However, I could now see the finishing post so just concentrated on getting there – still one-legged. My finishing time was 38 minutes 23 seconds but that didn't seem to matter – the atmosphere was fantastic and everyone felt a sense of achievement, whatever their time. I'm hooked, and want to give it another go. I've already signed up for my next open-water swim.

31 In the second paragraph, how did the writer feel?

    A disappointed by the difficult weather conditions
    B concerned by the other swimmers in the event
    C determined to be as tough as the people around her
    D relieved to have missed the most challenging event

32 What does 'it' refer to in line 12?

    A trying to swim so far
    B swimming in rough water
    C her new wetsuit
    D the open-air pool

33 Why does the writer mention the two people in the fourth paragraph?

    A to demonstrate how diverse the participants are
    B to show that most swimmers are very inexperienced
    C to explain the problems faced by those running the event
    D to justify her presence amongst the better swimmers

34 What is meant by 'Easy for him to say' in line 23?

    A He could have given her more useful tips.
    B He did not understand what it was like to be her.
    C He should have listened to her more carefully.
    D He was not even out of breath after his efforts.

35 What does the writer say about the swim in the sixth paragraph?

    A It would have been easier if she had taken other people's advice.
    B It was an effective way to prepare for more demanding swims.
    C It required less concentration after she had relaxed a little.
    D It turned out to be harder than she had been led to believe.

36 What does the writer express in the final paragraph?

    A her surprise at having managed to finish
    B her eagerness to repeat the experience
    C her pride at having swum so quickly
    D her confidence in her own ability

PAPER 1 Reading and
        Use of English
PAPER 2 Writing
PAPER 3 Listening
PAPER 4 Speaking

Part 1
Part 2
Part 3
Part 4
Part 5
Part 6
Part 7

You are going to read an article about prehistoric cave art in France. Six sentences have been removed from the article. Choose from the sentences **A–G** the one which fits each gap (**37–42**). There is one extra sentence which you do not need to use.

Mark your answers **on the separate answer sheet**.

Visiting prehistoric cave art in France

Exploring the mysteries of cave art in the Dordogne region of France.

At some point in remote prehistory, roughly 12,000 years ago, a group of men and women – no more than half a dozen, scientists believe – crawled into the narrow complex of tunnels of Rouffignac cavern in the Vézère valley, in the Dordogne region of France. Once in its deepest recess, they lay on their backs and, in flickering candlelight, started painting on the rock ceiling less than a metre above them. More than 60 images of mammoths, horses and ibex were outlined, each animal depicted in simple, confident lines that reveal startling artistic talent.

This is now known as the Great Ceiling of Rouffignac, one of the world's oldest and most beautiful art galleries. We have few clues as to who created it, though it was probably the work of the Cro-Magnons, the first members of *Homo sapiens* to settle in Europe 45,000 years ago and survivors of the Ice Age that later gripped the continent. **37** Fortunately, though, it can be reached far more easily today. A tiny electric train runs from Rouffignac's entrance to the Great Ceiling, the floor of which has been lowered to allow visitors to gaze up at its wonders.

The cavern train carries you past pictures of woolly rhinos, superbly rendered in black, and engravings of mammoths, carved into the soft walls by artists with their fingers. The cavern is also peppered with holes scratched by hibernating bears. **38** It is a stunning experience, one of many to be found in this remarkable area.

In the 25 km of the Vézère valley between the town of Montignac and the village of Les Eyzies there are 15 caves – including Rouffignac, Lascaux and others – which have been rated Unesco World Heritage sites because of their prehistoric art. The original Lascaux cave, outside Les Eyzies, was discovered in September 1940 and contains more than 600 prehistoric coloured paintings. **39**

Thousands flocked to see them, triggering changes to the cave's atmosphere that boosted the growth of algae and crystals on the artwork on its walls. In 1963 the cave was closed to the public and 20 years later an exact replica, Lascaux II, was opened. **40** Visitors can also see the hollowed stones they used as candle holders.

To judge from the bones they left there, our ancestors camped at cave entrances and enjoyed diets mainly made up of reindeer meat. **41** The artists concentrated instead on the more majestic animals – mammoths and woolly rhinos – that then populated the Dordogne. These painters fully understood perspective and exploited rock bulges and crevices to create works of art that would have shifted and shimmered in the flickering lamps they carried.

The reason why they were created is obscure, however. Some scientists believe they may have had a spiritual significance for the people who created them and their communities. **42** These works were created by full-time artists who would have required food, clothing and shelter from other community members in order to carry out their work. Visiting the end results, buried in these deep caverns, is an unforgettable experience – and a privilege.

A However, the trip's highlight is the Great Ceiling.

B This explains not only their artistic skills but their considerable knowledge of animal behaviour and anatomy.

C Whatever the case, it is clear that by this stage in our evolution art was now of critical importance to our species.

D Nor do we know why these artists picked such an inaccessible spot to display their genius.

E In addition to its vivid modern reproductions there are displays of the original artists' tools.

F Deep inside these caves, however, their minds moved to different matters.

G Many of these are of horses, deer and mammoths.

PAPER 1 Reading and ▶ Part 1
        Use of English   Part 2
                         Part 3

PAPER 2 Writing   Part 4

PAPER 3 Listening   Part 5

PAPER 4 Speaking   Part 6

Part 7

You are going to read an article in which a travel writer explains the way in which he approaches his trips. For questions **43–52**, choose from the paragraphs (**A–F**). The paragraphs may be chosen more than once.

Mark your answers **on the separate answer sheet**.

In which paragraph does the writer

explain how some of his colleagues approach a journey?	**43**
say he now understands what motivated him to make certain choices?	**44**
mention visits that failed to make a great impact on him?	**45**
accept that his advice will not always be followed?	**46**
give examples of how objects people value can be sources of inspiration?	**47**
say a particular distinction is crucial?	**48**
advise following up interests rather than trying to do unusual things?	**49**
emphasise thorough preparations for trips?	**50**
explain that something is bound to have a lasting effect?	**51**
say that people sometimes fail to recommend the most interesting places?	**52**

Traveling like a travel writer

Robert Reid has some good advice for travelers.

A I've spent a dozen years doing research for travel guidebooks, articles and videos on trips that have taken me to cities on stilts in Siberia, abandoned kingdoms in Burma, even my own hometown. And while I'm likely to remember the local people I meet more vividly than the history museums I breeze through, I've learned there's a resource that's better than anyone else you'll ever meet on your travels: you.

B It takes outsider eyes to really 'see' a place. I would have never found unexcavated ruins in the backwaters of Bulgaria or drunk coffee at classic farm-town diners in the Great Plains area of the US if I had passively relied on advice I got from locals on the ground. If we're being honest – at least in America – doing so often means being steered toward shopping malls, and cafés that are part of global chains. How did I find these places? I was visiting as a travel writer. That means not traveling 'like a local,' but in the company of locals – a subtle, but fundamental, difference.

C Travel writers – at least good ones – don't just drop into Bogotá or Brussels to see what happens, as fun as that can be. They do as much research as they can, devouring novels, articles, TV shows and films about where they'll be going to track down an angle, a hook or a mythology that grabs them. Then they use that angle as a lens that sets them on a path. And that path can lead to unexpected, marvelous things.

D It's time to play with what makes up 'travel.' The goal isn't being 'different' in what you do, it's being personal. Seriously, what do you like? Find ideas by looking at the 'most played' songs in your MP3 player, documentaries you have seen recently, or those old keepsakes you keep in a box under your bed. That chunk of volcano lava your dad got you when you were six? That old video tape or DVD of a band you still enjoy? Anything can turn into a makeshift guidebook if you approach it the right way.

E Looking back at my travel biography, I realise I've subconsciously used trips to do things I dreamt of being able to do as a child. I created a road-trip itinerary around the area of New York where one of my favorite singers grew up, based on lyrics he wrote about his hometown. I drove along roads he sings about in his songs, got coffee at his favorite café, and walked into the music room of his old high school. I even met a guy who used to live across the street from him and remembered hearing him practice the piano. I'll never hear those songs the same way again.

F Why do this? It's empowering. It's memorable. It builds on things that are already dear to you and introduces you to things you never knew you were looking for. It's also fun. You might not want to 'travel like a travel writer' on every trip you take, but you should try it at least once – as if the technique itself were a 'once in a lifetime' destination.

PAPER 1 Reading and
          Use of English
PAPER 2 Writing ▶ | Part 1 |
PAPER 3 Listening | Part 2 |
PAPER 4 Speaking

You **must** answer this question. Write your answer in **140–190** words in an appropriate style.

1 In your English class you have been talking about the clothes people wear. Now your English teacher has asked you to write an essay.

Write your essay using **all** the notes and give reasons for your point of view.

'People should not be judged by the clothes they wear.'

Do you agree?

Notes
Write about:

1. whether people's appearance is important
2. how people choose what to wear
3. .... (your own idea)

PAPER 1 Reading and
         Use of English

PAPER 2 Writing ▶ Part 1
                      Part 2

PAPER 3 Listening

PAPER 4 Speaking

Write an answer to **one** of the questions **2–5** in this part. Write your answer in **140–190** words in an appropriate style.

2   You see this announcement on an English-language website.

> **Articles wanted – An interesting person**
>
> We are looking for articles about interesting people. It could be someone you know, or someone famous. Tell us about the person, and why you think this person is interesting.
>
> The best articles will be posted on the website.

Write your **article**.

3   You see this announcement in an English-language magazine.

> **Reviews wanted – Shopping centres**
>
> Have you visited a shopping centre recently? Tell us about the shops, the places to eat, and any activities you can do there. Would you recommend this shopping centre to other people your age?
>
> The most interesting reviews will be published in the magazine.

Write your **review**.

4   (for FIRST candidates only)

Your English teacher has asked you to write a report on a day trip you have been on with your English class to a place in your area. Write about the place you visited, what you did there and how you travelled there. Was there anything about the trip that could have been better? How could future trips be improved?

Write your **report**.

(for FIRST FOR SCHOOLS candidates only)

You have seen this announcement in an English-language magazine for teenagers.

> **Stories wanted**
>
> We are looking for stories for our English-language magazine for teenagers. Your story must begin with this sentence:
>
> *Maria opened the front door and found a large box outside.*
>
> Your story must include:
> * a surprise
> * some instructions

Write your **story**.

5   (for FIRST FOR SCHOOLS candidates only)

Answer the following question based on the set text you have read.

Your English class has had a discussion about what happens in the book. Now your English teacher has given you this essay for homework.

What is the most important event in the book? Describe the event and explain its effect on the rest of the story. Why do you think the event is so important?

Write your **essay**.

PAPER 1   Reading and
            Use of English

PAPER 2   Writing

PAPER 3   Listening ▶

PAPER 4   Speaking

Part 1
Part 2
Part 3
Part 4

🎧 **Track 9**

You will hear people talking in eight different situations. For questions **1–8**, choose the best answer (**A**, **B** or **C**).

1   You hear part of a radio programme about people who can't hear musical beats.
    What does the man say about being 'beat deaf'?
    A   Many who believe they are beat deaf probably aren't.
    B   Beat deafness is connected with the speed of the music.
    C   Beat deaf people don't understand the idea of rhythm.

2   You hear two students talking about making a map of their local area.
    What do they agree about?
    A   how difficult it might be to use an online tool
    B   how helpful their geography teacher has been
    C   how important it is to do careful planning

3   You hear two friends talking about a TV programme they have seen.
    What does the woman say about the new salt product?
    A   It is not likely to be successful.
    B   It will not offer value for money.
    C   It may not taste as good as normal salt.

4   You hear a teacher telling her students about a historical novel.
    What is she doing?
    A   describing its relevance to her students
    B   providing detailed information about the plot
    C   explaining why she bought the book

5   You hear a man who is blind talking about experiencing travel through his sense of smell.
    Why is he talking about this?
    A   to persuade us to try out his technique
    B   to describe particular journeys he's made
    C   to explain how his skill makes him feel

6   You hear a sports coach talking to a cyclist.
    What is the coach doing?
    A   praising the cyclist for her progress
    B   explaining why the cyclist feels a certain way
    C   encouraging the cyclist to eat better foods

7   You hear an author talking to a friend about launching her new book.
    How does the author feel now?
    A   surprised by her publisher's behaviour
    B   worried about certain arrangements
    C   eager to carry out her plans

8   You hear a sea captain talking to trainees about finding the way at sea.
    What does he say sailors must do?
    A   learn from the mistakes of older sailors
    B   study relevant charts while sailing
    C   be aware of their location at all times

PAPER 1 Reading and
          Use of English
PAPER 2 Writing
PAPER 3 Listening ▶
PAPER 4 Speaking

Part 1
Part 2
Part 3
Part 4

 Track 10

You will hear a man called James Perry talking about growing olives, a kind of fruit used to make oil for food. For questions **9–18**, complete the sentences with a word or short phrase.

Olive farming

As James' olives were growing, some trees were affected by an unexpected

(**9**) ....

James says that a kind of (**10**) .... was one creature

found on his olive trees.

James decided to pick his olives by (**11**) .... when they

were ready.

James collected his olives using a (**12**) .... rather than

a traditional container.

James says he found cleaning (**13**) .... out of the

olives extremely boring.

After sorting them, James said that the olives had left

(**14**) .... over his kitchen.

At the olive press, James hadn't expected to wait in a

(**15**) ....

James' wife joked they could use his first oil in (**16**) ....

as well as for cooking.

James says that the olives need to be (**17**) .... when

you pick them.

James hopes next year's oil will have the flavour of

(**18**) .... , which he likes.

PAPER 1 Reading and
Use of English

PAPER 2 Writing

PAPER 3 Listening ▶
Part 1
Part 2
Part 3
Part 4

PAPER 4 Speaking

🎧 **Track 11**

You will hear five short extracts in which people are talking about why they studied astronomy, the scientific study of stars and planets. For questions **19–23**, choose from the list (**A–H**) the reason each speaker gives for choosing to study the subject. Use the letters only once. There are three extra letters which you do not need to use.

A to gain access to the latest equipment

B to follow a family tradition

                         Speaker 1   **19**

C to earn a good salary

                         Speaker 2   **20**

D to improve career opportunities

                         Speaker 3   **21**

E to prove something to other people

                         Speaker 4   **22**

F to apply knowledge of another subject

                         Speaker 5   **23**

G to increase the opportunity to travel

H to satisfy a childhood ambition

🎧 **Track 12**

You will hear an interview with a life coach called Mel Candy, who helps people to achieve a work-life balance. For questions **24–30**, choose the best answer (**A**, **B** or **C**).

24 Mel says that people who complain to her about being too busy
   A usually work in management positions.
   B want her to tell them precisely what to do.
   C enjoy the fact that it makes them seem important.

25 Mel thinks that people who live and work alone
   A tend to lose track of time.
   B worry about being isolated.
   C can lose their social skills.

26 What does Mel think about trying to do more than one task at a time?
   A She believes it's possible to learn to do it well.
   B She sees why people think it's a good technique.
   C She thinks it's important to research the idea.

27 According to Mel, the expert answer to gaining work-life balance is to
   A change your work routine.
   B achieve goals more quickly.
   C look ahead at forthcoming events.

28 Mel says it's difficult to achieve a work-life balance when people feel
   A concerned that others may judge them.
   B worried they'll miss something important.
   C scared of trying out new activities.

29 What does Mel say about the advice a client gave her?
   A It made a difference to her own life.
   B It confirmed why she likes to help people.
   C It's something she shares with other clients.

30 What does achieving a work-life balance mean for Mel?
   A feeling in control of her workload
   B having more time for social activities
   C achieving a state of physical relaxation

Part 1 (2 minutes)

The examiner (interlocutor) will ask each of you to speak briefly in turn and to give personal information about yourselves. You can expect a variety of questions, such as:

Do you live in a town or village?
Do you like living there? (Why?)
How can people spend their free time in the place you live?
What kind of jobs do people do where you live?

Part 2 (4 minutes)

You will each be asked to talk for a minute without interruption. You will each be given two different photographs in turn to talk about. After your partner has finished speaking, you will be asked a brief question connected with your partner's photographs.

1 Learning environments

Look at the two photographs on page 165 which show people learning in different environments.

Candidate A, compare these photographs, and say why you think the people might enjoy learning in these different environments.

Candidate B, which environment would you prefer to learn in? (Why?)

2 Travelling

Look at the two photographs on page 166 which show people travelling in different ways.

Candidate B, compare these photographs, and say why the people might prefer to travel in these ways.

Candidate A, which method of travel do you prefer? (Why?)

Part 3 (4 minutes)

You will be asked to discuss something together without interruption by the examiner. You will have a page of ideas and a question to help you.

Walking trips

Turn to the prompts on page 167 which show different objects people might use on a walking trip in the mountains. Talk to each other about how useful each object is for a walking trip. Then decide which **two** objects are the most useful and why.

Part 4 (4 minutes)

The examiner will encourage you to develop the topic of your discussion in Part 3 by asking questions such as:

Why do you think people enjoy walking in the mountains?
What preparations do you think people should make before they go on a long walk?
Is walking a popular activity in your country?
Apart from getting exercise, what other benefits of walking are there?
Do you think people should be encouraged to spend more time outdoors?
(Why / Why not?)

PAPER 1 Reading and Use of English

▸▸ PART 5

reservoir (n) man-made lake

imposing (adj) large and impressive

brave (v) to face something despite feeling a bit worried or afraid

descend on (v) to go to in large numbers

buzz with (v) to have a lively atmosphere because of

wetsuit (n) a tight body suit that people wear to stay warm in cold water

pop to (v) to quickly go somewhere

fare (v) to perform or manage

novice (n) someone who is just beginning to learn a skill or subject

opt for (v) to chose

elite (n) the very best

emerge (v) to come out of

acclimatisation (n) getting used to a new climate or conditions

flurry (n) a lot of / a short period of action

batter (v) to hit hard and repeatedly

cramp (v) to suffer the painful tightening of a muscle

calf (n) the muscle at the back of the lower leg

spasm (n) a sudden and usually painful tightening of a muscle

flex (v) to stretch

steward (n) an official employee whose job it is to guide the swimmers

kayak (n) a one-person boat with a paddle

drift (v) to be moved gradually by the water

off course (phr) away from the planned route

hooked (adj) addicted

▸▸ PART 6

remote (adj) distant

roughly (adv) approximately

recess (n) a hollowed out space in a wall

flickering (adj) (light or flame) not burning evenly, or going on and off

mammoth (n) a large, extinct woolly elephant with tusks

ibex (n) a mountain goat with long curved horns

depict (v) to represent in a picture

startling (adj) very surprising

grip (v) to have power or control over something

gaze (v) to look at something or someone for a long time in amazement

render (v) to represent, draw

woolly rhino (n) an extinct type of rhinoceros with a long woolly coat

pepper with (v) to cover with

hibernate (v) when animals sleep throughout winter to conserve energy

flock (v) to go to a place in large numbers

algae (n) a small, simple plant that grows in water or other wet places

replica (n) a copy

reindeer (n) a deer found in snowy areas

bulge (n) a bump or raised area

crevice (n) a narrow gap in rock or in a wall

shift (v) to move gradually

shimmer (v) to sparkle

privilege (n) honour

▸▸ PART 7

a dozen (phr) 12

stilts (n) poles used to support buildings that are built above the ground or above water

vividly (adv) clearly, with detailed mental images

breeze through (phr) to do something in a quick and relaxed manner

resource (n) something used for information

unexcavated (adj) something that has still to be dug up

backwater (n) remote quiet area

global chain (n) worldwide company that owns many shops of the same name

subtle (adj) small and not very noticeable

devour (v) to read quickly and in large numbers

angle (n) a particular way of approaching a problem

hook (n) something to catch your attention

mythology (n) a made up story

grab (v) to capture attention

keepsake (n) a small item of sentimental value

chunk (n) large piece

makeshift (adj) not the real thing, temporary

subconsciously (adv) without planning or thinking about it

lyrics (n) words to a song

empower (v) to give strength or power to

For questions **1–8**, read the text below and decide which answer (**A, B, C** or **D**) best fits each gap. There is an example at the beginning (**0**).

Mark your answers **on the separate answer sheet**.

Example:

| 0 | **A** | witnessed | **B** | participated | **C** | appeared | **D** | gazed |

| 0 | **A** | **B** | **C** | **D** |

Can you hear the lights?

If you've ever (**0**) .... the Northern Lights dancing in the night sky, you'll no doubt have been amazed by their beauty. These strange natural light displays are (**1**) .... by atmospheric energy, and a recent study has indicated that not only are they pretty to look at, but they may also produce certain distinct sounds. Researchers studying the phenomenon believe they have managed to (**2**) .... the sounds.

The Northern Lights appear most powerfully in Arctic (**3**) .... , where there have been tales told about the noises which (**4**) .... them for many years. People describe hearing hissing and crackling sounds, like the noises you hear when your radio is (**5**) .... for a signal.

The researchers recorded (**6**) .... but definite sounds during periods of intense atmospheric activity. They think that what might be creating the sounds are geomagnetic storms, which (**7**) .... large changes in the atmosphere. On the (**8**) .... , however, the scientific community remains puzzled.

1	**A** started	**B** resulted	**C** sourced	**D** caused
2	**A** capture	**B** obtain	**C** bring	**D** achieve
3	**A** neighbourhoods	**B** grounds	**C** regions	**D** districts
4	**A** approach	**B** accompany	**C** attend	**D** associate
5	**A** finding	**B** seeking	**C** trying	**D** searching
6	**A** clear	**B** faded	**C** faint	**D** remote
7	**A** generate	**B** get	**C** establish	**D** lead
8	**A** all	**B** whole	**C** majority	**D** principal

For questions **9–16**, read the text below and think of the word which best fits each gap. Use only **one** word in each gap. There is an example at the beginning (**0**).

Write your answers **IN CAPITAL LETTERS on the separate answer sheet**.

Example: | 0 | | O | N | | | | | | | | | | | | | | | | | | | | | | | | |

Diamonds: how to spot a fake

Trading in this beautiful gemstone is (**0**) …….. the increase. So how can you tell a real one apart (**9**) …….. a fake? Experts employ a number of tests to find out.

Diamonds bend light, in a process known (**10**) …….. refraction. Contrary to what you might (**11**) …….. expected, a real diamond's refraction is in shades of grey, while a fake diamond (**12**) …….. always display light in rainbow colours. Similarly, if the stone you're examining is very clear, it probably isn't original – real diamonds display flaws. Place the stone on a newspaper and if you're able to read newspaper print (**13**) …….. the diamond, it's probably fake.

Diamonds are the hardest natural substance, therefore if the one you're looking at is scratched and chipped, the chances (**14**) …….. it isn't genuine. Real diamonds also sink in water, whereas fake ones, (**15**) …….. are usually made of glass, tend to float. One final test involves passing a stone through fog – if (**16**) …….. surface clears quickly, it's genuine.

PAPER 1 Reading and ▶
         Use of English
PAPER 2 Writing
PAPER 3 Listening
PAPER 4 Speaking

Part 1
Part 2
Part 3
Part 4
Part 5
Part 6
Part 7

For questions **17–24**, read the text below. Use the word given in capitals at the end of some of the lines to form a word that fits the gap **in the same line**. There is an example at the beginning (**0**).

Write your answers **IN CAPITAL LETTERS on the separate answer sheet.**

Example: | 0 | V | I | S | I | T | O | R | S | | | | | | | | | | |

Shakespeare's Globe

Shakespeare's Globe Theatre in London attracts thousands of
(**0**) .... every year. It is in fact a reconstruction of the famous **VISIT**
theatre on its (**17**) .... site on the banks of the Thames. **ORIGIN**
(**18**) .... have been able to establish that the building that **ARCHAEOLOGY**
Shakespeare and his troupe acted in was not a true circle, but
was 20-sided. The 1599 theatre has been (**19**) .... using, as **BUILD**
far as possible, the techniques and (**20**) .... materials that **CONSTRUCT**
would have been used in Shakespeare's time. There are, of
course, extra exits, illuminated signs and other concessions to
comply with modern day fire regulations.

(**21**) .... , very little is known about something most people **SURPRISE**
would consider crucial in a theatre – the (**22**) .... of the **APPEAR**
stage itself. Almost nothing survives from the 1599 Globe to
suggest what it (**23**) .... looked like. The design of the stage **ACTUAL**
people see today was drawn from (**24**) .... provided by **EVIDENT**
existing buildings from the period.

For questions **25–30**, complete the second sentence so that it has a similar meaning to the first sentence, using the word given. **Do not change the word given.** You must use between **two** and **five** words, including the word given. Here is an example (**0**).

Example:

0 I've never seen a film as boring as this one.

SUCH

I've never seen .... as this one.

The gap can be filled by the words 'such a boring film', so you write:

Example: | 0 | SUCH A BORING FILM

Write **only** the missing words **IN CAPITAL LETTERS on the separate answer sheet.**

---

25 The meal cost a lot more than I'd expected.

FAR

The meal .... expensive than I'd expected.

26 Ben watched films on his laptop during the whole journey.

SPENT

Ben .... films on his laptop.

27 They're going to make a film of this book.

MADE

This book is .... a film.

28 'I'm sorry I didn't call yesterday,' Zena said.

APOLOGISED

Zena .... called the day before.

29 I remember my childhood when I smell roses.

REMINDS

The smell .... my childhood.

30 Harry was the only one who didn't bring a camera.

APART

Everybody .... Harry.

PAPER 1 Reading and Use of English ▸
  Part 1
  Part 2
  Part 3
  Part 4
  Part 5
  Part 6
  Part 7
PAPER 2 Writing
PAPER 3 Listening
PAPER 4 Speaking

You are going to read an article about the loss of darkness from our everyday lives. For questions **31–36**, choose the answer (**A, B, C** or **D**) which you think fits best according to the text.

Mark your answers **on the separate answer sheet**.

Bright nights, big problems

Author Paul Bogard discusses why we should turn off the lights and appreciate the dark.

Astronomers rate the darkness of our skies on a scale of 9 (brightest) to 1 (darkest). Most of us spend our lives in the radiance of levels 5 to 8, only rarely venturing into areas ranked 3 or darker. Because of the rapid growth of light pollution over recent decades, most Americans under 40 have never known real darkness. All over the globe our nights are growing brighter, and almost nowhere are they growing darker. We are just beginning to learn the true cost of all this light. Studies increasingly link our overuse of light at night with health concerns such as sleep disorders and disease. Other studies report the damaging ecological consequences, the tremendous waste of energy, and even the decrease in safety and security. But the steady loss of darkness from our lives is not easily measured, for like the similarly endangered qualities of solitude and quiet, the true value of darkness is something we are barely aware of.

Take a brilliantly starry sky. Since the beginning of time, a sky plush with stars was part of the common human experience. Everywhere on Earth, on most nights, our predecessors came face to face with the universe. This experience influenced their beliefs, mythologies, art – their very understanding of their place in the world. Today, because of light pollution, many of us live under skies which are polluted by light. For the tens of millions who live under a night sky showing 25 stars or fewer, it is nearly impossible to imagine a natural sky of some 2,500 individual stars backed by great swathes of uncountable billions. Our night sky continues to shape us, but now it is the absence of the universe around us that influences our beliefs, our myths, our impulse to create. We are being shaped by a diminished experience of darkness, and most of us don't even know what we are missing.

Our Milky Way galaxy is home to several hundred billion stars, and the universe home to several hundred billion other galaxies. A sky wiped clear of stars encourages us to exaggerate our importance, to imagine humanity as the centre of all things. Face to face with the endless immensity of the universe, we have the chance to know how insignificant we really are. But we might also realise the true largeness of our living on this planet, and realise that we have an enormous responsibility to care, that there is no other place to go, that home is here.

line 26 And what of beauty? 'Everyone needs beauty as well as bread,' wrote John Muir, American naturalist and author, and varied degrees of darkness are rich with this. Lighting designers in Paris understand that without darkness, there is no 'city of light', and work constantly to create their city's atmospheric beauty by subtly mixing artificial light with darkness. And with night's moonlit geographies, its scents of desert rain and autumn fires, its pulsing insect symphonies punctuated by a bird's solo call on a northern lake, natural darkness has many offerings of its own.

Yet we live immersed in artificial light. Much of this lighting is wholly unnecessary, born of habit and lack of awareness. So let us become aware: simply by shielding our existing lights we could significantly reduce their negative effects on our body, our mind, our soul. Artificial light at night is a miracle, a wonder, a quality that enriches our lives. But the same has always been true of darkness, and can be again.

31 What does the writer say about lack of darkness in the first paragraph?

    A   It is impossible to reverse its effects.
    B   It is something that many people are unhappy about.
    C   Its effects are something that need to be studied further.
    D   It can be compared with other things that people often fail to appreciate.

32 In the second paragraph, the writer says that because of light pollution we

    A   are considerably less creative than our ancient ancestors were.
    B   experience the world in a different way to previous generations.
    C   are aware that we are missing out on a great natural phenomenon.
    D   need a great deal of imagination in order to understand the universe.

33 What does the writer think about us/humans in the third paragraph?

    A   We ignore the need to look after our planet.
    B   We have an over-confident belief in our own value.
    C   We behave as though nothing exists apart from ourselves.
    D   We prefer to avoid thinking too deeply about our role on Earth.

34 What does 'this' refer to in line 26?

    A   beauty
    B   darkness
    C   variety
    D   lighting

35 Why does the writer include references to rain, fires and wildlife in the fourth paragraph?

    A   to describe what he enjoys least about night-time
    B   to explain why he some people think that lighting is necessary at night
    C   to provide an example of the attractive qualities of night-time
    D   to highlight the differences between urban and natural environments

36 In the final paragraph, we understand that the writer is

    A   irritated by people's lack of interest in darkness.
    B   understanding of the reasons why artificial light is essential.
    C   keen to draw comparisons between artificial light and darkness.
    D   hopeful that people are becoming aware of the negative impact of light.

PAPER 1 Reading and Use of English	Part 1
	Part 2
	Part 3
PAPER 2 Writing	Part 4
PAPER 3 Listening	Part 5
PAPER 4 Speaking	**Part 6**
	Part 7

You are going to read an article about chimpanzees and team work. Six sentences have been removed from the article. Choose from the sentences **A–G** the one which fits each gap (**37–42**). There is one extra sentence which you do not need to use.

Mark your answers **on the separate answer sheet**.

Chimps can be team players, too!

Maryann Mott reports on how chimps help each other – or not.

Providing help, without any benefit to yourself, is called altruism, and some scientists have proposed that it is a uniquely human behaviour. But two recent studies suggest that chimps may also lend a hand in human-like ways.

In the first study, researchers looked at altruistic behaviour in both 18-month-old human infants and young chimpanzees. Various scenes were acted out for the young in which an unknown adult had trouble achieving a goal. **37** Ten different situations were presented to 24 infants and three chimpanzees raised by humans.

The results showed that almost all of the children helped at least once and did so almost immediately. **38** They helped in all five tasks involving reaching, but not in more complex situations, like those involving physical obstacles.

The researchers believe both children and chimps are willing to help but that they differ in their abilities to interpret when help is needed. It has been claimed chimpanzees act mainly for their own ends, but in the experiment there was no reward, and they still helped. Anne Pusey, director of a university research centre which studies primates, says that helping depends on environment.' **39** ' As an example she points to a study that showed chimpanzee mothers did not assist their infants in learning how to catch insects called termites, which chimps like to eat. 'You would think that mothers watching their kids failing to get termites out of a mound might do this, but in fact they did not,' she said. Chimps raised by humans are considered by some to be behaviourally different from those which aren't, Pusey said. This might explain why the study's chimps offered help.

In a second study, researchers found that chimpanzees recognised when collaboration was necessary and chose effective partners. The researchers had never seen this level of understanding during cooperation in any other animal except humans. In the experiment, which took place at a chimpanzee sanctuary in Africa, two chimps had to pull a rope at the same time in order to drag a tray of food toward them. The researchers found that the chimpanzees only let a partner into the room, by opening a door, when the rope ends were too far apart to pull on their own. **40**

Just like people, some chimps were better cooperators than others. For example, a dominant chimpanzee, named Mawa, was impatient and missed opportunities to get the food. But another, named Bwambale, was a team player and was almost always successful. **41** But once they learned what a hopeless cooperator Mawa was, most chimps chose Bwambale in the next trial. The researchers concluded that clearly chimps could remember who was a good and who was a bad collaborator. Bad collaborators suffer by not being chosen next time.

The researchers also pointed out that there is no evidence that chimpanzees communicate with each other about a common goal like children do. **42** The studies just suggest that when chimpanzees cooperate they understand a bit more than was previously thought. Hopefully, future studies can show us what it is that makes human cooperation so unique.

A Neither can they learn how good a partner is by watching him or her interact with others.

B Not only did they know when they needed help, but they went out to get it.

C The chimps demonstrated similar, though less strong, motivation.

D This was a characteristic that wasn't even displayed by the humans involved in the study.

E At first the other chimps in the study chose them equally for help.

F These included things like stretching to get an object or stacking books.

G For example, in the wild, related chimps rarely help one another.

PAPER 1 Reading and
          Use of English
PAPER 2 Writing
PAPER 3 Listening
PAPER 4 Speaking

Part 1
Part 2
Part 3
Part 4
Part 5
Part 6
Part 7

You are going to read an article about four people who enjoy different forms of dance. For question **43–52**, choose from the people (**A–D**). The people may be chosen more than once.

Write your answers **on the separate answer sheet**.

Which person

says that her dance includes challenging movements from a different form of exercise?	43
says that dancing is the physical representation of her feelings?	44
appreciates the fact her dance form helps her to switch off from everyday routine?	45
admits that what first appealed about her dance form became less important over time?	46
enjoys the ability to use her creative skills more than anything else?	47
is keen to explain why her dance form should be recognised in the dance world?	48
compares herself to an artist in a different field from dance?	49
realised that her dance form required harder work than she'd expected?	50
was attracted to the dance form because of its modern appearance?	51
is pleased that she put so much into achieving her current status?	52

The challenge of dance

Four professional dancers talk about the forms of dance they love.

A Eva Smolienko: ballet dancer

I won't pretend the idea of wearing a tutu and satin shoes wasn't what attracted me to ballet as a girl, but through the years of demanding training that helped me become a ballerina, wearing beautiful costumes faded into insignificance, as love for the art form itself took over from the desire to look pretty. And far from skipping about pretending to be a butterfly, I discovered to my disappointment that ballet requires an enormous amount of self-discipline in order to meet its physical demands and mental challenges. Committing to ballet meant developing critical thinking skills, becoming musically aware and building stamina. The route to the fancy dresses was tough, involving anti-social hours, strain on the body, and intense mental focus. But the effort paid off, and I wouldn't have had it any other way, because I truly appreciate where I am today as a principal dancer in the company.

B Cherry Proctor: tap dancer

It was without doubt the percussive element of tap dance that attracted me to it, and I love the sound the metal on the shoes makes when it strikes the floor. I've always been attracted to rhythm and movement, and tap dance is the perfect combination of these. As a tap dancer I consider myself a musician, as essentially, I'm making music with my feet. Tap's fast and furious, and terrifically tricky, but the rewards that come with mastering the skill are worth all the effort of battling to get your head, or rather, feet, around the complicated beat patterns and speed. It's like my feet become musical instruments when I dance. Tap is excellent for developing coordination and mine has improved enormously. It also concentrates the mind when you're involved in performing challenging routines, which is certainly a welcome release from the pressures of daily life.

C Jenny Hardcastle: contemporary dancer

The fact that contemporary dance is an expressive dance form which combines several other forms is why I find it so fascinating. Contemporary dance focuses on the connection between mind and body, and nothing is more satisfying than exploring movement and making up my own dance sequences. Contemporary dance is more flexible and free than traditional dance forms like ballet, though like ballet, it helps the dancer work on balance and strength, as well as being aware of the space around them. Dancers aim for fluid movements and allow gravity to pull them to the floor – there's lots of floor work involved. When I'm dancing, I use my body to express my deepest emotions, from sadness to joy. Sometimes I feel exhausted afterwards, but I also feel as though a weight has been lifted from my shoulders.

D Tamara Whitely: street dancer

Street dance is still relatively new and it therefore comes under close examination from the critics in its field. But I would argue that there are elements of techniques and styles from all kinds of older disciplines wrapped up in street dance. Street is a loosely-structured form of dance and what first appealed to me was its 'street cred'. In other words, it's current, and it looks cool. It's easy to make the mistake of thinking that because it looks so unstructured, there's little real skill involved but that couldn't be further from the truth. While it may not conform to the strict principles of dances such as ballet, its choreography can be really quite complex. It often makes use of gymnastic elements which require strength, agility and coordination, which, as I found out, are not the easiest skills to acquire.

PAPER 1 Reading and
            Use of English

PAPER 2 Writing ▶   Part 1
                                    Part 2

PAPER 3 Listening

PAPER 4 Speaking

You **must** answer this question. Write your answer in **140–190** words in an appropriate style.

1 In your English class you have been talking about the importance of studying different subjects. Now your English teacher has asked you to write an essay.

Write your essay using **all** the notes and give reasons for your point of view.

Some people say it's a waste of time studying
subjects they are not interested in.

What do you think?

Notes
Write about:

1. passing on knowledge to others
2. talking to other people
3. .... (your own idea)

PAPER 1 Reading and
         Use of English

PAPER 2 Writing ▶   Part 1
                               Part 2
PAPER 3 Listening

PAPER 4 Speaking

Write an answer to **one** of the questions 2–5 in this part. Write your answer in
140–190 words in an appropriate style.

2   This is part of an email you have received from your English friend Sara.

> **From:** Sara
> **Subject:** My school project
>
> I'm doing a school project about how life has changed since our
> grandparents' generation. My grandparents grew up in the same town
> as me, but their life was really different from mine. How was your
> grandparents' life different to yours? Do you think life was better then,
> or now? I'd love to know more!
>
> Best wishes,
>
> Sara

Write your **email**.

3   You see this announcement in an English-language magazine.

> **Articles wanted – The difference between people**
>
> Do you think the world would be a boring place if everyone was the
> same? What makes people different from each other, and why does this
> make life more interesting? Tell us what you think.
>
> The best articles will be printed in our magazine next month.

Write your **article**.

4   Your English teacher has asked you to write a report about social activities in your
town which people can do for free. In your report, you should describe what free
activities are available and recommend the best ones for families to do together.

Write your **report**.

5   (*for FIRST FOR SCHOOLS candidates only*)

Answer the following question based on the set text you have read.

Your English class has had a discussion about the main characters in the book you
have read. Now your English teacher has asked you to write this essay for homework.

*Write about two of the main characters in the book you have read. Describe the
two characters and say what makes them similar and different from each other.
Which character are you most like?*

Write your **essay**.

Track 13

You will hear people talking in eight different situations. For questions **1–8**, choose the best answer (**A**, **B** or **C**).

1   You hear a woman talking about her driving instructor.
    What does she say about him?
    A   He sometimes talks too much.
    B   He has improved her confidence.
    C   He is good at explaining things.

2   You hear two friends talking about online learning.
    They agree that
    A   it is becoming very popular.
    B   it is an option some people can benefit from.
    C   it is not as good as other ways of learning.

3   You hear two colleagues talking about body language in job interviews.
    The man thinks that body language
    A   should be taken into account.
    B   can sometimes be misleading.
    C   is more important than people realise.

4   You hear a woman talking on the radio about a local chess club.
    What is she doing?
    A   reassuring potential new members
    B   explaining how competitions are run
    C   announcing a change of venue

5   You hear two friends discussing recycling.
    What opinion does the man express about recycling?
    A   People should make more of an effort to recycle things.
    B   It does not make sense to recycle most materials.
    C   There might be better ways to be environmentally friendly.

6   You hear a student talking about his English literature course.
    How does he feel now?
    A   relieved to have got onto the course he originally chose
    B   pleased to be in a seminar group with nice students
    C   eager to get feedback on his written work

7   You hear a woman talking about a new fabric her company is producing.
    What does she say about the fabric?
    A   It is remarkably cheap.
    B   It has taken a long time to develop.
    C   It will be used in many different ways.

8   You hear two friends talking about a problem caused by some plants.
    What does the man think about the problem?
    A   It will be impossible to solve.
    B   Its extent has been exaggerated.
    C   It is entirely caused by birds.

Track 14

You will hear an artist called Lukas Royle, who makes pictures in glass, talking about his life and work. For questions **9–18**, complete the sentences with a word or short phrase.

Making pictures in glass

Lukas says his parents wanted him to be a (**9**) ....

Lukas was inspired to become a glass artist when he saw a window in a

(**10**) .... centre.

Lukas' (**11**) .... encouraged him to go to art school.

Lukas got a job making glass (**12**) ....

while he was still a student.

After he graduated, Lukas was able to buy his own

(**13**) ....

A famous (**14**) .... bought some of Lukas' work at an

exhibition.

A journalist wrote a good review of Lucas' work for an arts

(**15**) ....

Lukas started to focus on (**16**) .... in his work.

At the moment Lukas is working on a window for a

(**17**) .... factory.

When Lukas isn't working he likes going

(**18**) .... with his friends.

Track 15

You will hear five short extracts in which professional tennis coaches are talking about their work. For questions **19–23**, choose from the list (**A–H**) what each speaker says. Use the letters only once. There are three extra letters which you do not need to use.

A I am honest about my mistakes.

B I can choose who I'm going to coach.

C I find the daily schedule demanding.

D I enjoy all the travelling involved.

E I've learned to hide what I'm thinking.

F I try not to push anyone further than they can manage.

G I have little time to spend with my family.

H I prefer working with difficult people.

Speaker 1	19
Speaker 2	20
Speaker 3	21
Speaker 4	22
Speaker 5	23

FIRST
TEST 4

Exam Essentials

PAPER 1 Reading and
Use of English

PAPER 2 Writing

PAPER 3 Listening ▶
Part 1
Part 2
Part 3
Part 4

PAPER 4 Speaking

Track 16

You will hear an interview with a concert violinist called Barry Green. For questions 24–30, choose the best answer (**A**, **B** or **C**).

24 Why did Barry become a professional violinist?
   A He was inspired by seeing other people play.
   B His parents thought it would be a good career.
   C He realised he was unable to play football professionally.

25 What does Barry say about his life at school?
   A It was difficult for him to find time to do his homework.
   B He was fortunate to find academic work relatively easy.
   C There was little understanding of his desire to be a violinist.

26 What did Barry do after leaving school?
   A He went straight to music college.
   B He studied different subjects for a year.
   C He travelled with other young musicians.

27 What does Barry say about going to music college?
   A He enjoyed the opportunity to take up another instrument.
   B He felt he was more talented than the other students.
   C He found it hard to adjust to the discipline.

28 Why did Barry start playing in public concerts?
   A He wanted the opportunity to play violin solos.
   B He was asked to after doing well in a competition.
   C He knew some of the musicians in the local orchestra.

29 What disadvantage of his current life does Barry mention?
   A He sometimes forgets what he is supposed to play.
   B He feels stressed when there are too many people on stage.
   C He has little time to visit the places where he gives concerts.

30 What does Barry say is positive about his professional life?
   A He appreciates having been able to fulfil his ambition.
   B He has the opportunity to spend time with interesting people.
   C He has a job that will keep him comfortable in retirement.

Part 1 (2 minutes)

The examiner (interlocutor) will ask each of you to speak briefly in turn and to give personal information about yourselves. You can expect a variety of questions, such as:

What sort of things do you like to do while you're on holiday? (Why?)
What did you do on your last holiday? (Did you enjoy it?)
What are you planning to do when you next have a few days off work / college / school? (Why?)

Part 2 (4 minutes)

You will each be asked to talk for a minute without interruption. You will each be given two different photographs in turn to talk about. After your partner has finished speaking, you will be asked a brief question connected with your partner's photographs.

1 Playing music

Look at the two photographs on page 168 which show people playing music in different ways.

Candidate A, compare these photographs, and say why you think the people enjoy playing music in these different ways.

Candidate B, which of these kinds of music would you prefer to listen to? (Why?)

2 Running

Look at the two photographs on page 169 which show people running in different situations.

Candidate B, compare these photographs, and say what you think the people enjoy about running in these different situations.

Candidate A, which of these ways of running do you think is more enjoyable? (Why?)

Part 3 (4 minutes)

You will be asked to discuss something together without interruption by the examiner. You will have a page of ideas and a question to help you.

Places to visit

I'd like you to imagine that a college is organising a day out for students in an English class. Turn to page 170 which has ideas for different places students can visit on a day out. Talk to each other about the advantages of visiting each place. Then decide which **two** of the places you think would the best ones for the students to visit.

Part 4 (4 minutes)

The examiner will encourage you to develop the topic of your discussion in Part 3 by asking questions such as:

Do you think students learn more in the classroom or when they are out on day trips? (Why?)
What are the most enjoyable ways of learning? (Why?)
Do you think people learn more when they are having fun? (Why / Why not?)
How were schools in your country different 50 years ago?
How do you think schools will change in the future? (What would be the advantages / disadvantages of these changes?)

PAPER 1 Reading and Use of English

▸▸ **PART 5**

radiance (n) brightness

venture (v) to dare to do or go

rank (v) to put in order

solitude (n) the state of being completely alone, especially when this is relaxing or enjoyable

plush with (phr) full of, in a luxurious or impressive way

mythology (n) a collection of myths (ancient traditional stories)

swathe (n) a large number of

impulse (n) a strong feeling that you must do something

diminish (v) to become less or smaller

pulsing (adj) regularly moving or making a sound in short bursts, like a heart beat

punctuated (adj) interrupted

immersed (adj) totally surrounded by

shield (v) to protect or cover

▸▸ **PART 6**

lend a hand (phr) to help

obstacle (n) something that makes it hard for you to do something, or an object that you must move or go around in order to move forward

collaboration (n) the process of working together with others to achieve something

sanctuary (n) a special area where animals live in a natural environment where they are protected from people or danger

dominant (adj) more important, powerful or stronger than the other people, animals or things of the same type

trial (n) a test

stack (v) to arrange in a pile, one thing on top of another

▸▸ **PART 7**

tutu (n) a short skirt worn by a female ballet dancer

insignificance (n) of no importance

skip (v) to leap or jump lightly

self-discipline (n) the ability to control your own behaviour so that you do what you think you should be doing

commit (v) to make a firm decision to do something

critical thinking (phr) judging and analysing

stamina (n) the ability to work hard or make a lot of physical or mental effort over long periods

anti-social (adj) not sociable, making it difficult to meet people and live a normal life

intense (n) very great or extreme

focus (n) concentration

percussive (adj) relating to percussion (striking two things together, like a stick and a drum)

fast and furious (phr) lively and exciting

terrifically (adv) very

master (v) to become extremely good at

coordination (n) the ability to use parts of the body together well

expressive (adj) something which enables you to show your feelings

sequence (n) a series of steps

fluid (adj) smooth

gravity (n) the force that attracts objects to the earth

principle (n) rule

choreography (n) the sequence of steps in a dance

agility (n) ability to move the body quickly and effectively

PAPER 1	Reading and ▶	Part 1
	Use of English	Part 2
PAPER 2	Writing	Part 3
		Part 4
PAPER 3	Listening	Part 5
PAPER 4	Speaking	Part 6
		Part 7

For questions **1–8**, read the text below and decide which answer (**A**, **B**, **C** or **D**) best fits each gap. There is an example at the beginning (**0**).

Mark your answers **on the separate answer sheet**.

Example:

0 **A** get   **B** bring   **C** call   **D** draw

0	A	B	C	D

Flowers from a 32,000-year-old seed!

We may not be able to (**0**) …….. dinosaurs back to life yet, but how about a flower? In 2012, flowering plants native to Siberia, in Russia, were grown from 32,000 year-old seeds, (**1**) …….. the previous record-holder by 30,000 years. Scientists found a number of seeds, probably buried by an ice-age squirrel, by the (**2**) …….. of the river Kolyma. The seeds, which were (**3**) …….. encased in ice, were dug up from 38 metres below the permafrost. Some of them had been (**4**) …….. , possibly by the squirrel itself, but others had the (**5**) …….. to generate new plants.

The scientists extracted plant tissue from the frozen seeds, and successfully germinated the plants. They grew, flowered, and after a year created seeds of their own. They were (**6**) …….. to each other but with different flower shapes from the modern (**7**) …….. of the same species. Experts say these results (**8**) …….. that any number of extinct plant species could now be found and grown again.

1	**A** succeeding	**B** gaining	**C** beating	**D** winning
2	**A** borders	**B** margins	**C** limits	**D** banks
3	**A** absolutely	**B** entirely	**C** properly	**D** utterly
4	**A** hurt	**B** damaged	**C** injured	**D** harmed
5	**A** expectation	**B** likelihood	**C** potential	**D** possibility
6	**A** identical	**B** same	**C** matching	**D** alike
7	**A** version	**B** type	**C** format	**D** style
8	**A** determine	**B** point	**C** indicate	**D** direct

PAPER 1 Reading and
         Use of English

PAPER 2 Writing

PAPER 3 Listening

PAPER 4 Speaking

Part 1
Part 2
Part 3
Part 4
Part 5
Part 6
Part 7

For questions **9–16**, read the text below and think of the word which best fits each gap. Use only **one** word in each gap. There is an example at the beginning (**0**).

Write your answers **IN CAPITAL LETTERS on the separate answer sheet**.

Example: 0 L I K E

My first day at university

My first day at university was rather (**0**) .... my first day at primary school, but without a helpful teacher to look after me. (**9**) .... I'd visited the campus before, and had a map, (**10**) .... took me 20 minutes to find my classroom. Everyone else seemed as lost as I was, so there was (**11**) .... point asking them for directions. Finally I saw a girl who looked as (**12**) .... she knew where she was going, so I asked her where room C25 was. (**13**) .... my surprise and relief, she was going there too, and we ended up having coffee in the student café together after the introductory talk. (**14**) .... had struck me about her when I'd first approached her was (**15**) .... confident she appeared, but she told me she was actually as nervous as I was! As we were on the same course, we spent the rest of the day together. We got (**16**) .... so well that now we're firm friends.

PAPER 1 Reading and ▶
           Use of English
PAPER 2 Writing
PAPER 3 Listening
PAPER 4 Speaking

Part 1
Part 2
Part 3
Part 4
Part 5
Part 6
Part 7

For questions **17–24**, read the text below. Use the word given in capitals at the end of some of the lines to form a word that fits the gap **in the same line**. There is an example at the beginning (**0**).

Write your answers **IN CAPITAL LETTERS on the separate answer sheet**.

Example: | 0 | S | A | Y | I | N | G | | | | | | | | | | | | | |

Elephants really don't forget

'Elephants never forget' is an old (**0**) .... that is supported   **SAY**
by evidence. It is (**17**) .... true of the matriarch – the   **PARTICULAR**
dominant female who leads each herd. These (**18**) ....   **POWER**
females develop a social memory over time, helping them
remember whether an outsider is a friend or an enemy.

The matriarch's (**19**) .... enables the group to feed and   **KNOW**
breed without fear: she will immediately signal to the rest of
the herd if danger is close by. This is essential for (**20**) .... :   **SURVIVE**
when elephants encounter an outside threat, they bunch
together to defend the group – so the matriarch's (**21**) .... is   **WARN**
vital for the herd's young.

The wiser and more (**22**) .... the matriarch, the more likely   **EXPERIENCE**
it is that a herd will produce more calves. The herd must
(**23**) .... that she stays close by: if she were separated   **SURE**
from the group, this would have a (**24**) .... impact on the   **CONSIDER**
reproductive capabilities of her family.

PAPER 1	Reading and Use of English ▶	Part 1
		Part 2
		Part 3
		Part 4
PAPER 2	Writing	Part 5
PAPER 3	Listening	Part 6
PAPER 4	Speaking	Part 7

For questions **25–30**, complete the second sentence so that it has a similar meaning to the first sentence, using the word given. **Do not change the word given.** You must use between **two** and **five** words, including the word given. Here is an example (**0**).

Example:

0 I've never seen a film as boring as this one.

SUCH

I've never seen .... as this one.

The gap can be filled by the words 'such a boring film', so you write:

Example: | **0** | SUCH A BORING FILM |

Write **only** the missing words **IN CAPITAL LETTERS on the separate answer sheet**.

---

25 The officials decided to postpone the match until a later date.

OFF

The match .... until a later date.

26 'I've never written an essay as good as this', said Mark.

BEST

Mark said it was .... ever written.

27 Naoko arrived late and she forgot her passport, too.

ONLY

Not .... late, but she also forgot her passport.

28 I believe Dennis is the best player on the team.

CONCERNED

As .... , Dennis is the best player in the team.

29 I haven't done any exercise for two weeks.

LAST

The .... any exercise was two weeks ago.

30 There's no way I can meet the deadline on this project.

IMPOSSIBLE

It's .... the deadline on this project.

PAPER 1	Reading and ▸	Part 1
	Use of English	Part 2
PAPER 2	Writing	Part 3
		Part 4
PAPER 3	Listening	**Part 5**
PAPER 4	Speaking	Part 6
		Part 7

You are going to read an article about why people put off doing things. For questions **31–36**, choose the answer (**A, B, C** or **D**) which you think fits best according to the text.

Mark your answers **on the separate answer sheet**.

Don't put it off, do it now!

Procrastination – or avoiding doing the jobs we know we should be doing – is a common problem.

Why do we spend so much of our time not doing the work we should be doing, or putting off minor tasks that have since piled up to create one enormous, insurmountable obstacle? Procrastinating, as putting things off like this is called, is in our genetic make-up; we avoid dull or difficult jobs, opting to browse the internet instead, until it's too late to do anything else. Some people, a fortunate and focused minority, seem born with the ability to just get on with things, but what about the rest of us?

'We often put things off despite knowing that it will make life harder and more stressful,' says Dr Piers Steel, the author of a book on procrastination and an authority on the science of motivation. 'If these tasks were fun, we'd just do them now, but we put off what is difficult or unpleasant.' Such as the paperwork that needs doing before leaving the office or cleaning the bits of your home that people can't see.

'You can put off anything,' Dr Steel continues. 'But we know that we really should get on and do these things. The fact is, the less people procrastinate, the more money they have, the better relationships they have, and the healthier they are.' This is obvious when you look at the couples who don't argue about whether anyone has cleaned the kitchen yet, the young go-getters who rise straight to the top at work, the health freaks who simply go for that run instead of endlessly rescheduling it in their own heads. And then, of course, there are the rest of us, who feel the chores piling up around us daily.

'We've evolved to respond to the moment, and not to set our sights too far in an uncertain world,' Dr Steel adds. 'We are not set up to appreciate long-term rewards, whether it's the benefit of a four-year degree, doing exercise or dieting. You feel the cost now and the reward comes much later. But humans value the short term.' Procrastination is often associated with unhappiness, so now is the time to unlearn your time-wasting techniques and work-avoidance tactics. 'You have two decision-making systems in your brain,' Dr Steel says, 'the limbic, which is responsible for the short term, and the prefrontal cortex, which deals with the future – it's responsible for civilisation. We bounce between long-term goals and short-term temptations, so we need goals that will translate our plans for the limbic system.'

line 24 For example, take students writing dissertations: they set themselves targets and word counts per day. These are thus turned from seemingly endless tasks into something concrete with easily measured progress. Dr Steel recommends such techniques, or 'pre-commitments', adding that engaging yourself and others a month or so before the 'deadline' makes it more likely a task will be completed. The added benefit is that you will want to avoid the embarrassment of not following up on something people are expecting you to do – telling everyone you are going to take up jogging makes you more likely to do so.

Overcoming procrastination ultimately comes down to planning, which, if you're not careful, becomes procrastination in itself. But it's worth making sure you have everything in place to change your strategies for the better – a separate computer log-on screen for work and for play, the former with a plain background, fewer applications and limited internet access. If you wish to check your personal emails, make sure they're a log-out, rather than a click, away and remember every time you disengage, that it takes 15 minutes fully to re-immerse yourself in the task at hand.

'Successful people don't pretend they don't procrastinate,' Dr Steel says. 'People who pretend they have willpower are less successful.' Instead, plan for procrastination: make your work environment a temple of productivity by cutting out all distractions, so you can really focus on moving forward.

31 What does the writer say about procrastinating in the first paragraph?

    A It is something people use as an excuse.
    B It is something many people can't help.
    C It is caused by the technology in people's lives.
    D It is more common when people have small jobs to do.

32 What is the writer's main point in the third paragraph?

    A There are plenty of examples that support Dr Steel's claims.
    B It is hard to understand people who manage not to put things off.
    C Dr Steel had difficulty finding people who never procrastinate.
    D Research shows that successful people enjoy their work.

33 In the fourth paragraph, Dr Steel says that people who procrastinate should

    A find out more about the way they make decisions.
    B be aware that their problem is relatively small.
    C attempt to overcome their natural tendencies.
    D take the advice of others in the same situation.

34 What does 'these' refer to in line 24?

    A students
    B dissertations
    C targets
    D word counts

35 Why does Dr Steel recommend making 'pre-commitments'?

    A They are an alternative to impossible goals.
    B They are an effective way of impressing others.
    C They allow people to achieve their aims sooner.
    D They make challenges feel more manageable.

36 What does the writer do in the sixth paragraph?

    A reminds the reader to take the time to focus properly on a task
    B warns the reader against spending too long getting organised
    C advises the reader to deal with non-work tasks quickly
    D encourages the reader to use breaks effectively

PAPER 1	Reading and ▶	Part 1
	Use of English	Part 2
PAPER 2	Writing	Part 3
		Part 4
PAPER 3	Listening	Part 5
PAPER 4	Speaking	**Part 6**
		Part 7

You are going to read an article about runners who also write blogs and post them on the internet. Six sentences have been removed from the article. Choose from the sentences **A–G** the one which fits each gap (**37–42**). There is one extra sentence which you do not need to use.

Mark your answers **on the separate answer sheet**.

Don't just run … get running and blogging!

There are thousands of running bloggers across the UK, from novice runners to world record holders.

I finished a marathon last month and set an 18-minute personal best. Before I'd written a text to my sister or friends who had asked me to let them know how I'd got on, I sent a message to around 2,000 people that I've never met.

Straightaway, the congratulatory replies came flooding in from all over the world; from people who understood what my achievement meant in terms of hard work, early nights and even earlier morning runs – people who had followed my progress through my blog and had offered encouragement and support. **37** The reply from my sister: 'Well done. That's good, right?'

I've kept a running blog for as long as I've been a runner – around five years – and I'm not the only one. There are thousands of running bloggers or blogging runners across the UK. Runners of all levels. Some people, like me, write for a living. **38** We're all sending out regular updates on our training and racing.

Non-runners struggle to comprehend why anyone would willingly head out on a cold, wet Sunday morning to run around for hours on end. **39** Why would anyone be interested in what you have to say? You're hardly a world-famous runner. Who cares how far you ran yesterday? Stop all the bragging.

Of course, there's money to be made from blogging; there's free stuff too, that brands will dish out to popular bloggers in the hope of a favourable review. **40** What we want to do is to connect with people like ourselves, get inspired by those who are a bit faster and share what we're doing.

With a friend I met through blogging, I recently hosted a conference for running bloggers. Write This Run saw 50 running bloggers come together in London to talk about running and blogging. We had a panel of expert speakers including an Olympic marathon runner and an ultra marathon multi-world record holder, as well as a bag full of free stuff for them all. **41**

Running and blogging can be solitary pursuits. **42** As one of our guests put it: 'It was a bit of a surreal experience – as if some of your favourite storybook characters had suddenly come to life and were in the same room as you! All these people whose faces I knew, whose running journeys I was familiar with, whose lives I caught glimpses of on a daily basis, there, in the flesh, in "3D".'

I believe one of the greatest things the internet can do for us is bring us together. To connect us with other people who like what we like, to share knowledge and experience. And though the connections and friendships we make online are no less valid because they haven't been made in person – when they are taken offline and into the real world it takes them to another level.

A But for all the bloggers I've met, the motivation for reading and writing blogs is simple.

B Others barely do so at all except for their blog.

C But what mattered most to everyone was the coming together.

D That's obvious, because new runners take comfort in the fact that other people have struggled too.

E Not because I'm an elite runner, but because I'm just like them.

F So we invited bloggers across the UK to come out from behind their keyboards and meet up in real life.

G Similarly, it's difficult for people who don't read or write running blogs to see the appeal.

PAPER 1 Reading and ▸ | Part 1
Use of English | Part 2

PAPER 2 Writing | Part 3

| Part 4

PAPER 3 Listening | Part 5

PAPER 4 Speaking | Part 6

Part 7

You are going to read an article in which four people talk about going to the cinema. For questions **43–52**, choose from the people (**A–D**). The people may be chosen more than once.

Mark your answers **on the separate answer sheet**.

Which person

mentions feeling confused at the cinema?	**43**
took advantage of an opportunity someone gave him?	**44**
was persuaded to see a film he didn't enjoy?	**45**
wishes he'd discovered his love of film earlier?	**46**
wanted to research something thoroughly?	**47**
hopes he will be able to turn his interest into a job?	**48**
explains the importance of regular visits he made to the cinema?	**49**
made a surprising discovery?	**50**
regrets taking something for granted?	**51**
states a preference for film over other media?	**52**

Going to the cinema

Four people talk about their experiences of going to see films at the cinema.

A Jonathan

My family went to the cinema every Saturday when I was a child. My parents both worked long hours, so we didn't see much of each other during the week, and going to the local Picture Palace meant a great deal to all of us. The habit stayed with me as I got older, and although I'm a great reader, and a fan of the arts in general, nothing comes close to the feeling I get when I'm fully absorbed in a film. That's not to say I'll watch anything, in fact I'm very critical of bad movies. I saw something just recently I wanted to walk out of, but had to sit through it to the end as a good friend of mine had talked me into going, and was laughing all the way through. When he asked me afterwards what I'd thought about it, I had to choose my words carefully!

B Ivan

Even though I've always loved films, I never went to the cinema much when I was younger – I preferred watching TV with my friends. There used to be three cinemas in the town I grew up in, and I suppose I just thought they'd always be there. They're long gone, of course, replaced by blocks of flats, and now I wish I'd been more often. These days, the nearest cinema is half an hour's drive away from my home. I go as often as I can, because watching a film on a big screen is the only way to truly appreciate it, in my opinion. I took a film studies course in my first year at university, because I'd decided to learn about the cinema industry in depth, and at that time I thought I might like to become a producer myself one day. I'm actually working in the music industry now!

C Liam

My interest in films dates back to a visit to the cinema with my father when I was about nine. We didn't go very often, tending to watch things like nature documentaries on TV at home. He'd picked the film and thought I'd like it because it was a spy drama, which I did, even though I hadn't really got a clue what was going on. There was something wonderful about the sense of occasion, and the thrill of watching a film in a crowd of other people. I was hooked. It also turned out that one of the actors lived in the next street to us, and I'd often seen him in our neighbourhood. I'd never had a clue who he was before then and was very impressed. A few years later, I started writing a film blog, and I'd like to make a living as a film critic one day.

D Simon

My parents rarely went to the cinema, so it was only as a teenager that I started going to the cinema with my friends, and realised what I'd been missing. Sadly, I'll never make up for losing out on the magic of seeing things on the big screen as a young child, but have done my best to make up for it ever since! I got a summer job in our local cinema, which I absolutely loved, because apart from selling tickets, I could see films for free. Then the manager asked me if I'd like to work at a week-long film festival in a neighbouring town. I met all sorts of amazing people with similar interests to mine, and a group of us ended up running our own independent film festival a few years later.

PAPER 1 Reading and
Use of English

PAPER 2 Writing ▶ Part 1
Part 2

PAPER 3 Listening

PAPER 4 Speaking

You **must** answer this question. Write your answer in **140–190** words in an appropriate style.

1 In your English class you have been talking about travel. Now your English teacher has asked you to write an essay.

Write your essay using **all** the notes and give reasons for your point of view.

Some people say they can discover everything about other countries without ever going there, so there's no point in foreign travel these days.

What do you think?

Notes
Write about:

1. making friends with different people
2. finding out about other cultures
3. .... (your own idea)

PAPER 1   Reading and
          Use of English
PAPER 2   Writing   ►
                              Part 1
                              Part 2
PAPER 3   Listening
PAPER 4   Speaking

Write an answer to **one** of the questions **2–5** in this part. Write your answer in **140–190** words in an appropriate style.

2   You see this announcement on an international website.

> **Articles wanted – What makes you laugh?**
>
> What do you think is funny?
> Do your friends and family laugh at the same things as you do?
> What do you think people all over the world might agree is funny?
>
> Write us an article answering these questions. The best articles will be
> posted on our website.

Write your **article**.

3   You see this advertisement in a local English-language newspaper.

> We need someone to help in our busy sports shop this summer.
> Our customers come from all over the world, so speaking English is
> essential. We are looking for people who know about sport, so they can
> give useful advice to customers.
>
> Apply in writing to the manager, Mrs Gina Jones, saying why you
> would be the right person for the job.

Write your **letter**.

4   (*for FIRST candidates only*)

Some English students are coming to visit your college for two days. Your English teacher has asked you to write a report saying what the students should see and do while at the college and suggesting what they could do in the evenings.

Write your **report**.

(*for FIRST FOR SCHOOLS candidates only*)

You have seen this announcement in an English-language magazine for teenagers.

> **Stories wanted**
>
> We are looking for stories for our English-language magazine for
> teenagers. Your story must begin with this sentence:
>
> *When I realised who was next to me on the bus, I just couldn't believe it!*
>
> Your story must include:
> * a phone call
> * a party

Write your **story**.

5   (*for FIRST FOR SCHOOLS candidates only*)

Answer the following question based on the set text you have read.

Write a **review** of the book you have read. Your review should include information about the story and the characters. Would you recommend this book to other people?

PAPER 1 Reading and Use of English

PAPER 2 Writing

PAPER 3 Listening ▶ Part 1

PAPER 4 Speaking

Part 2
Part 3
Part 4

🎧 **Track 17**

You will hear people talking in eight different situations. For questions **1–8**, choose the best answer (**A**, **B** or **C**).

1   You hear two friends talking about a hiking trip.
    What is the man worried about?
    A   lack of adequate climbing experience
    B   lack of oxygen on the mountain
    C   lack of appropriate equipment

2   You hear two students talking about maintaining traditions.
    They agree that
    A   we should come up with new celebrations.
    B   it is important to learn from the past.
    C   too many customs are outdated.

3   You hear two students talking about a website.
    What does the girl think about it?
    A   It is less helpful than she'd hoped.
    B   It is a good place to hold discussions.
    C   Its specialist advice is interesting.

4   You hear a man talking to his friend about the cookery school she runs.
    What are the friends doing?
    A   talking over ways to attract new business
    B   expressing disappointment in a staff member
    C   discussing why the school is successful

5   You hear part of a radio programme about modern zoos.
    The zoo-keeper says that he
    A   understands why some people dislike zoos.
    B   believes animals enjoy their lives in zoos.
    C   encourages people to take part in zoo projects.

6   You hear a football coach talking to his team about winning and losing.
    How does he feel?
    A   surprised that the team feels so positive
    B   proud of the team's recent success
    C   disappointed by his team's behaviour

7   You hear two people talking about a sports event they are organising.
    What is the purpose of their discussion?
    A   to decide how to increase sales of certain tickets
    B   to confirm the timetable of sports events
    C   to reach agreement about entry prices

8   You hear two friends discussing a newspaper article about physics.
    What surprised the man about it?
    A   how interested it made him in the subject
    B   how inspired it made him feel
    C   how excited he was to understand it

PAPER 1 Reading and
         Use of English
PAPER 2 Writing
PAPER 3 Listening   ▶ Part 1
                        Part 2
                        Part 3
                        Part 4
PAPER 4 Speaking

 Track 18

You will hear an online talk by a man called Thomas Booth about how to restore old furniture. For questions **9–18**, complete the sentences with a word or short phrase.

Restoring old furniture

Thomas took a long time to clean the (**9**) ....
on the first item he restored.

Thomas recommends looking for any (**10**) .... on an
item, to find out whether it's valuable.

If the restored item is valuable, Thomas suggests setting yourself a
(**11**) .... before starting work.

Thomas reminds listeners to put a (**12**) .... on every
part to help re-build an item.

According to Thomas, first-time restorers should refer to a
(**13**) .... while working.

Thomas always wears a particular item of clothing, glasses and a
(**14**) .... while he works.

Thomas uses a (**15**) .... to clean
smaller parts of an item.

Thomas was lucky to find a replacement
(**16**) .... the same as one
missing from an item he was working on.

Thomas uses the word '(**17**) ....' to describe an old
finish which doesn't come off easily.

Using a certain tool made from (**18**) ....
will prevent damaging a restoration item.

PAPER 1 Reading and
　　　　　Use of English

PAPER 2 Writing

PAPER 3 Listening ▶

PAPER 4 Speaking

Part 1
Part 2
Part 3
Part 4

🎧 **Track 19**

You will hear five short extracts in which people are talking about leaving school. For questions **19–23**, choose from the list (**A–H**) how each speaker says they felt on their last day at school. Use the letters only once. There are three extra letters which you do not need to use.

A　surprised by one teacher's comments

B　proud to have gained a particular qualification

　　　　　　　　　　　　　　　　　　　　　　Speaker 1　｜　**19**

C　relieved not to have to study further

　　　　　　　　　　　　　　　　　　　　　　Speaker 2　｜　**20**

D　excited about starting work

　　　　　　　　　　　　　　　　　　　　　　Speaker 3　｜　**21**

E　sad to be leaving friends behind

　　　　　　　　　　　　　　　　　　　　　　Speaker 4　｜　**22**

F　impatient to start their next course of study

　　　　　　　　　　　　　　　　　　　　　　Speaker 5　｜　**23**

G　uncertain about what to do next

H　upset to have missed a special ceremony

PAPER 1 Reading and
            Use of English

PAPER 2 Writing

PAPER 3 Listening ▶

PAPER 4 Speaking

Part 1
Part 2
Part 3
Part 4

🎧 **Track 20**

You will hear an interview with a man called Ben Chadwick, who is a mathematician, talking about the work he does. For questions **24–30**, choose the best answer (**A**, **B** or **C**).

24 When people find out Ben is a mathematician, they are
    A interested to find out more about his job.
    B unsure of what they should talk to him about.
    C disappointed he doesn't do what they expected.

25 When asked about the maths–music link, Ben expresses
    A annoyance at people's lack of desire to work hard.
    B understanding of people's hope that a link exists.
    C confusion over some people's fear of maths.

26 When asked for his opinion, Ben says the link between maths and music
    A is not as complex as it first appears.
    B is demonstrated in schoolwork results.
    C is different to what people might expect.

27 To prove that mathematicians are better than other people at music, Ben will
    A research mathematicians' backgrounds.
    B consider who to involve in a study.
    C learn more about music himself.

28 What does Ben want to know about mathematicians who play the piano?
    A which structures they prefer music to have
    B why they prefer the piano to other instruments
    C which composers' music they would rather play

29 When comparing maths and languages, Ben says that people
    A find the connection between them uninteresting.
    B think languages are more emotional than maths.
    C prefer studying languages to maths.

30 What does Ben say about liking maths?
    A He enjoys discovering the truth.
    B He wants to inspire other people.
    C He finds it a good mental challenge.

Part 1 (2 minutes)

The examiner (interlocutor) will ask each of you to speak briefly in turn and to give personal information about yourselves. You can expect a variety of questions, such as:

What kind of events do you celebrate with your family and friends?
What do you do to celebrate special occasions?
Do you enjoy large or small celebrations? (Why?)
What's the last celebration you had? (Did you enjoy it?)

Part 2 (4 minutes)

You will each be asked to talk for a minute without interruption. You will each be given two different photographs in turn to talk about. After your partner has finished speaking, you will be asked a brief question connected with your partner's photographs.

1 Helping others

Look at the two photographs on page 171 which show people helping each other in different ways.

Candidate A, compare these photographs, and say why you think the people have chosen to help others in these different ways.

Candidate B, what things do you do to help other people?

2 Reading

Look at the two photographs on page 172 which show people reading.

Candidate B, compare these photographs, and say why you think the people have chosen to read these different things.

Candidate A, which do you prefer to read? (Why?)

Part 3 (4 minutes)

You will be asked to discuss something together without interruption by the examiner. You will have a page of ideas and a question to help you.

English classes

Imagine your teacher has asked you to think of ways to improve your English classroom. Turn to page 173 which shows some ideas for how your classroom could be improved. Talk to each other about how useful each improvement might be for students studying English in your classroom. Then decide which **two** of the improvements you think should be made to your classroom.

Part 4 (4 minutes)

The examiner will encourage you to develop the topic of your discussion in Part 3 by asking questions such as:

What other improvements could be made to an English classroom?
What is the main reason people learn English in your country?
Do you think English should be a compulsory subject at school?
What benefits are there of learning a foreign language?
Do you think it's better to learn a language in the country where it's spoken? (Why / Why not?)
What other things can you do to improve your English?

▶▶ **PART 5**

insurmountable (adj) impossible to overcome

genetic make-up (n) the way DNA is arranged in a human body

browse (v) to look for information, especially on a computer

motivation (n) a feeling of enthusiasm or interest that makes someone want to do something

go-getter (n) someone who takes opportunities and works hard

freak (n) someone who behaves in a strange way

reschedule (v) to change the date or time of something

chore (n) an ordinary or boring job that must be done regularly

set our sights (phr) aim for

dissertation (n) a long essay which a student must write in order to obtain a degree

concrete (adj) real, defined

disengage (v) to take your mind off, or stop thinking about something

(re-)immerse yourself (v) to completely focus your attention on one thing (again)

at hand (phr) that you are currently working on)

▶▶ **PART 6**

novice (adj) someone who is just beginning to learn a skill or subject

best (n) highest achievement

blog (n) regular comment article, written online

comprehend (v) to understand

head out (phr v) to set off

brag (v) to boast, to proudly tell people what you have done

brand (n) the official identity of a company

dish out (phr) give

host (v) to organise (an event) and/or invite people (to an event)

panel (n) group of invited speakers

solitary pursuit (phr) activity that you do on your own

surreal (adj) unreal, not normal

glimpse (n) a brief view of something

in the flesh (phr) in person, present here and now

valid (adj) genuine

take to another level (phr) make even better

appeal (n) attraction

elite (adj) one of the best

▶▶ **PART 7**

talked me into (phr) persuaded me to

choose my words carefully (phr) to think carefully about what to say

to be long gone (phr) to have disappeared a long time ago

on a big screen (phr) in the cinema

in depth (phr) in a lot of detail

pick (v) to choose

have not got a clue (phr) to have no idea

thrill (n) excitement

hooked (adj) so attracted to, or interested in something that you want to do it all the time

blog (n) regular comment article, written online

PAPER 1	Reading and Use of English	▶	Part 1
			Part 2
PAPER 2	Writing		Part 3
			Part 4
PAPER 3	Listening		Part 5
			Part 6
PAPER 4	Speaking		Part 7

For questions **1–8**, read the text below and decide which answer (**A**, **B**, **C** or **D**) best fits each gap. There is an example at the beginning (**0**).

Mark your answers **on the separate answer sheet**.

Example:

0 **A** mutter   **B** speak   **C** praise   **D** threaten

0	**A**	B	C	D

Why we don't like the sound of our own voice

'That doesn't sound like me ...' This is what many of us (**0**) .... when we hear our recorded voices. Well, yes, it does – and it's what everyone else hears, too.

When someone speaks to us, or we hear a recording of our voice, the sound is air-conducted. Sounds (**1**) .... on the air are transmitted through our eardrums, making the small bones in our inner ears (**2**) .... In turn, these vibrations are (**3**) .... by our brains.

When we speak, the sound doesn't all enter our ears from the outside, and what we hear is (**4**) .... different. The vibrations are sent directly to our inner ear, and as they travel, their frequency is lowered.

The reason our recorded voice doesn't (**5**) .... us is that we've grown up hearing ourselves in a (**6**) .... way, so it's difficult to (**7**) .... that isn't how we sound to the outside world. We've (**8**) .... got used to what we sound like inside.

1	**A** carried	**B** travelled	**C** fetched	**D** reached
2	**A** wave	**B** beat	**C** bounce	**D** tremble
3	**A** decided	**B** interpreted	**C** explained	**D** settled
4	**A** likely	**B** hardly	**C** slightly	**D** little
5	**A** please	**B** cheer	**C** invite	**D** tempt
6	**A** thorough	**B** right	**C** particular	**D** real
7	**A** approve	**B** agree	**C** allow	**D** accept
8	**A** well	**B** simply	**C** quite	**D** mostly

PAPER 1	Reading and ▸	Part 1
	Use of English	Part 2
PAPER 2	Writing	Part 3
		Part 4
PAPER 3	Listening	Part 5
PAPER 4	Speaking	Part 6
		Part 7

For questions **9–16**, read the text below and think of the word which best fits each gap. Use only **one** word in each gap. There is an example at the beginning (**0**).

Write your answers **IN CAPITAL LETTERS on the separate answer sheet**.

Example: `0` `B` `E` `E` `N`

What's in a colour?

Psychologists have long (**0**) …….. aware that our emotions are affected by colour. Certain colours are thought to have (**9**) …….. calming effect, while others are said to stimulate our appetite or make us feel more positive.

The fact that certain colours trigger particular feelings (**10**) …….. led to institutions, companies and artists using colour to influence (**11**) …….. way we feel. For example, relaxing colours might be applied to hospital walls; colours encouraging us (**12**) …….. eat faster might be used in fast food restaurants; and colours (**13**) …….. inspire confidence might be incorporated into a company logo.

Colours have different meanings culturally. The colour red is a symbol (**14**) …….. love, passion or danger in some societies, whereas in others, it may represent happiness and good luck. Yellow can make us feel joy or sadness, depending on where we live in the world. (**15**) …….. remains the same wherever we live is that colours do have an effect on us, (**16**) …….. we're aware of it or not.

PAPER 1	Reading and ▸	Part 1
	Use of English	Part 2
PAPER 2	Writing	**Part 3**
		Part 4
PAPER 3	Listening	Part 5
PAPER 4	Speaking	Part 6
		Part 7

For questions **17–24**, read the text below. Use the word given in capitals at the end of some of the lines to form a word that fits the gap **in the same line**. There is an example at the beginning (**0**).

Write your answers **IN CAPITAL LETTERS on the separate answer sheet**.

Example: | 0 | K | N | O | W | N | | | | | | | | | | | | | | |

The Challenger Deep

Our planet's deepest (**0**) …….. place is called the Challenger   **KNOW**
Deep, nearly 11 kilometres below the surface of the Pacific
Ocean. The Challenger Deep is in the Mariana Trench, a
deep crack in the Earth's crust more than 2,550 kilometres in
(**17**) …….. .   **LONG**

The water pressure at the bottom of the Challenger Deep is
about a thousand times the standard (**18**) …….. pressure at sea   **ATMOSPHERE**
level. It is in constant darkness and the temperature is just a few
degrees above freezing. It was (**19**) …….. thought that in these   **INITIAL**
conditions, it was (**20**) …….. for any life to exist.   **POSSIBLE**

In 1960, two (**21**) …….. men went down into the Challenger   **COURAGE**
Deep in a special underwater vessel, but (**22**) …….. the water   **FORTUNATE**
was too cloudy for them to take photographs. In 2012, another
man made the descent without finding any (**23**) …….. of life.   **EVIDENT**
However, unmanned robotic sample collectors have now found
tiny micro-organisms in the sediment at the bottom, and the
discovery has caused considerable (**24**) …….. for scientists.   **EXCITED**

For questions **25–30**, complete the second sentence so that it has a similar meaning to the first sentence, using the word given. **Do not change the word given.** You must use between **two** and **five** words, including the word given. Here is an example (**0**).

Example:

0   I've never seen a film as boring as this one.

   SUCH

   I've never seen .... as this one.

The gap can be filled by the words 'such a boring film', so you write:

Example: | 0 | SUCH A BORING FILM

Write **only** the missing words **IN CAPITAL LETTERS on the separate answer sheet.**

---

25   Someone is fixing my car for me this week.

   HAVE

   I've arranged .... this week.

26   I only came because you asked me to.

   COME

   I .... you hadn't asked me to.

27   You should use the sports facilities available here.

   ADVANTAGE

   We advise you .... the sports facilities here.

28   Why is there never any orange juice left when I want some?

   RUN

   Why have we always .... orange juice when I want some?

29   Could you take me to the station in your car, please?

   LIFT

   Would you mind .... to the station, please?

30   When someone told Jane the good news, she rang her father immediately.

   SOON

   Jane rang her father .... been given the good news.

PAPER 1 Reading and ▶
       Use of English

PAPER 2 Writing

PAPER 3 Listening

PAPER 4 Speaking

Part 1
Part 2
Part 3
Part 4
Part 5
Part 6
Part 7

You are going to read an article about why people do extreme sports. For questions **31–36**, choose the answer (**A**, **B**, **C** or **D**) which you think fits best according to the text.

Mark your answers **on the separate answer sheet**.

Success and risk in extreme sports

What is it that drives some to take extreme risks, while the rest of us hurry for the safety of the sidelines?

Lester Keller, coach and sports-psychology coordinator, says that not everyone has the mental makeup to excel in extreme sports. 'It takes a certain kind of person,' he says. He notes that most of us hit a natural ceiling that limits our appetite for extreme risk and, as a result, our ability to perform well in tricky conditions.

But others have a much higher tolerance, if not desire, for risk. Keller points to Daron Rahlves, a top ski racer who spends the summer off-season racing in motocross competitions. 'He enjoys the challenge and the risk,' Keller said. Rahlves has told Keller that 'the high element of risk makes you feel alive, tests what you are made of and how far you can take yourself'. Rahlves said in a previous interview, 'I'm in it for the challenge, my heart thumping as I finish, the feeling of being alive'. He went on to point out that he would definitely get nervous on some of the courses, but that this would just make him fight more. The more difficult the course, the better, he reported. 'That's when I do best,' he said.

Psychologists note that some people seem to have a strong desire for adrenaline rushes as a thrill-seeking behaviour or personality trait. Like many extreme athletes, Emily Cook's appetite for risk appeared at a young age. 'I was both a skier and a gymnast,' said the former ski champion. 'I was one of those kids who enjoyed and excelled at anything acrobatic, anything where you were upside down. It was just kind of a part of Emily.' Cook noted that as her expertise grew, so did the stakes. As she started doing harder tricks, she was increasingly drawn to the challenge. 'There are definitely moments when you're up there doing a
line 18 new trick and it seems like the stupidest thing in the world. But overcoming that is just the coolest feeling in the world. Doing something that you know most people wouldn't do is part of it.'

Shane Murphy, sports psychologist and professor, has worked with Olympians and other athletes. He says he is struck by the way they redefine risk according to their skills, experience and environment. 'I've worked with groups climbing Everest, including one group without oxygen. To me that just seems like the height of risk. But the climbers took every precaution they could think of,' he said. 'To them it was the next step in an activity that they've done for years.' Murphy said the perspective of extreme athletes is very different from our own. 'We look at a risky situation and know that if we were in that situation we would be out of control,' he said. 'But from the athletes' perspective, they have a lot of control, and there are a lot of things that they do to minimise risk.'

Climbing and other 'dangerous' activities are statistically not as risky as outsiders assume. Another key aspect of risk perception may be something referred to as 'the flow', a state in which many athletes become absorbed in pursuits that focus the mind completely on the present. 'Something that makes you try doing a tougher climb than usual, perhaps, is that your adrenaline flows and you become very concentrated on what you're doing,' mountaineer Al Read has said. 'After it's over there's exhilaration. You wouldn't have that same feeling if the risk hadn't been there.'

People of different skill levels experience flow at different times. As a result, some may always be driven to adventures that others consider extreme. 'I can enjoy hitting a tennis ball around, because that's my skill level,' Murphy says. 'But others might need the challenge of Olympic competition.'

31 By using the term 'natural ceiling', Lester Keller is

    A pointing out that many people don't actually want to do extreme sports.
    B explaining why some people aren't as good as they'd like to be at sport.
    C suggesting a point at which extreme sportspeople should stop taking risks.
    D highlighting the level of skill many extreme athletes aim to reach.

32 Daron Rahlves said that for him, taking risks

    A was something that forced him to face difficulties he usually avoided.
    B wasn't always worth what he had to put himself through physically.
    C was a way for him to continue to be excited by his place in the world.
    D was something he wouldn't do unless he knew he could overcome them.

33 What does 'that' refer to in line 18?

    A trying to do more difficult tricks
    B Emily's sense that she is being foolish
    C doing things that other people don't
    D Emily's desire to do acrobatic activities

34 What does Shane Murphy think about the mountain climbers he mentions?

    A They are more ambitious than other sportspeople he has encountered.
    B They are willing to put in huge amounts of preparation for challenges.
    C They use arguments that non-climbers can't easily understand.
    D They don't deliberately seek out very difficult challenges.

35 What point is made in the fifth paragraph?

    A Extreme athletes use techniques other people don't use.
    B Most people lack the focus required to do extreme sports.
    C A certain state of mind makes attempting an activity more likely.
    D Non-athletes are probably wise not to try extreme sports.

36 What does the article as a whole tell us?

    A Those who take risks are more likely to be successful in life.
    B Taking part in extreme sports is not as difficult as people think.
    C Extreme athletes are driven by a need to be better than others.
    D Risk-taking is something you either naturally want to do or avoid.

PAPER 1	Reading and	▶	Part 1
	Use of English		Part 2
PAPER 2	Writing		Part 3
			Part 4
PAPER 3	Listening		Part 5
PAPER 4	Speaking		**Part 6**
			Part 7

You are going to read an article about a bird called the Great Snipe. Six sentences have been removed from the article. Choose from the sentences **A–G** the one which fits each gap (**37–42**). There is one extra sentence which you do not need to use.

Mark your answers **on the separate answer sheet**.

The world's fastest bird?

A fat little shore bird called the Great Snipe has smashed the record for the fastest long-distance, nonstop flight in the animal kingdom.

In a recent study, scientists discovered that the Great Snipe can complete a transcontinental flight across Europe, from Sweden to sub-Saharan Africa, in as little as two days without resting. **37** To track the birds, biologists captured and tagged ten Great Snipes with geo-locators – a small device which would record the birds' geographical location – at their breeding grounds in western Sweden. Tracking data for three of the birds was retrieved after their recapture in Sweden a year later.

At first glance, Great Snipes don't look especially speedy or well equipped for such a difficult journey. **38** But it's these plentiful fat reserves that allow the birds to fly such long distances without stopping, said study leader and biologist Raymond Klaassen. 'The birds almost double their body weight before the flight,' Klaassen said. 'But all this will be burned during the flight, and they will arrive thin and exhausted in Africa.'

It's a rare bird that can fly both far and fast. For example, the Arctic Tern clocks up as many as 80,000 kilometres during its yearly migration from the Arctic to the Antarctic and back again. **39** At the other end of the scale, Peregrine Falcons can reach speeds of up to 322 kilometres an hour – but only in short bursts to catch prey. The only other bird that comes close to matching the Great Snipe's abilities is the Godwit, a wading bird (a bird that walks in water to find food).

Scientists have recorded these birds flying more than 11,500 kilometres, on their route from Alaska to New Zealand, in nine days at an average speed of about 56 kilometres an hour.

'One difference between the Godwits and the Snipes is that the Godwits travel over the ocean, and thus have no opportunity to stop,' Klaassen said. '**40** ' By contrast, Snipes have several rest-stop options during their autumn migration to Africa but choose not to take advantage of them. The reasons for this are unclear, especially since the birds make several stops during their return flights to Sweden in the spring.

As with other migratory birds that fly long distances, it's unclear how Great Snipes can apparently fly for such long periods with little or no sleep. '**41** We now believe that half of their brain sleeps at a time, alternating between the left and the right side. Or they do not sleep at all, but this seems impossible regarding the importance of sleep in general,' said Klaassen.

Klaassen said that so little is known about bird-migration strategies that he wouldn't be surprised if the Great Snipe's record is broken soon. 'Generally we know rather little about the performances of different species, as many have not yet been tracked,' he said. 'I foresee many surprises in the near future. **42** The field of bird migration is currently going through a revolution, and these are certainly very exciting times for us.'

A This is one of the unsolved mysteries of long-distance flights.

B Indeed, the world's longest migration is two times longer than this.

C The birds travelled up to 6,760 kilometres at an average speed of 97 kilometres an hour.

D However, the bird spreads the flight out over several months and stops to fish along the way.

E That's because their bodies are small and chubby, not aerodynamic, and in the autumn the birds become rather well rounded.

F For this reason, their amazing flights are not their choice.

G Without doubt, these will be due to the recent development of tiny recording devices.

PAPER 1 Reading and ▶
Use of English

PAPER 2 Writing

PAPER 3 Listening

PAPER 4 Speaking

Part 1
Part 2
Part 3
Part 4
Part 5
Part 6
Part 7

You are going to read five reviews about websites that are useful for students. For questions **43–52**, choose from the reviews (**A–E**). The reviews may be chosen more than once.

Mark your answers **on the separate answer sheet**.

In which review does the journalist

comment on how easy it is to find the required information quickly? | **43** | |

highlight the site's missing explanation for the importance of certain skills? | **44** | |

suggest the website could be improved in terms of ability to locate information? | **45** | |

explain that this website includes detailed information that other websites don't? | **46** | |

praise the website's variety of features when compared to other websites of its kind? | **47** | |

highlight the practical advice that the website's users can receive from specialists? | **48** | |

say that the website is only likely to be useful for people of a particular character? | **49** | |

recommend the website for people who have no experience in a certain area? | **50** | |

admit that the website helps students think about what they've done? | **51** | |

mention how the website fails to provide users with practical skills? | **52** | |

Great websites for students

Education editor Tom Gardner reviews useful websites for students.

A Info-pics

The Info-pics website is an up-to-the-minute website which incorporates a useful tool for creating 'information graphics', with the intention of allowing students to present complex, or potentially less interesting, information in a clear and attractive way. The tool allows users to input data into a choice of different templates, helping them to present their history project or science presentation however they wish. I haven't come across any similar site with such a wide range of charts, graphs and graphics to choose from. But although the visuals are exciting and high quality, finding your way around the site isn't straightforward, meaning it's probably better left to older students.

B Readwell

Readwell allows users the freedom to review books, share opinions and make recommendations about the best reads of the moment with their contemporaries. One thing many reading websites fail to do is provide a comprehensive portfolio of an author's work and biographical information, something Readwell does with style. One of the highlights of the site is the chance to get involved in discussion groups, which is an interesting way for students to form and communicate arguments, while learning to understand and react to different opinions. Some of the comprehension quizzes aren't as challenging as I'd like to have seen for the intended audience, but at least they get users to carefully consider what they've read.

C School Search

One of the best tools available for practising research skills, School Search offers access to a vast range of academic publications. What I found particularly refreshing about the site is how user-friendly it is, despite the amount of data available. Also impressive is that information about each publication is presented clearly and concisely, which helps users to locate relevant and useful material as background reading for any assignment they're working on. All you have to do is enter keywords on the topic of your choice, and in a moment you'll gain access to hundreds of articles and papers which you can read online or print. In my opinion, there's no better site for first-time researchers.

D Speakright

Speakright is geared towards helping students prepare a forthcoming class presentation. The site's main aims are to assist students in developing oral presentation skills and building confidence. The website contains lists of useful phrases for sequencing and signalling. Students will have to rely on memorising these phrases, as there are no practice exercises to develop understanding of how to apply them correctly. Also lacking is any focus on why being able to do a presentation may be useful beyond the classroom; instead, the website is geared towards simply getting students through their next talk. What is outstanding about this site, however, is the record function. Students can record themselves speaking, watch themselves back, and post their talk so that their peers and expert advisors can give detailed feedback on their performance.

E Writeway

This free resource is intended as a reference for any student wishing to improve their writing skills in a relatively short period of time. It covers all aspects of writing, from how to include references to background reading, to effective use of punctuation and style. The different topics are accessible, though without examples of how to apply the information to a particular piece of writing, the site is less successful. There are no interactive elements either, which means users don't have the opportunity to communicate with others or seek answers to any questions they might have. This is one for the independent-minded out there, who will still find the site useful for learning how to express their ideas better in writing.

PAPER 1 Reading and
          Use of English

PAPER 2 Writing ▶ | Part 1 |
                     | Part 2 |

PAPER 3 Listening

PAPER 4 Speaking

You **must** answer this question. Write your answer in **140–190** words in an appropriate style.

1 In your English class you have been talking about personal appearance. Now your English teacher has asked you to write an essay.

Write your essay using **all** the notes and give reasons for your point of view.

> 'Some people worry too much about the way they look. They should concentrate on becoming more interesting instead.'
>
> Do you agree?

Notes
Write about:

1. why people care about the way they look
2. spending money
3. .... (your own idea)

PAPER 1 Reading and
Use of English

PAPER 2 Writing ▶
| Part 1
| **Part 2**

PAPER 3 Listening

PAPER 4 Speaking

Write an answer to **one** of the questions 2–5 in this part. Write your answer in **140–190** words in an appropriate style.

2   You see this announcement in an English-language magazine.

> **Articles wanted – Are you a sports fan?**
>
> What's the best game or match you've ever watched? Tell us about it!
>
> What makes a sports game or match exciting?
>
> We'd love to receive your articles. The best ones will be printed in our magazine next month.

Write your **article**.

3   This is part of an email you have received from your English friend Robert.

> **From:** Robert
> **Subject:** My school project
>
> In class we've been talking about different kinds of communication, such as spoken language and body language. I'm doing a project about how we can communicate with people who don't speak the same language. Can you give me some ideas about how people can do this?
>
> Thanks!
>
> Robert

Write your **email**.

4   Your local tourist office wants to publish information in English for visitors from other countries. In order to do this, they need reports about interesting places to visit. You have been asked to write about a historical building or monument in your town. In your report you should explain why the place is important, and suggest ways in which the experience of visiting the place could be improved.

Write your **report**.

5   (for *FIRST FOR SCHOOLS* candidates only)

Answer the following question based on the set text you have read.

> **Articles wanted!**
>
> We are looking for articles about characters in books.
>
> *Which character from the book you have read do you think many readers would have something in common with? Why? Do you have anything in common with the character yourself?*

Write your **article**.

🎧 **Track 21**

You will hear people talking in eight different situations. For questions **1–8**, choose the best answer (**A**, **B** or **C**).

1   You hear two travel agents talking about the holidays people choose.
    What do they agree about?
    A   People like travelling in groups.
    B   Good accommodation is important.
    C   Cities are the most popular places to visit.

2   You hear a writer talking about his job.
    What does he say about it?
    A   It is the perfect job for him.
    B   It is not as difficult as people think.
    C   It is the only thing he ever wanted to do.

3   You hear two people talking about a TV programme they both watched.
    What sort of TV programme was it?
    A   a travel documentary
    B   a comedy series
    C   a sports programme

4   You hear a woman talking about her first day working as a restaurant chef.
    How does she feel now?
    A   anxious about her performance
    B   irritated with her colleagues
    C   worried about her job prospects

5   You hear two members of local government talking about a park.
    What does the man say about it?
    A   It is very well looked after.
    B   It is pleasant to sit in.
    C   It is a good place to see wildlife.

6   You hear a decorator talking to his colleague about moving some furniture.
    What is he doing?
    A   requesting help from his colleague
    B   agreeing with his colleague's suggestion
    C   giving his colleague advice on something

7   You hear two chemistry students talking about their course.
    What is the woman's opinion of it?
    A   It is taught in an interesting way.
    B   All the topics are thoroughly covered.
    C   They are being well prepared for future jobs.

8   You hear a student talking about the room she rents.
    According to the woman, the room is
    A   too small for all her things.
    B   too noisy in the evenings.
    C   too expensive for her.

Track 22

You will hear a woman talking to new students about the university music society. For questions **9–18**, complete the sentences with a word or short phrase.

University music society

The society was started by music (**9**) ....
50 years ago.

To join the (**10**) .... , simply turn up at a practice
session.

Everyone is invited to attend the talk on (**11**) .... this
evening.

There will be a jazz performance in the (**12**) .... Hall
next Wednesday.

The society's next social event is a (**13**) ....

The theme for the composer competition is (**14**) ....
this year.

Membership of the society includes free (**15**) .... to
concerts around the country.

The music practice rooms' (**16**) .... are currently being
restored.

Society members also do things in the local area, such as giving concerts in
(**17**) ....

The weekly (**18**) .... is a good way of finding out
about society events.

PAPER 1 Reading and
          Use of English

PAPER 2 Writing

PAPER 3 Listening ▶

PAPER 4 Speaking

    Part 1
    Part 2
    Part 3
    Part 4

Track 23

You will hear five short extracts in which people are talking about why they entered a young engineers' competition. For questions **19–23**, choose from the list (**A–H**) what each speaker says. Use the letters only once. There are three extra letters which you do not need to use.

A I was told about it by a lecturer.

B I think I could do very well.

C I felt I needed a challenge.

D I need publicity for my invention.

E I want to meet people with similar interests.

F I was encouraged to by someone I know.

G I nearly won another competition.

H I hope it will help me get a job.

Speaker 1   **19**

Speaker 2   **20**

Speaker 3   **21**

Speaker 4   **22**

Speaker 5   **23**

PAPER 1 Reading and
         Use of English

PAPER 2 Writing

PAPER 3 Listening   ▶

PAPER 4 Speaking

Part 1
Part 2
Part 3
Part 4

 Track 24

You will hear an interview with a man called Matt Brown, who has recently trained as a sailing instructor. For questions **24–30**, choose the best answer (**A**, **B** or **C**).

24 Why did Matt decide to become a sailing instructor?
    A He had wanted to do it since he was a child.
    B It would allow him to pay for his studies.
    C A friend of his recommended he should.

25 What does Matt say about choosing somewhere to train as a sailing instructor?
    A It was difficult to find a place on a course.
    B He was warned against going on certain courses.
    C There were few courses he could afford.

26 What surprised Matt about the other people on his course?
    A the ages they were
    B the experience of sailing they had
    C their enthusiasm for learning to sail

27 How did Matt react when he saw some dolphins?
    A He took as many photographs as he could.
    B He worried that they might cause problems.
    C He tried to hide his excitement.

28 What does Matt say he missed after his course was over?
    A learning something new every day
    B being able to sail as often as he wanted
    C being awake early enough to see the sun rise

29 Matt thinks that he will enjoy
    A training other people to be instructors.
    B working with people with similar interests.
    C teaching teenagers something useful.

30 What is Matt going to do next?
    A do another course
    B apply for a job
    C go on holiday

Part 1 (2 minutes)

The examiner (interlocutor) will ask each of you to speak briefly in turn and to give personal information about yourselves. You can expect a variety of questions, such as:

How often do you watch films?
Have you seen a good film recently? (What did you see? / Did you enjoy it?)
Is there a film that you would like to see soon? (What is it?)

Part 2 (4 minutes)

You will each be asked to talk for a minute without interruption. You will each be given two different photographs in turn to talk about. After your partner has finished speaking, you will be asked a brief question connected with your partner's photographs.

1 Museums

Look at the two photographs on page 174 which show people in different types of museum.

Candidate A, compare these photographs, and say what you think the people might enjoy about being in these different museums.

Candidate B, which museum would you prefer to visit? (Why?)

2 Working environments

Look at the two photographs on page 175 which show people in different types of workplace.

Candidate B, compare these photographs, and say how you think the people feel about working in these different environments.

Candidate A, in which of these places would you prefer to work? (Why?)

Part 3 (4 minutes)

You will be asked to discuss something together without interruption by the examiner. You will have a page of ideas with a question to help you.

Short film about your area

Imagine you have been asked to make a short film for tourists about your area. Turn to page 176 which shows some ideas for some things that you could show in the film. Talk to each other about whether each idea would be good to put in the film. Then decide which **two** of the ideas would be the best ones to include.

Part 4 (4 minutes)

The examiner will encourage you to develop the topic of your discussion in Part 3 by asking questions such as:

What are the advantages of a city or town being a popular tourist destination? (Why?)
What are the disadvantages? (Why?)
What do you think the main reasons are for people travelling abroad?
What do you think people learn by travelling to other countries?
How can people learn about other countries without actually visiting them? Do you think this is effective? (Why? / Why not?)

PAPER 1 Reading and Use of English

▸▸ PART 5

mental makeup (phr) qualities of the mind

excel (v) to do very well

tolerance (n) the ability to experience something that may be difficult, unpleasant or painful without being harmed or complaining about it

thump (v) to bump, bang

adrenaline rush (phr) a sudden burst of energy that is caused by a chemical that is produced by your body, usually at times of danger or excitement

thrill-seeking (adj) looking for excitement

personality trait (phr) a characteristic

expertise (n) expert knowledge

stake (n) interest, involvement

be drawn to (phr v) to be attracted to

be struck by (phr v) if you are struck by something it seems interesting or impressive to you

precaution (n) a safety measure

perspective (n) the way you think about something

pursuit (n) enjoyable or leisure time activity

exhilaration (n) excitement, extreme happiness

▸▸ PART 6

transcontinental (adj) across continents

tag (v) to label

breeding ground (n) the place where animals breed (reproduce, have young)

retrieve (v) to collect

clock up (phr v) to achieve, record or register

migration (n) the process when an animal or bird moves to another place, usually seasonally

burst (n) a period of intense activity

prey (n) an animal that is hunted by another animal

chubby (adj) fat

aerodynamic (adj) having the shape/ability to move efficiently through air

▸▸ PART 7

incorporate (v) to include

tool (n) a useful resource

template (n) a document with a particular format which is used as a pattern or an example for other documents

contemporary (adj) someone alive at the same time as a particular event or person

comprehensive (adj) including everything

portfolio (n) a collection of work

concisely (adv) expressed in only a few words, but in a way that is easy to understand

assignment (n) a piece of work that you must do as part of a course of study or your job

be geared towards (phr) to be aimed at

sequence (v) to put in order

signal (v) to indicate

peer (n) someone of the same age, or belongs to the same social, educational or professional group as another person

PAPER 1	Reading and Use of English	▶	Part 1
			Part 2
PAPER 2	Writing		Part 3
			Part 4
PAPER 3	Listening		Part 5
			Part 6
PAPER 4	Speaking		Part 7

For questions **1–8**, read the text below and decide which answer (**A**, **B**, **C** or **D**) best fits each gap. There is an example at the beginning (**0**).

Mark your answers **on the separate answer sheet**.

Example:

0 **A** fell **B** resulted **C** grew **D** became

0	A	B	C	D

The dodo, a bird that couldn't fly

The dodo is a bird that (**0**) .... extinct in the 17th century. It lived on the island of Mauritius in the Indian Ocean, and had evolved and (**1**) .... to its unique island habitat. There were no predators to hunt it on the island, and plenty of fruit lying on the ground, so (**2**) .... millions of years, the dodo eventually (**3**) .... its ability to fly. It also became bigger to (**4**) .... it to store enough fat to survive when food was scarce.

In the 16th and 17th centuries, European sailors started arriving on the island. Accounts written at the (**5**) .... describe the birds as trusting and friendly, and having no reason to (**6**) .... human beings because they had no experience of people, the giant birds were easy to catch and kill for food. (**7**) .... , it was the animals the sailors brought with them – especially rats and monkeys – that posed the greatest (**8**) .... to the dodo, eating their eggs and chicks.

1	**A** adapted	**B** changed	**C** suited	**D** transformed
2	**A** with	**B** across	**C** over	**D** around
3	**A** rejected	**B** lost	**C** dropped	**D** threw
4	**A** ensure	**B** make	**C** enable	**D** let
5	**A** time	**B** moment	**C** point	**D** occasion
6	**A** frighten	**B** scare	**C** panic	**D** fear
7	**A** Even	**B** However	**C** Despite	**D** Although
8	**A** concern	**B** threat	**C** problem	**D** trouble

For questions **9–16**, read the text below and think of the word which best fits each gap. Use only **one** word in each gap. There is an example at the beginning (**0**).

Write your answers **IN CAPITAL LETTERS on the separate answer sheet**.

Example: `0` `T` `O` ☐☐☐☐☐☐☐☐☐☐☐☐☐☐☐☐☐☐☐☐☐

Learn to play the piano online

Do you want (**0**) …….. play the piano, but can't afford or find a teacher? There is another option available to you, as (**9**) …….. as you can use a computer somewhere with internet access, that is. You can learn online. There are even a number of websites (**10**) …….. allow you to do this for free. Some provide expert and detailed lessons, and as you work (**11**) …….. way through them – taking as long as you wish, which is rarely (**12**) …….. option in a conventional lesson, it feels just (**13**) …….. being guided by an experienced teacher who knows exactly what they are doing. Believe (**14**) …….. or not, some of the websites are very good fun to use, and even quite addictive. (**15**) …….. fast and effectively you progress will of course depend (**16**) …….. the time you are prepared to put into your online piano lessons, and whether or not you put in the practice – but after all, this applies to most things in life.

PAPER 1 Reading and
Use of English

PAPER 2 Writing

PAPER 3 Listening

PAPER 4 Speaking

Part 1
Part 2
Part 3
Part 4
Part 5
Part 6
Part 7

For questions **17–24**, read the text below. Use the word given in capitals at the end of some of the lines to form a word that fits the gap **in the same line**. There is an example at the beginning (**0**).

Write your answers **IN CAPITAL LETTERS on the separate answer sheet.**

Example: | 0 | W | O | O | D | E | N | | | | | | | | | | | | | | |

Making your house a home

Whether it's a concrete apartment in a city or a (**0**) .... house	**WOOD**
on the water, what matters most isn't your home's outward	
(**17**) .... , but how it makes you feel when you step inside.	**APPEAR**
Home is where we can (**18**) .... be ourselves, and it provides us	**TRUE**
with a private space away from the world. A house is (**19**) .... –	**FUNCTION**
it's where we rest, eat and entertain; but a home is where we feel	
safe and create memories with those we share it with.	
As we change and grow, our home should reflect our (**20**)	**DEVELOP**
It's easy to stay stuck in our ways: the furniture sits in the same	
place, and so do we. But there's nothing wrong with (**21**)	**ARRANGE**
things from time to time. Change reminds us we're (**22**)	**LIVE**
creatures. Giving your home a new look doesn't (**23**) .... mean	**NECESSARY**
spending money; it simply means putting a bit of (**24**) .... into	**THINK**
who you are and what you need right now.	

For questions **25–30**, complete the second sentence so that it has a similar meaning to the first sentence, using the word given. **Do not change the word given.** You must use between **two** and **five** words, including the word given. Here is an example (**0**).

Example:

0   I've never seen a film as boring as this one.

   SUCH

   I've never seen .... as this one.

The gap can be filled by the words 'such a boring film', so you write:

Example: | **0** | SUCH A BORING FILM |

Write **only** the missing words **IN CAPITAL LETTERS on the separate answer sheet**.

---

25   'I'll drive Tim to the airport,' Martin insisted.

   INSISTED

   Martin .... to the airport.

26   I'm not sure whether David took the house keys with him or not.

   MIGHT

   David .... the house keys with him, but I'm not sure.

27   I wasn't allowed to enter the building without showing some identification to the security guard.

   LET

   The security guard .... enter the building without showing him some identification.

28   Let me know when you've decided what you want to do.

   MIND

   Tell me when you have .... about what you want to do.

29   Jodie thinks it's a good idea to make copies of the files.

   FAVOUR

   Jodie is .... copies of the files.

30   I don't understand why Bob's going to study science.

   SENSE

   It doesn't .... why Bob's going to study science.

PAPER 1   Reading and ▸   Part 1
          Use of English   Part 2
PAPER 2   Writing   Part 3
                              Part 4
PAPER 3   Listening   **Part 5**
                              Part 6
PAPER 4   Speaking   Part 7

You are going to read an article about a photographer called Mary McCartney. For questions 31–36, choose the answer (**A**, **B**, **C** or **D**) which you think fits best according to the text.

Mark your answers **on the separate answer sheet**.

Mary McCartney, photographer

Journalist Tim Lewis met photographer Mary McCartney to talk about her work.

This is what Mary McCartney, portrait photographer, says about her approach to taking pictures: 'I'm always trying to make a connection with the person I'm photographing. I don't want to just come away with a shot that I think is interesting – I also want the subject to like that shot of themselves. I won't go: "That's great, it doesn't matter what you think, it's going in." I want it to have a real sense of them.' It is an empathetic, sensitive approach to photography, but it is one that produces some stunning results. Subjects – particularly celebrities – appear to relax when McCartney turns her lens on them. The images often feel intimate and genuinely spontaneous, as if we are peering in on a private, unguarded moment.

McCartney was inspired to become a photographer in her mid-20s, sifting through contact sheets taken by her mother, who also photographed celebrities. 'My mum was quite a wanderer,' says Mary. 'She had a real sense of adventure and a cheekiness to her, which is something I like and that I try
line 12 to take into my style of work. I remember once we went out for lunch and I grilled her about her early career in photography and particularly about the people she was hanging out with. I wanted to know all about what she'd done. I was like: "I can't believe you photographed Jimi Hendrix!" I was so jealous.'

When it comes to working with exceptional individuals, Mary does not fare too badly herself. She has taken portraits of famous artists, actors and singers. Is there anyone she is still desperate to photograph? McCartney names a famous singer, almost squealing. 'I love her; I love her voice, her music. I imagine she's quite done – she'd probably arrive camera-ready – but I just find her life so intriguing. I've always been drawn to strong women. When I like what they do, it makes me quite proud to be photographing them, and I feel an extra responsibility to show how cool I think they are or something.'

McCartney has photographed many of her subjects on multiple occasions, but she finds it can often get harder rather than easier after the first time. 'When you know someone, you have to get into a different headspace – it's easy to get distracted if it's too friendly,' she says. One exception, though, is her father. 'Dad's really good fun to take pictures of, because he likes to make it interesting for himself, he doesn't just want to do a straight portrait. So he'll mess around or say, 'Let's do something crazy with my hair.' If I'm doing it, he knows it's a safe environment and he can go further than he would otherwise, so you may get that one unexpected shot.'

If Mary McCartney's professional life is dominated by women, then at her home in north London – where she lives with her four sons and her husband, it is strictly men only. 'There's not a lot of pink in my home, definitely,' she says. 'But I like the chaos, luckily.'

McCartney has written a vegetarian cookbook titled *Food*, but she is adamant that her priority remains photography. She is currently working on a stills and video project that focuses on people who dedicate their bodies and lives to their vocations. Two of the sets she has already completed are the dancers of the corps de ballet at the Royal Opera House and some actresses in a musical. They're very contrasting groups, I suggest. 'Actually there's not very much difference between the pictures,' says McCartney. 'A lot of the actresses, their background is ballet. It's the same gruelling schedule and time commitments. You couldn't necessarily tell them apart.'

31 What point does Mary make about her approach to her work?

    A She cares about the opinions of the people she photographs.
    B The equipment she uses depends on who she's photographing.
    C She prefers taking photographs of people who interest her.
    D The lack of privacy that comes with fame inspires her photography.

32 What does 'grilled her' mean in line 12?

    A teased her a great deal
    B asked her a lot of questions
    C reminded her repeatedly
    D told her some stories

33 What does Mary suggest in the third paragraph?

    A It would be difficult to take an unusual photograph of the singer.
    B Actually meeting the singer might make Mary rather nervous.
    C The singer would have high expectations of Mary's photograph.
    D Taking the singer's photograph might boost Mary's career.

34 Mary says that photographing her father

    A is more successful if she keeps him occupied.
    B involves preparations to make sure he looks good.
    C has the potential to produce unpredictable results.
    D requires her to make a special effort to concentrate.

35 What is the writer doing in the fifth paragraph?

    A explaining why Mary likes photographing women so much
    B describing Mary's attempts to balance work and family life
    C illustrating the problems Mary faces every day
    D showing the differences between certain aspects of Mary's life

36 What do we learn about the photographs Mary has taken recently?

    A They are less important to her now than writing cookery books.
    B They are part of a project to explore the differences between people.
    C They reveal characteristics shared by people doing different jobs.
    D They have been more complicated to produce than she had expected.

PAPER 1 Reading and ▶   Part 1
        Use of English   Part 2
PAPER 2 Writing   Part 3
                          Part 4
PAPER 3 Listening   Part 5
PAPER 4 Speaking   **Part 6**
                          Part 7

You are going to read an article about someone who made their own bicycle out of bamboo. Six sentences have been removed from the article. Choose from the sentences **A–G** the one which fits each gap (**37–42**). There is one extra sentence which you do not need to use.

Mark your answers **on the separate answer sheet**.

Making my own bicycle – out of bamboo!

In a London warehouse, people are being taught how to build bamboo bicycles.

It was 8 a.m. on a Saturday morning and I was standing in a freezing cold warehouse in London. By the end of the weekend, I was meant to have turned some bamboo into a bicycle frame. I was at the Bamboo Bicycle Club, founded by friends James Marr and Ian McMillan, ready for my bamboo bike building course.

Preparations for the workshop had begun the week before, with a discussion about what style of bike I wanted to build. **37** [   ] That's why I'd opted for a frame that contrasted with the stiff geometry of my existing one.

When I arrived at the workshop, the precise list of body measurements requested from me had already been transferred onto a personalised diagram of my frame. **38** [   ]

The first step was setting up the jig – the structure used to hold the frame in place – then to select the bamboo. Things I was told to watch out for were cracked pieces and pieces that were too thin. Of course, finding pieces that were the colour I wanted was just as important. **39** [   ] James and Ian are strong believers in making your bike look exactly how you want. 'But don't get too attached to your pieces,' James warned, as we raised our saws. The fibres on the outer layer of bamboo have a tendency to flake off, weakening it so much it can't be used.

The rest of the afternoon was spent fixing each piece of the frame into the jig, slotting in the bottom bracket, seat tube and handlebar tube. The particular qualities of bamboo as a construction material means unexpected adjustments can suddenly become necessary. At one point a problem lining up my two chain stays (the narrow tubes running alongside the back wheel) threatened to make my frame useless. **40** [   ] There was just enough space to fit a wheel.

Besides, most things can be fixed by a spot of whittling with a special craft knife. **41** [   ] Spare pieces are turned into pen pots, bike racks and stands for MP3 players. It seems bikes are not the only thing you can make out of bamboo.

On Sunday morning we returned to the workshop bright and early to complete the final process; binding. After a shaky start, we began to tightly wrap each joint on the frame with natural fibres soaked in a special glue. After two layers, the binding was wrapped tightly with electrical tape, to keep it firm and ensure a smooth finish. **42** [   ] In a few hours I would be an official member of the bamboo bicycle club.

While we waited, I took the opportunity to test ride Ian's bike to find out what it was really like to ride a bamboo bike. It felt just as capable as any bike, but softer, more relaxed. I rode past a group of people who looked surprised, but in a pleasant way. 'Every time I get on my bike I can't help smiling,' said James. 'It reminds me of when I built it.'

A Luckily, however, after some careful checks, Ian confirmed that it was alright.

B This was the plan that I would follow.

C If all else fails you simply have to cut off another length.

D I can proudly say I managed to do it even more effectively.

E Personally, I felt that any bicycle made out of organic matter should be a relaxed one, something to cruise around on rather than race.

F Some people like the frame to be consistent, others like a mix of light, dark or speckled.

G All that was left now was for it to dry.

PAPER 1 Reading and ▶   Part 1
         Use of English   Part 2
PAPER 2 Writing   Part 3
                          Part 4
PAPER 3 Listening   Part 5
                          Part 6
PAPER 4 Speaking
                          Part 7

You are going to read an article in which four students talk about the fashion design courses they are doing. For questions **43–52**, choose from the people (**A–D**). The people may be chosen more than once.

Mark your answers **on the separate answer sheet**.

Which person

is looking forward to working on a student project in the fashion industry?	43
comments on the friendly atmosphere at their college?	44
has become more interested in fashion since starting their course?	45
enjoys the freedom they are given on how to approach their projects?	46
mentions being able to use as much material as they like?	47
values input from people outside the college working in the fashion industry?	48
says the main emphasis is on the practical aspects of the course?	49
points out that they will be able to use what they have learned in a number of different ways?	50
chose their course because of a job they had?	51
comments on how the variety of activities offered prevents them getting bored?	52

Fashion design courses

Four first-year fashion design students talk about their courses in clothes design.

A Greg

My course involves research, design, and a lot of experimenting with different materials and techniques. We also do cultural studies and academic writing, but the focus is on actually making things. In the first year we don't have any contact with the fashion industry, but do projects that are assessed and monitored by our tutors. They're very helpful and experienced, and when we're working on a project, they give us a topic, and then let us go wherever we like with it. It's an opportunity to experiment within a supportive environment, which is ideal. My classmates come from a wide variety of backgrounds and some of them already have experience of working in the industry. We're all part of a community, and it's a great feeling to walk into the building every morning and see lots of people I know and like.

B Kara

I've always wanted to be a fashion designer, and I think that by the time I graduate, I will have all the skills I need, as well as having had a wonderful time at college. No two weeks are the same, which is what I love about this course. There are so many different things to do that it never feels dull. I'm working on a project at the moment where we are asked to design a range of casual wear and imagine we are doing it for a famous brand. This helps us learn about meeting real-world requirements and understanding the process that designers and their work go through. I've always found the college technicians incredibly helpful, and so are all the tutors, of course. There's no limit to the amount of fabric we can use, which of course will be different when we have jobs later on. I'll enjoy that while it lasts!

C Tom

I've always loved fashion, but had a number of different jobs in the car industry before deciding to follow my dream. My course has been very interesting so far, and I'm sure it will become even more so when we are sent out to get work experience in a company in our second year. We'll report back to our college tutors on how our project is progressing, and they'll be able to advise us and support us while we're doing it. At the moment I'm thinking of specialising in children's leisurewear, but the skills we're acquiring can be adapted to any area of fashion so my options are very open. I've been amazed to find out about the range of textiles and fabrics available to designers these days, and it's been great to be shown and to practise so many different techniques. I feel we're all being well prepared for our future careers in the industry.

D Mary

My hobby is surfing, and I love everything to do with sports and the outdoors. I spent a year working in a sportswear shop, which is where I became interested in the way sports clothes are designed, and all the different materials available. I realised it was an area I wanted to explore further, and since enrolling at my college, I've never looked back. Sports clothes have to work practically, and help improve the wearer's performance. I've also found that the fashion side of things appeals to me, though I'd never thought about that very much before. I've been doing a project with a famous sportswear company this term, and the designers there have been very friendly and helpful. They add a different perspective to that of the college tutors, and I really appreciate that.

You **must** answer this question. Write your answer in **140–190** words in an appropriate style.

1 In your English class you have been talking about working life. Now your English teacher has asked you to write an essay.

Write your essay using **all** the notes and give reasons for your point of view.

Is earning money the only good reason for working?

Notes
Write about:

1. training and studies
2. colleagues
3. .... (your own idea)

PAPER 1 Reading and
         Use of English
PAPER 2 Writing ▶   Part 1
                     Part 2
PAPER 3 Listening
PAPER 4 Speaking

Write an answer to **one** of the questions 2–5 in this part. Write your answer in **140–190** words in an appropriate style.

2   This is part of an email you have received from an English-speaking friend.

> As you know, I love reading! How about you? What sort of things do you read – books, magazines, online articles, or something else? Why do you read them? How important is reading in your life? I think people our age read less than older people – is that true in your country?
>
> Write soon
>
> Alex

Write your **email**.

3   You see this announcement on an English-language website.

> **Articles wanted – An unexpected event**
>
> We need articles about surprising things that have happened to people.
> Has anything unexpected ever happened to you?
> Tell us what happened, and why it was so unexpected.
> What happened as a result of the event?
>
> The best articles will appear on our website next week.

Write your **article**.

4   (*for FIRST candidates only*)

Your teacher has asked you to write a report for the college English-language magazine on places to eat in your area. Include information about:

• the types of places where people can eat
• the different kinds of food people can eat when they eat out
• how the choice available in your area could be improved

Write your **report**.

(*for FIRST FOR SCHOOLS candidates only*)

You have seen this announcement on an English-language website for teenagers.

> **Stories wanted**
>
> We are looking for stories to publish on our website next month. Your story must begin with this sentence:
>
> *James saw a light ahead of him and walked towards it.*
>
> Your story must include:
> •   a river
> •   a happy ending

Write your **story**.

5   (*for FIRST FOR SCHOOLS candidates only*)

Answer the following question based on the set text you have read.

Write an **essay** about two characters in the book you have read. Describe the two characters and the relationship between them, and explain what part each character plays in the story.

Track 25

You will hear people talking in eight different situations. For questions **1–8**, choose the best answer (**A**, **B** or **C**).

---

1   You hear a flight attendant talking about taking long flights.
       What is he doing?
       A   warning against certain passenger behaviour
       B   explaining why passengers should do certain things
       C   complaining about a certain kind of passenger

2   You hear a patient talking to a diet expert about taking vitamins.
       The expert thinks that the patient should
       A   approach a doctor for further advice.
       B   focus his efforts on cooking healthy food.
       C   be aware of the expense of taking vitamins.

3   Your hear two friends talking about a yoga class they have attended.
       What do they agree about?
       A   how unfamiliar the exercises were
       B   how tiring the exercises were to do
       C   how likely they are to practise the exercises

4   You hear a university student leaving a message for a department secretary.
       What is the purpose of the student's call?
       A   to apologise for missing a class
       B   to request feedback on her presentation
       C   to arrange a meeting with her tutor

5   You hear a woman talking to her colleague about leaving her job.
       How does the woman feel?
       A   proud of what her colleagues have achieved
       B   satisfied she has made a success of her role
       C   pleased she has made some good friends

6   You hear a student talking about his idea for a project with his tutor.
       The tutor is concerned that the student.
       A   will need to widen his topic area.
       B   has forgotten about part of the process.
       C   hasn't done enough background reading.

7   You hear a man telling a friend about his work.
       What does he say about it?
       A   It is often misunderstood.
       B   It isn't as creative as he'd like.
       C   He'd prefer to do something else.

8   You hear part of a radio talk about training horses.
       The woman is of the opinion that
       A   horse-training is better left to experts.
       B   training a horse isn't as hard as it seems.
       C   horses can react well to training.

🎧 **Track 26**

You will hear a woman called Mandy Butler talking about the production of candles. For questions **9–18**, complete the sentences with a word or short phrase.

Candle making

Mandy was surprised to learn that (**9**) .... , nuts and olive oil were first used to make wax.

Mandy tried to reproduce a time-keeping stick that burned a different (**10**) .... every 60 minutes.

Mandy was unaware that a weight such as a (**11**) .... could be used in candles as a timing device.

Mandy discovered that in the 13th century, candle making was banned because of its (**12**) ....

Mandy thinks the best improvement to candles was limiting the (**13**) .... they produced.

Mandy has seen a (**14**) .... at a museum, which demonstrated candle manufacturing.

Mandy wrote an article on how wax was produced from (**15**) .... in the mid 19th century.

Because of how it burned, Mandy explains that (**16**) .... was used for the central 'wick' in a candle.

Mandy now enjoys using candles for (**17**) .... purposes at home.

Today's workshop will focus on experiments with mixtures of (**18**) ....

PAPER 1 Reading and
Use of English

PAPER 2 Writing

PAPER 3 Listening ▶

PAPER 4 Speaking

Part 1
Part 2
Part 3
Part 4

🎧 **Track 27**

You will hear five short extracts in which people are talking about travelling abroad for work. For questions **19–23**, choose from the list (**A–H**) what each speaker thinks is most helpful when travelling frequently. Use the letters only once. There are three extra letters which you do not need to use.

A Use a car hire company with a good reputation.

B Take a copy of important documents with you.

Speaker 1 ☐ **19**

C Pack your bag as lightly as possible.

Speaker 2 ☐ **20**

D Always fly with the same airline.

Speaker 3 ☐ **21**

E Read up on local business customs.

Speaker 4 ☐ **22**

F Learn some useful phrases.

Speaker 5 ☐ **23**

G Order your foreign currency in advance.

H Have a bag ready-prepared with essentials.

PAPER 1 Reading and
        Use of English

PAPER 2 Writing

PAPER 3 Listening ▶

PAPER 4 Speaking

Part 1
Part 2
Part 3
Part 4

Track 28

You will hear a psychologist called Sheena Smith talking about studying human behaviour. For questions **24–30**, choose the best answer (**A**, **B** or **C**).

24 What does Sheena like about studying behaviour now?
   A noting the differences between people
   B getting to understand herself more
   C learning about human emotion

25 When Sheena talks about her father's 'telephone voice', she remembers
   A the excitement she felt about a discovery.
   B the pride she felt in the way her father spoke.
   C the amusement she felt at her mother's reaction.

26 During her time at university, Sheena wrote about how we
   A aren't as intelligent as we like to think.
   B don't like to question our cultural habits.
   C are unable to change the way we behave.

27 When Sheena took part in an experiment in a lift she felt
   A surprised by people's lack of interest in conversation.
   B disappointed by how awkwardly others behaved.
   C concerned about doing the wrong thing.

28 What does Sheena think about the work she is currently doing?
   A It isn't as interesting as her previous projects.
   B It isn't as useful as she thought it might be.
   C It isn't as easy to do as she had assumed.

29 The project Sheena has most enjoyed working on
   A had an unexpected outcome.
   B helped her to progress in her career.
   C changed her opinion about the value of research.

30 Sheena says that what she'd like to study in the future will be
   A unlike anything she's tried before.
   B rewarding for the participants.
   C difficult to achieve.

Part 1 (2 minutes)

The examiner (interlocutor) will ask each of you to speak briefly in turn and to give personal information about yourselves. You can expect a variety of questions, such as:

What kind of food do you enjoy eating?
Do you enjoy cooking? (Why / Why not?)
Do you prefer eating out or eating at home? (Why?)
What kind of things do you talk about when you're sharing a meal with friends or family?

Part 2 (4 minutes)

You will each be asked to talk for a minute without interruption. You will each be given two different photographs in turn to talk about. After your partner has finished speaking, you will be asked a brief question connected with your partner's photographs.

1 Talking to friends and relatives

Look at the two photographs on page 177 which show people chatting to friends or relatives in different ways.

Candidate A, compare these photographs, and say why you think the people have chosen to chat to their friends or relatives in these different ways.

Candidate B, how do you prefer chatting to your friends and relatives?

2 Cinema

Look at the two photographs on page 178 which show people in different situations.

Candidate B, compare these photographs, and say what the people might enjoy about watching these different types of film.

Candidate A, which of these films would you prefer to see? (Why?)

Part 3 (4 minutes)

You will be asked to discuss something together without interruption by the examiner. You will have a page of ideas with a question to help you.

English class party

Imagine that your teacher has asked you to plan an end-of-year party for your English class. Turn to page 179 which shows some ideas for things to do at the party. Talk to each other about how enjoyable each idea might be for your class. Then decide which **two** of the ideas you should choose for the party.

Part 4 (4 minutes)

The examiner will encourage you to develop the topic of your discussion in Part 3 by asking questions such as:

What other things could you do at a party with your English class?
Why do you think people celebrate finishing a course of study?
Do people in your country celebrate when they finish a course of study? (How do they celebrate?)
Do you think it's important to hold social events like parties? (Why / Why not?)
What are some good ways to get to know new people?
Why do you think friendships are important?

▶▶ PART 5

portrait (n) a drawing, painting or photograph of a person, especially of the face

shot (n) a photograph

empathetic (adj) understanding of someone else's feelings

spontaneous (adj) unplanned

peer in (v) to look at closely from outside

unguarded (adj) relaxed because you are in private

sift through (phr) sort through

contact sheets (n) pages of small versions of all the photographs from a photography session

wanderer (n) someone who travels without a particular goal

cheekiness (n) being slightly disrespectful, but in a funny, attractive way

hang out with (phr) to spend time with socially

fare (v) to be successful / unsuccessful in a particular situation

squeal (v) to make a high-pitched noise

intriguing (adj) very interesting, fascinating

drawn to (phr) attracted to

headspace (n) state of mind, way of seeing things

adamant (adj) very certain

still (n) photograph

vocation (n) a job that you do because you feel it is your purpose in life, or because you have special skills

corps de ballet (phr, French) a group of ballet dancers

gruelling (adj) very tough

▶▶ PART 6

bamboo (n) a tall tropical plant that has hard, hollow stems that are used for making furniture, poles, etc

warehouse (n) a large building used for storage

stiff (adj) rigid, unbending

saw (n) a tool used for cutting wood or metal

flake off (phr) to break off gradually in thin pieces

slot in (v) to fit something into a long narrow hole

bracket (n) L-shaped strong structure used to hold things in place

line up (v) to move objects to make them fit correctly

whittle (v) to cut a piece of wood into a smaller size by gradually removing very small pieces

cruise around (phr) travel around for pleasure

speckled (adj) spotted

▶▶ PART 7

assess (v) to mark or grade

monitor (v) to watch the progress of something or someone

brand (n) the official identity of a company

leisurewear (n) informal clothes

textiles (n) woven or knitted fabric, material

enrol (v) to put your name down on the official list to go to a college, university or other organisation

perspective (n) the way in which someone sees something

PAPER 1 Reading and ▶
          Use of English

PAPER 2 Writing

PAPER 3 Listening

PAPER 4 Speaking

Part 1
Part 2
Part 3
Part 4
Part 5
Part 6
Part 7

For questions **1–8**, read the text below and decide which answer (**A, B, C** or **D**) best fits each gap. There is an example at the beginning (**0**).

Mark your answers **on the separate answer sheet**.

Example:

0 **A** appear   **B** grow   **C** spring   **D** rise

| 0 | **A** | **B** | **C** | **D** |

'Living' walls reduce pollution in cities

Buildings covered in greenery are starting to (**0**) …….. in cities around the world. These living walls are the outside surfaces of buildings, bursting all over with vegetation. They certainly look pretty, but there's a far more interesting (**1**) …….. for their existence.

According to biogeochemists, the green walls – which are covered with pre-planted panels – offer several (**2**) …….. besides disguising an ugly façade. They have been (**3**) …….. to cool the building down, reduce noise, and make the block more energy (**4**) …….. .

But what's really exciting is that green walls could potentially reduce air pollution in the 'corridors' between tall buildings on a street. As the wind (**5**) …….. through these man-made canyons, carrying with it traffic fumes and other environmental pollutants, the green walls appear to (**6**) …….. large amounts of the most (**7**) …….. chemicals in the air. This could be the perfect (**8**) …….. to the difficulty of improving air quality in some of the planet's most polluted cities.

1	**A** idea	**B** reason	**C** excuse	**D** argument
2	**A** profits	**B** values	**C** benefits	**D** positives
3	**A** demonstrated	**B** convinced	**C** accepted	**D** proven
4	**A** efficient	**B** practical	**C** economical	**D** appropriate
5	**A** runs	**B** travels	**C** rolls	**D** flies
6	**A** soak	**B** breathe	**C** take	**D** absorb
7	**A** painful	**B** hurtful	**C** harmful	**D** unhelpful
8	**A** solution	**B** action	**C** result	**D** reaction

For questions **9–16**, read the text below and think of the word which best fits each gap. Use only **one** word in each gap. There is an example at the beginning (**0**).

Write your answers **IN CAPITAL LETTERS on the separate answer sheet**.

Example: | 0 | I | S | | | | | | | | | | | | | | | | | | | | |

Smile, please!

Photographers always insist that we smile when our photo (**0**) …….. being taken. But what (**9**) …….. we don't feel like smiling? Yet few of us would dare not to when we hear the words, 'Smile, please!'

(**10**) …….. do we expect other people to smile for the camera? Because we feel uncomfortable if they don't. When we look (**11**) …….. a photo of an event, we want to remember the occasion as having been (**12**) …….. happy one. How can you tell whether someone's smile is genuine (**13**) …….. not? Well, cheeks and lips will be raised, and eyes will crinkle at (**14**) …….. corners.

We don't just smile when we're happy, however. We also smile in order (**15**) …….. appear open to new acquaintances, provide a positive first impression of ourselves, or soften awkward situations. (**16**) …….. is nothing like smiling to help us get ahead both personally and professionally, and its positive effects can even help us live longer.

PAPER 1 Reading and ▶ Part 1
        Use of English Part 2

PAPER 2 Writing **Part 3**

PAPER 3 Listening Part 4

PAPER 4 Speaking Part 5

      Part 6

      Part 7

For questions **17–24**, read the text below. Use the word given in capitals at the end of some of the lines to form a word that fits the gap **in the same line**. There is an example at the beginning (**0**).

Write your answers **IN CAPITAL LETTERS on the separate answer sheet**.

Example: | 0 | L | O | C | A | T | E | D | | | | | | | | | | |

The world's oldest open-air museum

The Skansen museum, (**0**) ……… on an island near Stockholm, **LOCATE**
the capital of Sweden, is the world's oldest open-air museum. It
was founded in 1891 by a man called Artur Hazelius. Hazelius'
(**17**) ……… was to bring the traditional culture of his native **INTEND**
countryside to (**18**) ……… by exhibiting furnished houses and **LIVE**
farms, with small fields and gardens around them, as well as
domesticated and wild animals.

Around 150 houses and farms of (**19**) ……… interest have been **HISTORY**
moved to Skansen over the years, some of which might otherwise
have (**20**) ……… . The history of Sweden is reflected both in **APPEAR**
the buildings and their (**21**) ……… . Visitors can learn about the **SURROUND**
(**22**) ……… conditions in which people in Sweden lived between **SOCIETY**
the 16th and the mid-20th centuries. The (**23**) ……… of exhibits **MAJOR**
are from the 18th, 19th and early 20th centuries. Urban life in
Sweden is also represented, consisting (**24**) ……… of buildings **PRINCIPAL**
from Stockholm that were moved to Skansen during the 1920s
and 1930s.

For questions **25–30**, complete the second sentence so that it has a similar meaning to the first sentence, using the word given. **Do not change the word given.** You must use between **two** and **five** words, including the word given. Here is an example (**0**).

Example:

0   I've never seen a film as boring as this one.

   SUCH

   I've never seen .... as this one.

The gap can be filled by the words 'such a boring film', so you write:

Example: | **0** | SUCH A BORING FILM |

Write **only** the missing words **IN CAPITAL LETTERS on the separate answer sheet**.

---

25   Nobody has ever cleaned that statue while I've been working at the museum.
   BEEN
   That statue .... I first started working at the museum.

26   All Ian's friends know he prefers eating at home to eating in a restaurant.
   RATHER
   All Ian's friends know .... at home than in a restaurant.

27   Despite investing in faster technology, our production is slow.
   EVEN
   Our production is slow, ... in faster technology.

28   There's no way Bethany will resign from her job.
   INTENTION
   Bethany .... resigning from her job.

29   The cat would never go outside in the rain.
   WHEN
   The cat always refused .... was raining.

30   I didn't take a picture of that bird before it flew away, and now I regret it!
   SHOULD
   I .... a picture of that bird before it flew away!

PAPER 1	Reading and ▸	Part 1
	Use of English	Part 2
PAPER 2	Writing	Part 3
		Part 4
PAPER 3	Listening	**Part 5**
PAPER 4	Speaking	Part 6
		Part 7

You are going to read an article about learning to play the drums. For questions **31–36**, choose the answer (**A**, **B**, **C** or **D**) which you think fits best according to the text.

Mark your answers **on the separate answer sheet**.

Finding the beat

Will Jill Tunstall be able to keep up with the rhythm of her ten-year-old niece, Emma, as they learn how to play the drums?

In my family there are some with no musical ability (me) and others with plenty (virtually everybody else). I know why. As a teenager, piano lessons at the highly inconvenient time of 3 p.m. on a Saturday were always going to end quickly and badly. My niece, ten-year-old Emma, however, is at the top of the musical league. She is so rhythmically intelligent she can tell you in a nanosecond what dance she can do to any piece of music. I name a popular rock song. 'Oh, you can cha-cha-cha to that,' Emma tells me en route to our lesson in drumming. This is a first for both of us, so I'm hoping for some sort of level playing field.

Emma and I are about to spend two hours playing the noisiest of instruments. The drum is also the oldest instrument in the world, after the voice, says our teacher, Steve Hignett. He runs a UK music project that includes a weekly community drumming circle dedicated to world rhythm drumming. He introduces us to a small hand drum called the doumbek. Depending on where you whack it, and how, it produces a variety of sounds. Tapping away at random, I think I might finally have found my music. As the rest of the class arrive, they assure us that we'll fit in no problem. Even the most inexperienced can sit alongside those with a drumming track record. Drumming is also said to help with stress, anxiety and depression. The noise and the focus involved certainly blot everything else out as far as I'm concerned.

Steve bangs out basic beats and we follow suit. I start well, I think, but it isn't long before I go wrong. I make the mistake of looking at Emma and we burst into laughter. As the round comes to an end, at the signal blow of Steve's whistle, we both finish a loud and embarrassing beat behind everyone else. Steve is fine with this, and the whole group smile supportively at us, so with renewed energy I join in as we start again.

Some minutes later I'm feeling really into it when I look at Emma once more. She gives me that smile that mothers normally reserve for small children struggling with their lines in their first school play. Then, nodding enthusiastically, she urges me to pull back and just use one hand in a basic stroke. I listen to what *line 23* I'm playing and realise it is out of time with everybody else in the group, so I take her unspoken advice and concentrate hard before bringing in the other hand.

By now my arms and shoulders are aching like crazy and I feel as if I've done a tough work-out session. Emma holds up pink palms and we pull pained faces at each other. But there's no time to sit back. Steve pulls us out of the circle to play two huge drums. We get sticks with these, and they make a really big booming sound. Emma's young brain gets it straight away but I just cannot get the rhythm right. Nobody notices. That's the thing about playing the drums in a group with these volume levels. It's a far cry from standing out during a violin solo in a professional orchestra.

'We'll try an Arabic style now,' says Steve. I really concentrate and start to feel a bit more confident, even if I'm not in time. Emma, meanwhile, is on a roll, trying her hand at all sorts of drums. By the end of the evening, our arms throb, our hands are red and our ears are ringing. But we have enjoyed ourselves. Drumming rocks, we agree. And even though I'm hardly able to lift a spoon at breakfast next morning, we still find ourselves drumming on the table. I can't wait to go back.

31 What is the writer doing in the first paragraph?

    A expressing regret at not having continued with her music lessons
    B describing the kind of music she is usually interested in
    C highlighting the difference between her musical skills and those of her niece
    D explaining how her niece has developed such impressive musical skills

32 What does the writer say about drumming in the second paragraph?

    A It is known to help people boost their attention levels.
    B It has been shown to consistently improve people's mood.
    C It has become the most popular instrument to play in the UK.
    D It is a type of music that can be played without previous experience.

33 How does the writer feel when she and her niece make an obvious mistake?

    A guilty about spoiling the performance for others
    B amused by the group's reaction to their mistake
    C grateful for the encouragement of the others
    D ashamed of ignoring the teacher's advice

34 What does 'it' refer to in line 23?

    A the rhythm she is playing
    B the group of drummers
    C her niece's advice
    D her drum

35 What is participating in the drumming class compared to in the fifth paragraph?

    A completing a mental challenge
    B doing hard physical exercise
    C being a part of an orchestra
    D competing with professionals

36 By the end of the drumming session, the writer is

    A disappointed the class is over.
    B enthusiastic about the activity.
    D frustrated by her lack of progress.
    C glad she can follow one drumming style.

PAPER 1 Reading and ▶   Part 1
         Use of English   Part 2
PAPER 2 Writing   Part 3
                           Part 4
PAPER 3 Listening   Part 5
PAPER 4 Speaking   **Part 6**
                           Part 7

You are going to read an article about how body language can be the same all over the world. Six sentences have been removed from the article. Choose from the sentences **A–G** the one which fits each gap (**37–42**). There is one extra sentence which you do not need to use.

Mark your answers **on the separate answer sheet**.

Blind Olympic athletes show the universal nature of body language

A fascinating study has shown that the way people demonstrate pride is the same the world over.

Tune into any sports coverage on TV and you will see many an athlete proudly raise their arms and head in victory, while a much larger number hang their shoulders and necks in defeat. We've all shown the same body language ourselves and studies have revealed why – they are innate and universal behaviours, performed by humans all over the world in response to success and failure.

The discovery came from Jessica Tracy from the University of British Columbia and David Matsumoto from San Francisco State University, who wanted to see how people across different cultures expressed feelings of pride and shame. **37** ☐

But how to find out? We humans are very good at picking up behaviours from each other, which makes it very hard for a researcher to tell if an action is learned or innate. **38** ☐ And it was critically important that some of these subjects had never seen other people reacting to success or failure before – if they had, it would be impossible to confirm if the actions are inborn. Where could such a group of people be found?

The answer was Athens, during the 2004 Olympic Games. Its sister competition – the Paralympics – included many athletes who were born blind. **39** ☐ Working with a professional photographer (who wasn't briefed on the experiment's goals), Tracy and Matsumoto compared the body language of 108 judo competitors, 41 of whom had lost their sight, and

12 of whom were blind from birth. The Olympics being an international tournament, the fighters hailed from 37 nations across the world, from North Korea to Algeria to the United States.

The photographer repeatedly snapped the athletes after their competitions, and the researchers painstakingly recorded the positions of their head, arms and bodies. **40** ☐ The winners tilted their heads up, smiled, lifted their arms, clenched their fists and puffed out their chests, while slumped shoulders and narrowed chests were the hallmarks of losers.

The results provide strong evidence that these actions are indeed inborn. **41** ☐ And while it's possible that parents may have taught their blind children some of these behaviours (like raising their hands over their heads during play), it's very unlikely that they could have imparted the full set in this way, particularly the expansion or narrowing of the chest.

The stances were also remarkably consistent between men and women, and between contestants from every part of the world. **42** ☐ These results showed that behaviours associated with shame and pride are universal, and Tracy and Matsumoto argue that these emotions deserve a place alongside other primary emotions, such as happiness, fear, anger, surprise, sadness and disgust. Like these other sentiments, pride and shame are innate behaviours that transcend human cultures and are accompanied by their own distinct sets of actions.

A Therefore, they could not possibly have witnessed how their peers reacted to winning and losing.

B In particular, they wanted to know whether these expressions were instinctive, or whether they were culturally determined and learned through observation.

C After analysing this data, they found that the sighted and sightless athletes behaved in almost exactly the same ways.

D In fact, the athletes' culture was found to have only a very small effect on their body language.

E That strongly suggests that the sighted fighters were demonstrating their pride in accordance with their national values.

F Men and women who have never seen other people behave in these ways still make exactly the same movements.

G What Tracy and Matsumoto needed was a large group of people from all over the world, whom they could watch as they experienced success and failure.

PAPER 1 Reading and ▸   Part 1
       Use of English   Part 2
                      Part 3

PAPER 2 Writing   Part 4

PAPER 3 Listening   Part 5

PAPER 4 Speaking   Part 6

                      Part 7

You are going to read an article about an artist. For questions **43–52**, choose from the paragraphs (**A–E**). The paragraphs may be chosen more than once.

Mark your answers **on the separate answer sheet**.

Which paragraph mentions

the reasons why the artist uses a range of materials in her paintings?   **43**

the artist's belief that the way she works is bound to be connected to her character?   **44**

the artist's argument that her work is more serious than it might appear?   **45**

the capacity of painting to demonstrate a range of ideas and emotions?   **46**

why the artist changed her mind about the approach she takes to her work?   **47**

ongoing adjustments the artist makes that lead her to use a particular type of paint?   **48**

the fact that the artist enjoys seeking out new painting processes?   **49**

the artist's admiration for a particular artistic technique?   **50**

the artist's desire for her work not to go unnoticed?   **51**

the artist's lack of detailed planning when she works?   **52**

Artist Fiona Rae loves to show off in paint

Fiona Rae tells us how she develops her bold contemporary paintings.

A What I love about painting is that it embodies a series of thought and feeling processes. It's all there on the canvas as a record. I can put something on the canvas, consider it, adjust it, remove it, replace it, add to it, conceal it, reveal it, destroy it and repair it. I can be in a good mood, a bad mood or a cheerful mood – it's all useful. I tend to make up what I do on the canvas as I go along. I have a vague idea in mind, but usually abandon it pretty quickly. I use canvas on wooden stretchers, prepared with a couple of coats of primer and I then paint the canvas a flat colour in acrylic paint. Acrylic is a good base for oil colours, providing an even, non-absorbent surface.

B If I want to paint a hard-edged graphic symbol such as a letter, I usually do this in acrylic paint as well. Occasionally I use gouache paint on some of the little images I include, in order to have a different kind of look to the paint. Each type of paint has a different quality and texture, and I think it adds to the visual richness to apply colours using different paint media. I use oil paint for all the brushstrokes and drawing – this is because oil paint is so flexible that I can adjust what I'm doing almost endlessly. Oil paint is the most fantastically adaptable substance: once you've figured out how not to turn everything into an ugly grey, oil paint remains wet long enough for countless changes of mind, and because of the way the pigment is held in the oil, it shines beautifully.

C Source imagery can come from anywhere, although I'm still hooked on 15th-century German artist Dürer's woodcuts for the way he uses line so inventively to describe everything from patches of grass to cloudbursts. I also have a collection of symbols that I'm using at the moment – little angels, hearts, pandas ... I used to think I could only use something once, but I'm now realising that some of the ways I use paint, and some of the images I've come up with, are my own personal building blocks, and that each painting develops the theme further.

D The way I make paintings reflects the way I experience the world, and what I'm like as a person. I think this is unavoidable. I have never wanted to limit myself to one or two kinds of mark-making – I find it exciting and challenging to find different ways of using paint, both by looking at art history, and through the process of using paint itself. My paintings have an invented space that holds all the contents together – but I think that anything can go into that space, from heartfelt expressive marks to deliberate brushstrokes to graphic signs and symbols, and images.

E Just because I'm able to do lots of different things in paint, it doesn't mean I don't mean it. The paintings are not simply an exercise in being cool and turning the world on its head, they're a sincere attempt to make sense of the world and the joy and despair I feel at being alive. I also have to admit I enjoy showing off in paint. I don't want to make paintings that sit quietly in the corner of the room – I want to make paintings that are surprising and that have something new to add to the history of painting.

You **must** answer this question. Write your answer in **140–190** words in an appropriate style.

1   In your English class you have been talking about activities that people do in their free time. Now your English teacher has asked you to write an essay.

Write your essay using **all** the notes and give reasons for your point of view.

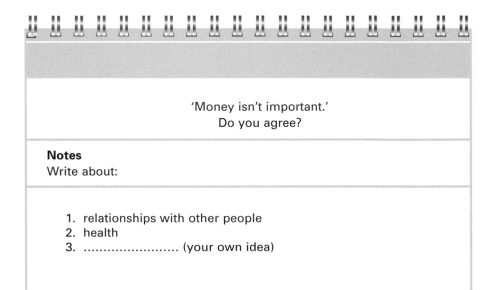

'Money isn't important.'
Do you agree?

Notes
Write about:

1. relationships with other people
2. health
3. .... (your own idea)

PAPER 1 Reading and
         Use of English

PAPER 2 Writing   ▶   Part 1

PAPER 3 Listening   Part 2

PAPER 4 Speaking

Write an answer to **one** of the questions **2–5** in this part. Write your answer in **140–190** words in an appropriate style.

2   You see this announcement in an English-language magazine.

> **Reviews wanted: An interesting documentary programme**
>
> Write a review about an interesting documentary programme you have seen on TV recently.
>
> The best reviews we receive will be published next month!

Write your **review**.

3   This is part of a letter you have received from your English friend, Paula.

> I'm going to go travelling with my family in August and we're going to visit a few different countries. I'd like to learn a few phrases in different languages so that I can communicate with local people. What kinds of phrases do you think I should learn and why?
>
> Thanks, Paula

Write your **letter**.

4   (*for FIRST candidates only*)

Your English teacher has asked you to write a report for students about how they can become healthier. Your report should include information about the services or places to go in your town which can help people to become healthier. You should also say which other service or place should be made available.

Write your **report**.

(*for FIRST FOR SCHOOLS candidates* only)

You have seen this notice on an English-language website.

> **We want your stories!**
>
> We're going to post a weekly story on our website and we'd love to post a story written by you! Your story must begin with this sentence:
>
> *I could see that my brother was really excited about something.*
>
> Your story must include:
> •   an unusual gift
> •   a trip to a city

Write your **story**.

5   (*for FIRST FOR SCHOOLS candidates* only)

Answer the following question based on the set text you have read.

Write an **essay** about the ending of the book you have read. Describe what happened in this part of the story and explain how the other events in the book led to this ending. Was the ending what you expected to happen? Why / Why not?

PAPER 1 Reading and Use of English

PAPER 2 Writing

PAPER 3 Listening   ▶

PAPER 4 Speaking

Part 1
Part 2
Part 3
Part 4

Track 29

You will hear people talking in eight different situations. For questions **1–8**, choose the best answer (**A**, **B** or **C**).

1   You hear an office manager talking about someone in her team.
    What does she say about him?
    A   He appreciates the advice she offers.
    B   He produces work of a high standard.
    C   He enjoys taking on challenging work.

2   You hear two people in a university swimming team talking about a recent training session.
    How does the woman feel now?
    A   pleased with her performance during training
    B   relieved she has been selected for a competition
    C   keen to increase the time she spends training

3   You hear a scientist talking on the radio about a medical development.
    What is he doing?
    A   criticising others in his field
    B   announcing a new discovery
    C   explaining a misunderstanding

4   You hear two psychology students talking about people who are famous.
    They agree that famous people
    A   prefer socialising with other celebrities.
    B   dislike being recognised everywhere.
    C   often become bored with their lifestyle.

5   You hear a shop assistant talking to a store detective about a customer.
    The shop assistant says the customer
    A   was polite.
    B   talked a great deal.
    C   had expert knowledge.

6   You hear two university students talking about their new football kit.
    What is the woman's opinion?
    A   It should have been less heavy.
    B   It should have been provided free of charge.
    C   It should have been a different colour.

7   You hear a maths teacher talking about what makes his job enjoyable.
    He says his job is enjoyable because
    A   his pupils are motivated.
    B   he has pleasant colleagues.
    C   the school is well-equipped.

8   You hear two tourist information officers talking about a tourist attraction.
    What does the man say about it?
    A   It needs advertising more widely.
    B   There are few places to buy food.
    C   Tourists consider it old-fashioned.

PAPER 1 Reading and
         Use of English

PAPER 2 Writing

PAPER 3 Listening   ▶

PAPER 4 Speaking

Part 1
Part 2
Part 3
Part 4

🎧 **Track 30**

You will hear a student called Jane Stubbs talking to a group of other students about a geography field trip she went on as part of her course. For questions **9–18**, complete the sentences with a word or short phrase.

Geography field trip

Jane says the geography field centre is in what is known
as a (**9**) ' .... area'.

Jane heard a talk on the first day about
(**10**) .... that live near the centre.

On the walk Jane saw a (**11**) ....
made of iron that was 100 years old.

On the second day the groups had to decide which
(**12**) .... they wanted to do
during their time at the centre.

Jane's (**13**) .... could no longer be used
after it blew away.

Jane went to the (**14**) .... to collect water samples.

Jane found the (**15**) .... she had
learned at school was useful.

On the last day, the students gave their presentations in order
of (**16**) ....

Jane enjoyed the presentation on farms involved in
making (**17**) .... products.

The students gave some (**18**) ....
to the field centre staff before leaving.

PAPER 1 Reading and
             Use of English

PAPER 2 Writing

PAPER 3 Listening ▶

PAPER 4 Speaking

Part 1
Part 2
Part 3
Part 4

 Track 31

You will hear five short extracts in which people are talking about digital books. For questions **19–23**, choose from the list (**A–H**) what each speaker says. Use the letters only once. There are three extra letters which you do not need to use.

A I can see the words very clearly.

B I only read digital books when I travel.

C I can't always find what I want in digital format.

D I wouldn't consider replacing all my paper books with digital books.

E I always have a new digital book ready to read next.

F I like the quality of the pictures.

G I don't find digital books particularly convenient.

H I appreciate all the extra features.

Speaker 1	19
Speaker 2	20
Speaker 3	21
Speaker 4	22
Speaker 5	23

Track 32

You will hear a radio interview with a student architect called Claire Hirst. For questions **24–30**, choose the best answer (**A**, **B** or **C**).

24 What does Claire say she has enjoyed learning on her course?
    A how to explain her ideas to her fellow students
    B how construction workers actually put up a building
    C how architects combine practical and creative skills

25 Claire says that in their final year of studies students find they
    A work on their own more than previously.
    B get more advice from the tutors.
    C have fewer projects to do.

26 How does Claire say doing work placements has helped her?
    A It has allowed her to make a decision about the future.
    B It has developed most of the skills she already had.
    C It has confirmed what she imagined about the job.

27 What does Claire say about the project she is currently working on?
    A She knows the building will be constructed one day.
    B She is pleased with the work she has done on it.
    C She is glad the materials she chose have reduced costs.

28 Claire says that when designing people's homes, architects should
    A imagine living there themselves.
    B try to make them interesting.
    C consider who will live in them.

29 What does Claire say about finding a job as an architect?
    A Having interview experience is useful.
    B Phoning architects' offices is effective.
    C Recommendations by tutors can help.

30 What does Claire say people thinking of studying architecture should know?
    A Make sure you can afford the extra course materials.
    B You can expect to socialise a lot on your course.
    C It is a very long course and the work is difficult.

Part 1 (2 minutes)

The examiner (interlocutor) will ask each of you to speak briefly in turn and to give personal information about yourselves. You can expect a variety of questions, such as:

What sort of leisure activities are available for young people in your area?
Have you used any of your local leisure facilities recently? (Where did you go?)
Would you like to try a new leisure activity in the future? (What would you like to do?)

Part 2 (4 minutes)

You will each be asked to talk for a minute without interruption. You will each be given two different photographs in turn to talk about. After your partner has finished speaking, you will be asked a brief question connected with your partner's photographs.

1 Cooking

Look at the two photographs on page 180 which show people cooking in different ways.

Candidate A, compare these photographs, and say why you think the people are cooking in these different ways.

Candidate B, which meal would you prefer to eat? (Why?)

2 Shopping

Look at the two photographs on page 181 which show people shopping in different ways.

Candidate B, compare these photographs, and say why you think the people prefer to shop in these different ways.

Candidate A, how do you prefer to shop? (Why?)

Part 3 (4 minutes)

You will be asked to discuss something together without interruption by the examiner. You will have a page of ideas with a question to help you.

Improving your college

Imagine you have been given enough money to build one new thing for your college. Turn to page 182 which shows some ideas for things you could spend the money on. Talk to each other about how each idea would improve the college. Then decide which **two** of the ideas would be the best ways to improve your college.

Part 4 (4 minutes)

The examiner will encourage you to develop the topic of your discussion in Part 3 by asking questions such as:

How important is it for people to have access to computers at college? (Why?)
Do you think children should be allowed to take their own computer to school if they have one? (Why? / Why not?)
Are libraries still necessary these days now that people can download books so easily from the internet? (Why?)
Is good teaching the only important thing at a school or college? (Why? / Why not?)
What are the most important subjects for people to study at college? (Why?)

▶▶ **PART 5**

nanosecond (n) a very short period of time

en route (adv) on the way

level playing field (phr) at an equal level

dedicated to (v) focused on, giving energy and time to

whack (v) to hit with a lot of force

at random (phr) with no method

track record (phr) reputation, experience

blot out (phr v) make you completely ignore or forget

follow suit (phr) to do what everyone else does

supportively (adv) encouragingly

urge (v) to insist, encourage strongly

stroke (n) a hit, beat

pained (adj) hurt, as if experiencing pain

booming (adj) loud, with a deep loud sound that continues for some time

be a far cry from (phr) be very different to

be on a roll (phr) having a successful period

throb (v) if a painful part of your body throbs, the pain comes and goes again and again in a regular pattern

rock (v) to be really good

▶▶ **PART 6**

innate (adj) born within us

shame (n) a feeling of embarrassment or guilt that you have when you have behaved badly

critically (adv) very

inborn (adj) born within us

hail from (phr) come from

snap (v) to take a photo

painstakingly (adv) slowly and with great care

tilt (v) to lift upwards

clench (v) to tighten the muscles in a part of the body

puff out (v) to push up and outwards

hallmark (n) a typical sign

expansion (n) increase in size

primary (adj) main, most important

sentiment (n) a feeling

instinctive (adj) natural feeling

determined (adj) decided by

▶▶ **PART 7**

embody (v) to represent an idea

canvas (n) a kind of fabric which artists use to paint on

conceal (v) to hide

vague (adj) unclear

abandon (v) to stop doing

stretcher (n) a frame for a canvas painting

primer (n) a preparation substance

acrylic (n) a kind of paint commonly used by artists

gouache (n) a kind of paint used by artists which is mixed with water and a kind of glue

texture (n) the way something feels when you touch it

media (n) substances used in creating artworks, such as paint, pencil, etc.

pigment (n) natural colour

imagery (n) visual images

be hooked (phr) if you are hooked on something, you find it so interesting or enjoyable that you want to do it all the time

patch (n) an area

heartfelt (adj) deep, strong, sincerely felt

CAMBRIDGE ENGLISH
Language Assessment
Part of the University of Cambridge

Do not write in this box

Candidate Name
If not already printed, write name
in CAPITALS and complete the
Candidate No. grid (in pencil).

Candidate Signature

SAMPLE

Examination Title

Centre

Supervisor:

If the candidate is ABSENT or has WITHDRAWN shade here ▭

Centre No.

Candidate No.

Examination Details

0	0	0	0
1	1	1	1
2	2	2	2
3	3	3	3
4	4	4	4
5	5	5	5
6	6	6	6
7	7	7	7
8	8	8	8
9	9	9	9

Candidate Answer Sheet

Instructions
Use a PENCIL (B or HB). Rub out any answer you wish to change using an eraser.

Part 1: Mark ONE letter for each question.

For example, if you think **B** is the right answer to the question, mark your answer sheet like this:

`0  A  B̶  C  D`

Parts 2, 3 and **4:** Write your answer clearly in CAPITAL LETTERS.

For Parts 2 and 3 write one letter in each box. For example:

`0  E X A M P L E`

Part 1

1	A	B	C	D
2	A	B	C	D
3	A	B	C	D
4	A	B	C	D
5	A	B	C	D
6	A	B	C	D
7	A	B	C	D
8	A	B	C	D

Part 2

Do not write below here

9		9 1 0 u
10		10 1 0 u
11		11 1 0 u
12		12 1 0 u
13		13 1 0 u
14		14 1 0 u
15		15 1 0 u
16		16 1 0 u

Continues over ➡

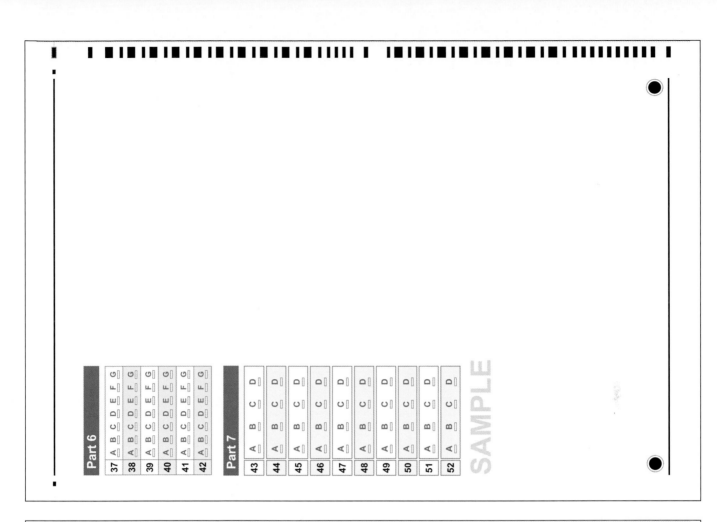

Part 6

37	A	B	C	D	E	F	G
38	A	B	C	D	E	F	G
39	A	B	C	D	E	F	G
40	A	B	C	D	E	F	G
41	A	B	C	D	E	F	G
42	A	B	C	D	E	F	G

Part 7

43	A	B	C	D
44	A	B	C	D
45	A	B	C	D
46	A	B	C	D
47	A	B	C	D
48	A	B	C	D
49	A	B	C	D
50	A	B	C	D
51	A	B	C	D
52	A	B	C	D

SAMPLE

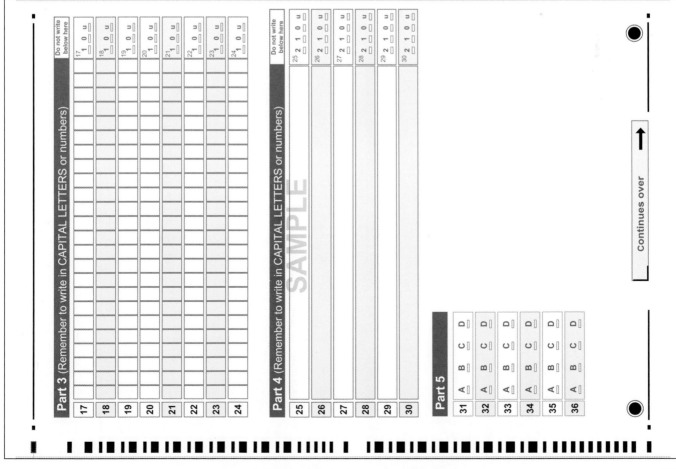

Part 3 (Remember to write in CAPITAL LETTERS or numbers)

Do not write below here

17	1	0	u
18	1	0	u
19	1	0	u
20	1	0	u
21	1	0	u
22	1	0	u
23	1	0	u
24	1	0	u

Part 4 (Remember to write in CAPITAL LETTERS or numbers)

Do not write below here

25	2	1	0	u
26	2	1	0	u
27	2	1	0	u
28	2	1	0	u
29	2	1	0	u
30	2	1	0	u

SAMPLE

Part 5

31	A	B	C	D
32	A	B	C	D
33	A	B	C	D
34	A	B	C	D
35	A	B	C	D
36	A	B	C	D

Continues over ↑

157

Paper 3 Listening

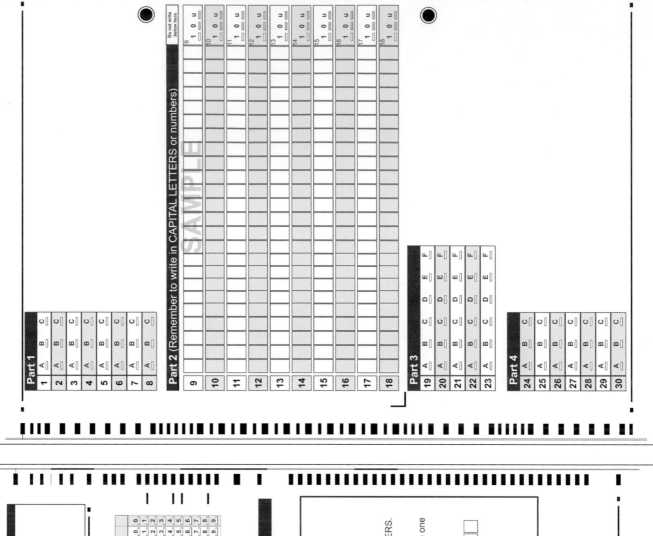

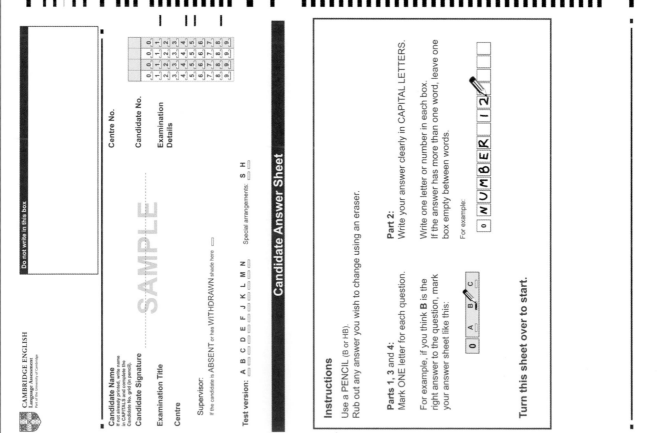

CAMBRIDGE ENGLISH
Language Assessment
Part of the University of Cambridge

Do not write in this box

Candidate Name
If not already printed, write name
in CAPITALS and complete the
Candidate No. grid (in pencil).

Candidate Signature

Examination Title

Centre

Supervisor:
If the candidate is ABSENT or has WITHDRAWN shade here ☐

Test version: A B C D E F J K L M N   Special arrangements: S H

Centre No.

Candidate No.

Examination
Details

Candidate Answer Sheet

Instructions

Use a PENCIL (B or HB).
Rub out any answer you wish to change using an eraser.

Parts 1, 3 and 4:
Mark ONE letter for each question.

For example, if you think **B** is the
right answer to the question, mark
your answer sheet like this:

Part 2:
Write your answer clearly in CAPITAL LETTERS.

Write one letter or number in each box.
If the answer has more than one word, leave one
box empty between words.

For example:

Turn this sheet over to start.

Part 1
1 A B C
2 A B C
3 A B C
4 A B C
5 A B C
6 A B C
7 A B C
8 A B C

Part 2 (Remember to write in CAPITAL LETTERS or numbers)

Do not write
below here

9
10
11
12
13
14
15
16
17
18

Part 3
19 A B C D E F
20 A B C D E F
21 A B C D E F
22 A B C D E F
23 A B C D E F

Part 4
24 A B C
25 A B C
26 A B C
27 A B C
28 A B C
29 A B C
30 A B C

TEST FIRST 1

▶▶ **PART 2**

Candidate A

Language bank

The first picture shows a man sitting in his living room and eating pizza out of a box. It looks like he's watching the football on TV. Maybe he lives alone, so he's eating this way because the TV keeps him company. It's quite a relaxed way of eating. I think it might be boring to sit at the table on your own, so that's possibly why he chooses to eat like this. In the second picture there's a family sitting around a table and eating a meal together. They appear to be in their kitchen and the food looks nice and healthy. They look relaxed and happy and seem to be having a conversation. They probably enjoy catching up with each other after a busy day at school or work, and sitting at the table eating a meal together is a great opportunity to do this.

Why do people enjoy eating in these different places at home?

▶ **1**

▶ **2**

▶▶ **PART 2**

Candidate B

Language bank

In the first picture, there's a family at home in their living room watching television. It looks like they're watching a football match. The kids are sitting very near their parents and they look really relaxed, but also very interested in the game. Quite often families support the same football team, so this is an excellent way for them to spend time together doing something they all enjoy. In the second picture, the family is playing some sort of board game. They're laughing and it looks as though the little boy has won the game because he seems to be cheering. Playing a game together can be really good fun, and it gives family members a chance to interact with each other in a non-serious way, so I think that's why they're doing this together.

Why might the families be doing these different activities together?

▶▶ **PART 3**
Candidates A and B

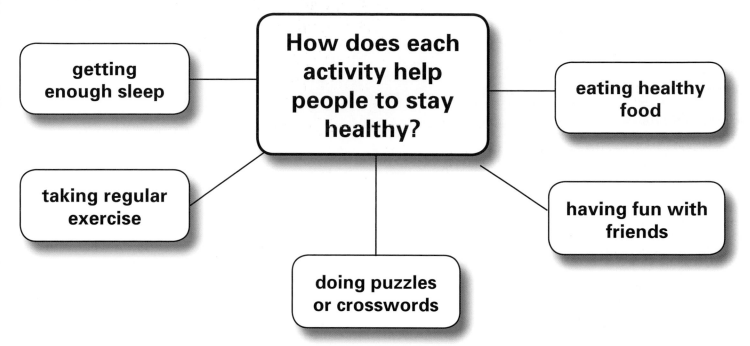

Language bank

So, first of all, we have to talk about how each activity helps people to keep healthy. It's really important to get enough sleep, isn't it?

Yes, it is. If you don't, it can affect you physically and mentally. You need sleep to feel refreshed and give your body and mind time to rest. Taking exercise is essential, too. It helps you to keep fit, doesn't it?

Exactly, and I think eating healthy food is vital to keep ourselves in good shape and avoid disease. What about having fun with friends? How do you think that helps us to stay healthy?

Maybe because if we share problems and have a laugh, we'll feel better emotionally, won't we?

I see what you mean. And I think doing puzzles or crosswords is a good way to keep your brain active.

OK, now we need to decide which two activities to include in the talk. I think we should go for things we know plenty about. I do a lot of exercise, so we could talk about that. What do you think?

Good idea. And I know some good healthy recipes, so we could include those, too. Do you agree?

Yes, I do. So let's choose 'taking regular exercise' and 'eating healthy food' then.

▶▶ PART 2

Candidate A

Language bank

In the first picture, there are two people skiing in the mountains. There are no other people around them, and there's lots of snow. They look as if they're setting off down a steep slope and it looks very exciting. They might have chosen to go skiing because it's their hobby. They certainly seem to know what they are doing! In the second picture, I can see two people wearing what appears to be scuba diving equipment – at least I think that's what it is. There is a large number of small silver fish swimming around them, and the two people are standing or kneeling on the seabed, under some kind of rock, or maybe it's a reef. These people have probably decided to go diving so they can see and experience new things and maybe also because it's quite a relaxing thing to do in warm waters.

Why have the people chosen to do these different holiday activities?

▶ 1

▶ 2

▶▶ **PART 2**

Candidate B

Language bank

Both the pictures show young women sitting down, but in one picture the woman has a laptop and looks as if she's somewhere quite busy – like a park in a city centre, perhaps. There are trees in the background and people walking past. It doesn't look very comfortable, because she's sitting on a pavement or path of some kind, but maybe she likes sitting there and working or just browsing the internet. If she works in a busy office, maybe that's what she enjoys doing in her lunch break. In the other picture, the woman is completely on her own, by the sea. She also looks relaxed and happy, but she's more casually dressed than the other woman. Maybe she's on holiday or having a day out at the seaside. She probably enjoys the peace and quiet, the view and all the fresh air.

What might the people like about being where they are?

▶ **1**

▶ **2**

▶▶ **PART 3**
   Candidates A and B

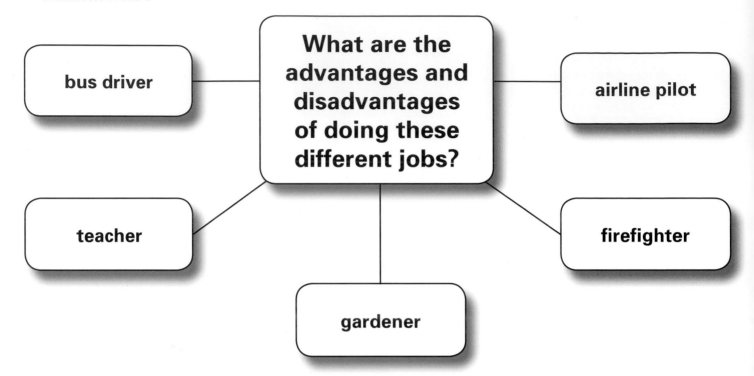

bus driver

What are the advantages and disadvantages of doing these different jobs?

airline pilot

teacher

firefighter

gardener

Language bank

OK, let's start with being an airline pilot. If you're a pilot, you get to travel a lot, and your work may take you to exotic places. It's well paid, but it's also very stressful.

You're right. Some of the other jobs aren't as exciting, but they must be satisfying to do, because you can help other people.

Do you mean being a teacher or a firefighter?

Yes, and they're essential jobs for society. I think being a teacher can sometimes be difficult, but it's an important job.

I wouldn't mind being a gardener, because although it's physically demanding, you get to work outdoors, and you're not working under pressure like in the other jobs. What do you think? Which two jobs would you like to do?

Well, I'd quite like to be a gardener too, but I've also always thought it would be good to be a bus driver. It isn't very well paid in my country, but I'd like to drive around my city all day. But I wouldn't like to deal with awkward passengers!

No, I wouldn't either.

▸▸ PART 2
Candidate A

Language bank

In the first picture there's a man who looks like he's in his fifties. He must be a teacher because he's at the front of the classroom and it looks like he's explaining something on the board. He's in a wheelchair and he's teaching a group of adults. There are both women and men in the class I think. It looks like they could be studying maths. In the second picture there's a child and someone who looks like she's teaching him. She could be a private teacher, or perhaps the boy's mother. It looks like the boy is learning at home. Both methods of learning have their advantages and disadvantages and are enjoyable in different ways. I think learning in a group is good because you can talk to the other students and discuss your ideas, whereas in a private class you get more attention from the teacher, and you probably learn more quickly this way.

Why might the people enjoy learning in these different environments?

▸ 1

▸ 2

> ▶ **PART 2**
>
> **Candidate B**

Language bank

In the first picture you can see a man, who may be about 40, riding a bike. He's wearing a coat or a suit with a helmet and it looks like he might be on his way to work. He's carrying something on the back of his bike and there's a bag in the basket on the front. That could be work or perhaps even his lunch. It looks like people are going to work in the second picture, too, because they seem to be wearing work clothes. I think they're on a train and it looks quite full. The man might prefer to travel by bike because it's a way of exercising and it's good for the environment too. Bikes don't cause pollution. The people on the train have probably chosen to travel this way because it's more relaxing and comfortable. Another advantage is that it's probably faster, especially if they have a long way to travel. They're also protected against bad weather and it's a more sociable way to travel.

Why might the people prefer to travel in these ways?

▶ 1

▶ 2

▶▶ **PART 3**

Candidates A and B

a water bottle

How useful is each object for a walking trip in the mountains?

some sandwiches

a detailed map of the area

a waterproof jacket

strong walking boots

Language bank

Going on a walking trip certainly needs some planning, doesn't it? Water is essential, don't you think? You can't survive without that.

Yes, I agree. And strong boots are a must as well – they protect your feet and ankles against mud or rocks.

And they make walking comfortable, too. You don't want to get blisters. What about sandwiches? Well, food's important for energy if you're doing a long walk, especially uphill.

Absolutely. What about a map? That would be really useful if you don't know the route and you aren't with a guide.

Yes, and you can find you way back if you get lost. What else? A waterproof jacket might be useful if you're likely to be walking in wet weather.

The weather can change really quickly in the mountains, can't it? So which two things do you think are most useful? I think water would be our first choice from what we've said.

I totally agree with you. And I'd take the map, though you might not agree with me there.

I think good boots are more important because they make so much difference when you're walking.

OK, let's go with water and boots then. I think we've reached an agreement, haven't we?

▶▶ **PART 2**

Candidate A

Language bank

The pictures both show people who look as if they're enjoying what they're doing, but they're playing music in very different settings. In one picture, there are three teenage boys in what appears to be the garage of a house. One of them is playing the drums, and the other two are playing electric guitars – they might be playing rock or pop. They probably enjoy experimenting with music together in this relaxed way. In the other picture I can see a young male piano player, very formally dressed in a black suit. He could be in a concert hall – I can just make out a few members of the audience in the front rows. I imagine he's playing classical music and he looks as though he's enjoying himself as much as the people in the band in the other picture, but unlike them he's playing on his own. He might be enjoying the fact that the audience is listening to him.

Why do the people enjoy playing music in these different ways?

▶▶ **PART 2**

Candidate B

Language bank

In one picture there's a woman jogging on her own along the side of a main road. She looks as if she may be crossing a bridge and I think she must be in a city. I'd say she enjoys running on her own, because by running alone she can go at her own pace and choose the route she wants to take. She may well run every day early in the morning or after work. In the second picture there's a very large group of men running up a hill on some grass, so they're likely to be in the countryside. They're all wearing numbers and I think they're in a long-distance cross-country race. They're all close together, so I'd imagine they've only just set off. They probably enjoy competing against each other, but I expect that they train for their races by running on their own like the woman in the other picture.

What do the people enjoy about running in these different situations?

▶ 1

▶ 2

▶▶ **PART 3**

Candidates A and B

an art gallery

Which places would be good for the students to visit?

a science exhibition

a sports centre

a historical building

a food festival

Language bank

I think these are all good places to visit, don't you?

Yes, I do. The students are in an English class, though, do you think that matters?

Well I imagine that wherever they go with their English teacher, they'll all have to speak English together as much as possible anyway. But now I come to think about it, I'm not sure a sports centre is really such a good idea.

Oh, why's that?

It's not really somewhere they can all do things together all day.

I'm not sure I agree. I mean they could take part in team games and compete in groups against one another.

Yes, you're right. But I still think that maybe somewhere like a historical building would be better. Then the teacher could tell the students about it in English and the students could ask questions. Which of the other places do you think would be good?

I'd enjoy the food festival myself. I think that would be both fun and interesting. How about you?

Yes, I couldn't agree with you more! So let's go for the historical building and the food festival as the two best places, shall we?

Sure. That's a good combination.

▶▶ **PART 2**

Candidate A

Language bank

In the first picture I can see a man and a woman by a car. They look about the same age. The man is helping the woman to stand up from or get into her wheelchair. He must have helped her to get out of the car or is about to help her get into the car because she probably isn't mobile enough to do this on her own. He might have chosen to help her because she's a friend who is ill and perhaps lives on her own. In the second photo it looks as if the younger woman is helping the older woman to do something on the computer. The younger woman is pointing at the screen. The women could be members of the same family, or neighbours, and they appear to be in someone's home. I notice that there are some brochures or something similar on the table, so perhaps the elderly woman wants to book a holiday. The younger woman probably knows more about using computers than the older woman as she's more likely to have grown up with them, so that might be why she's chosen to help.

Why have the people chosen to help others in these different ways?

▶▶ **PART 2**

Candidate B

Language bank

In the first photo there's a boy reading what looks like a magazine or comic book. He's smiling at something, so he must be enjoying what he's reading. It's quite an informal setting – it looks like he's in the garden. The second picture is more serious. A businesswoman is reading a newspaper. She must be in her office or at work because she's wearing smart clothes and is sitting at a desk, I think. People read different thing for different reasons, don't they? The boy is probably reading his comic for fun and entertainment in his free time, whereas the businesswoman could be catching up on important news that might affect the work she does. She could be a banker, for example, and wants to know what's going on in that world.

Why have the people chosen to read these different things?

▶ 1

▶ 2

▸▸ **PART 3**
   Candidates A and B

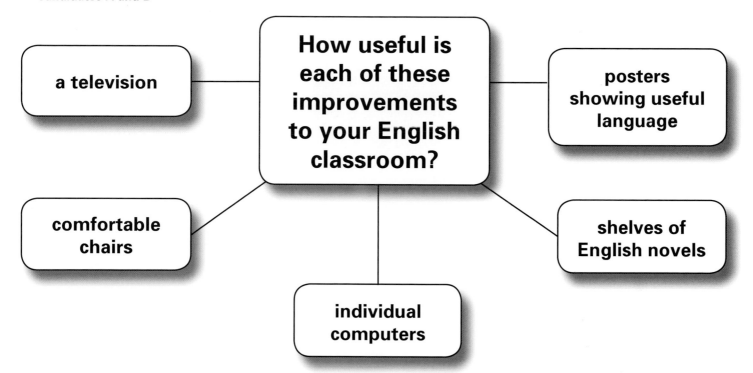

Language bank

I think the room could definitely be improved with these things! A TV would be great – we could watch films and programmes in English.

I'm not sure that would be very helpful unless your English is really good. I find it quite difficult to follow things in English on TV. The posters sound like a good idea. You could refer to them while you're working.

Yes, I'm with you on that, especially if they show verb patterns or tenses. I always get those confused. What else? It would be nice to have individual computers, so we could all use the internet at the same time.

Comfy chairs would be good as well – though if you get too comfortable, you might not want to do any work! What about novels? They're stories, aren't they?

That's right, yes. I'm not keen on reading, even in my own language, but I know it's useful for learning vocabulary and improving your writing. We need to choose two things now. What would be your choice?

I think I'd go for the computers and the posters, because you'd have good access to accurate and natural English with those.

Well, I think we've reached a decision. Posters and computers.

▶ ▶ PART 2

Candidate A

Language bank

The pictures both show people looking at things in museums, but the museums are quite different. In the first picture there's a young woman looking at a gold necklace, I think, in a glass case. I think she may be interested in history and enjoy finding out about how people lived and dressed in the past. In the other picture, an older man is pointing at or touching something on a computer screen. He must be in a more modern type of exhibition, where people can use technology to learn more about the things in the exhibition. Some people find more old-fashioned museums like the one the woman's in a bit boring, but more and more museums nowadays tend to have interactive exhibits like the one in the second picture. A lot of people prefer that kind of exhibition because it's more exciting and varied, and you learn in an active way, so maybe that's what the man likes about the museum he's in.

What might people enjoy about being in these different museums?

▶ 1

▶ 2

▶▶ PART 2
Candidate B

Language bank

The two pictures are of people at work, but in very different working environments. In one picture, the people are wearing more casual clothes and are sitting round a table with cups of what looks like tea or coffee. They appear to be discussing something in quite a relaxed way and it looks as if they all get on well together and enjoy working there. The other workplace is very different. I can see a woman in the foreground wearing a smart blouse and there are two more people in the background, who seem to be doing the same thing as the woman. She has headphones on and is typing something on a keyboard. Perhaps this place is a call centre. She doesn't look as relaxed as the people in the other picture, but she doesn't look unhappy. I suppose she might feel a bit isolated sometimes, since it doesn't look like the sort of office where you could easily chat to your workmates.

How do the people feel about working in these different environments?

▶ 1

▶ 2

▶▶ **PART 3**
  Candidates A and B

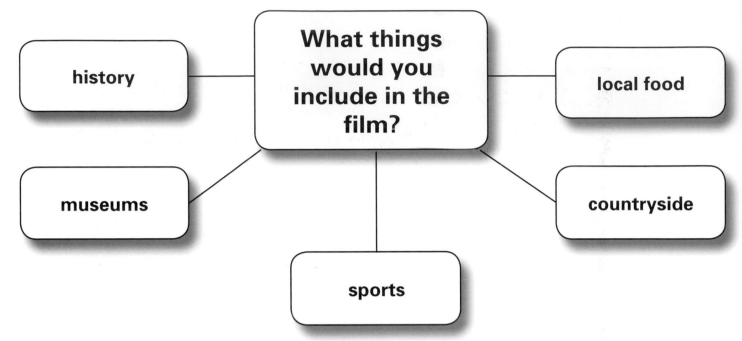

Language bank

There are so many things to include in a film about our area that it's a little hard to choose, isn't it?

Absolutely! I think these would all be worth putting in. Shall we look at each one before we decide?

Good idea. So, let's take history to start with. Why don't we show some of the historical buildings and talk about the famous people who lived here in the past?

OK. It would also be good to include people making typical dishes from round here. Yes, and also where the food is grown – then there'd be shots of all the beautiful countryside around here.

That's right. And then we wouldn't need to include the countryside as a separate topic – it could come under food, couldn't it?

Good thinking! I like that idea.

Thanks! So what else? I'm not sure if we need to include sports – it isn't as if sports are particularly important in our region, really.

Well there's the football team. I'd forgotten about that.

Oh no, I want to include everything, but we have to decide on just two! We haven't talked about museums, but I suppose they could come under history.

Yes, why not? So shall we go for history and food, then?

OK.

▸▸ **PART 2**

Candidate A

Language bank

The first photo shows a group of girls chatting. They're about the same age, so they must be friends, rather than relatives, though I suppose they could be cousins, perhaps. I think they're sitting on the steps of a monument or something like that. They look like they're having a nice time and enjoying each other's company. In the second picture the man is talking to a woman on screen. It looks like he's using a sort of computer tablet to do this. The woman looks older than him, so she might be his mum or aunt. I think the girls are together because they probably live in the same area, so it's easy for them to meet and spend time with each other. It could be that the man and woman don't live close to each other and that's why they're using the internet to keep in touch.

> **Why have the people chosen to chat to friends or relatives in these different ways?**

▸ 1

▸ 2

▶▶ **PART 2**

Candidate B

Language bank

In both of the photographs, I can see people at the cinema, but it looks as if they're watching very different types of film. In the first picture, the people in the audience look rather scared, whereas in the other photo they're laughing. I think the family who look so frightened must be watching a scary film, though it can't be that scary because the children seem quite young. They could be watching an adventure film, and this might be a really frightening bit. I imagine that people like these films because they find them exciting. On the other hand, people also love comedy films because everybody likes to have a good laugh from time to time. It's a good way of relaxing and spending time with your friends or family.

What might the people enjoy about watching these different types of film?

▶ **1**

▶ **2**

▶▶ **PART 3**
  Candidates A and B

	How enjoyable might each of these activities be for a class party?	
watching a film in English		**sharing food**
doing a quiz about things you've learned		**playing board games**
	listening to music	

Language bank

Do you think it would be difficult to organise a party for our English class?

I don't think so. There are some good ideas about things to do here. Everyone loves music, don't they? So, in my opinion, it would be a good idea to have some music on. It helps create a party atmosphere.

It does, but I doubt everyone would agree on what kind of music to play! Food's always a nice thing to have at a party. Everyone could make a different dish and bring it to share.

That's a good idea. I don't know about watching a film. Everyone would have to sit quietly, wouldn't they?

Yes, it wouldn't really be a party if we watched a film, would it? And personally, I don't really like quizzes. I'm always worried I won't know the answers.

I know what you mean – I'm not that keen on them either. Playing board games is a nice idea.

Depending on which game it can be a bit boring, though, don't you think?

Anyway, let's decide which two things to choose for our party. I'd vote for the food and the music, though you might not agree with me about the music.

Well, I think the games would be better, because they're good fun. Otherwise it might get a bit boring just standing around and chatting.

I see what you mean. OK. Let's go for the food and the games, then.

▶▶ **PART 2**

Candidate A

Language bank

In the two photographs, there are men cooking, or at least preparing food. The man in the first photograph is putting a ready meal into a microwave. The second picture shows a man chopping vegetables, and I think he's following a recipe on his tablet. The first man is probably going to eat quite an unhealthy meal. In contrast, the one who's doing the cooking is using a lot of healthy ingredients: a variety of fresh vegetables and a chicken. Maybe he's about to put it into the oven with the vegetables. He's putting quite a lot of effort into what he's doing, probably because he wants to eat healthily. He might be cooking for more than person – possibly his family or a few guests. On the other hand the man with the ready meal may be in a hurry, and he's cooking something he'll be able to eat almost straightaway.

Why are the people cooking in these different ways?

▶ **1**

▶ **2**

▶▶ **PART 2**

Candidate B

Language bank

The two photos show people shopping, but in different ways. In the first picture, the woman is holding a credit card and is doing something on her laptop. I imagine that means she's just bought something online, or is in the process of entering her card details. She looks quite pleased with herself, so she must be happy with what she's decided to buy. The second photo shows two people in a department store. They look like mother and daughter. Maybe the girl's mum is buying her some new clothes. They look like they're talking about the dress the girl's holding up. I can't tell whether they like it or not from their expressions, though. People shop online because it's convenient – you don't even have to leave the house. The downside is that you can't see the product before you pay for it. If you go to a shop you can try things on and decide whether you like them before you buy them. You do have to make more effort, but at least you save yourself some trouble if the product isn't right.

Why do the people prefer to shop in these different ways?

▶ 1

▶ 2

▶▶ PART 3

Candidates A and B

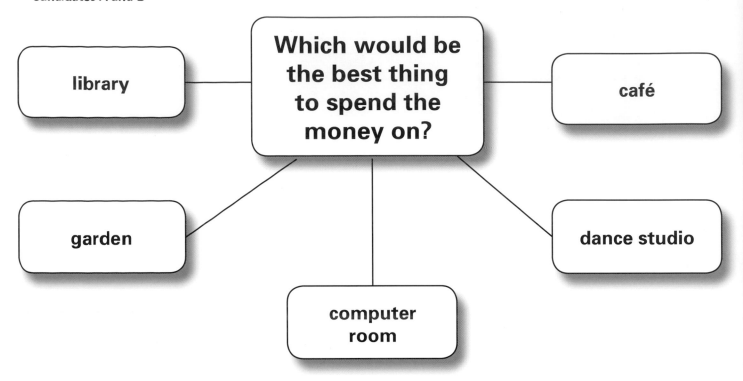

library

Which would be the best thing to spend the money on?

café

garden

dance studio

computer room

Language bank

What do you think the most useful thing would be for the college?

We already have a library, don't we, but all the other things would be good, wouldn't they? Personally, I don't think we really need to spend money on a garden. But a dance studio would be fantastic.

In my opinion, that wouldn't be such a good idea. After all, not everybody's interested in dance. Don't you think it would be better to spend the money on something that everyone could use?

I suppose you may be right. How about a new computer room? The one we have is a bit too small, and it would be nice to have some new computers, too.

I'm not so sure about that. I mean lots of people can use the computers in the library, too, so it doesn't seem to me that a new computer room is really necessary.

That's true. Well what about a café, then? We don't have anywhere to sit and relax during our breaks, and when it's raining we can't go outside.

Yes, I think a café's a great idea.

All right, let's go for the café, then.

Preparing, planning and checking

▶▶ Preparing for the Writing Paper

One of the best ways to improve your writing skills is to read as widely as possible. This will help you to expand your range of vocabulary and grammatical structures. You also need to study the basic text types which you may be asked to produce in the exam, and have a good understanding of their basic features: layout, organisation, style and register (level of formality). You should also practise completing writing tasks in the time allowed in the exam. Remember the criteria the examiners will use in awarding marks:

- Has the candidate achieved the purpose stated in the instructions?
- Does the text have a positive general effect on the target reader?
- Does the text cover all the content points?
- Is the text well organised and are ideas linked appropriately?
- Has language been used accurately?
- Does the text show a good range of vocabulary and grammatical structures?
- Is the register appropriate for the task?
- Is the layout appropriate?

If possible, ask an experienced teacher to provide feedback on pieces of writing you produce when you are practising for the exam. This will help you to learn what kind of mistakes you frequently make so that you can avoid them. For example, if you often make mistakes with a certain tense, you can ask your teacher to explain it to you again, or you can use a good grammar guide to help you. It's also a good idea to make a list of expressions that you can include in your exam text, such as the useful phrases you find with the model answers in this section.

▶▶ Planning your answer

The most useful lesson to learn about writing is the importance of planning what to write before you actually start writing. In the exam you will only have time to write your text once, so you should make time to write a plan before you begin writing. This will help you to write your exam text more easily.

Always read the question carefully and make sure you understand the following:

- Who are you writing for (a friend, a teacher, other students)?
- What are the points you must include in your answer?

- Does the text type (an email, an article, a report, a review) have any particular layout requirements?
- Do you have the necessary vocabulary to answer the question on the topic?

When you are sure you understand what you have to do to answer the exam task, prepare a plan of what you are going to write. It doesn't matter if you change your plan or cross things out – nobody will read it. But it has to show clearly the different sections of your writing and which points you must include in which section (i.e. in the introduction, main body, and conclusion). When you look at the plan carefully, you might want to change it; for example, one point might be better in a different paragraph, or you might realise you will be repeating yourself. When you are satisfied with your plan, you will find it much quicker to write your text. Give yourself five minutes to make your plan before you start writing.

▶▶ Question 5, the set text task (*FIRST FOR SCHOOLS only*)

If you choose to write about one of the set texts, remember that the question may ask for an essay, article, email or letter. You may be asked to write about the characters, relationships or themes in the book. Make sure you know the story well, as you will need to support your views with examples from the book. When answering the question, think carefully about the target reader, and plan your answer accordingly.

Remember: Do **NOT** answer the set text question if you have not read the book.

▶▶ Checking

Most people make more mistakes than usual when they are writing under exam conditions. Always give yourself at least five minutes at the end to read through your work. First, check that you have answered the question correctly and that you have included all the information that was required. Second, check for mistakes in grammar, spelling, punctuation, etc. You should have enough writing experience by now to know where you often make mistakes – spelling certain words, for example, or using a particular type of punctuation.

If you need to change something in your text, make the correction carefully and make sure it is still easy for the examiner to read your work. If you need to cross out something you have written, just put one line through the word or words.

1 Essay

▶▶ **Exam task – Part 1**

You **must** answer this question. Write your answer in **140–190** words in an appropriate style.

In your English class you have been talking about eating habits. Now, your English teacher has asked you to write an essay.

Write an essay using **all** the notes and give reasons for your point of view.

Some people say that eating together regularly is the best way of staying close to family and friends.
What do you think?

Notes
Write about:

1. how much time people have to cook and eat
2. special occasions
3. .... (your own idea)

Useful phrases

Introducing the topic
The first point I would like to make is ...
Some people believe ...
Many people think ...
Most people would agree that ...

Expressing opinions
In my opinion ...
From my point of view, ...
It is certainly true that ...
I (do not) believe / think ...
I feel strongly that ...

Discussing pros and cons
On the one hand, ... / On the other hand, ...
Although ... , ...
However, ...
Whereas, ...

Adding more arguments for or against
Furthermore, ...
Moreover, ...
In addition, ...

Giving examples
For example / instance, ...
One example of ... is ...
... such as ...
... like ...

Conclusion
Overall, my personal opinion is ...
To conclude, ...
On balance, ...

▶▶ **Approach**

▶ Organise your writing clearly into paragraphs. Introduce the topic at the beginning in your introduction and summarise your opinion at the end in your conclusion.

▶ Read the question carefully and look at the notes, so you know exactly what you have to write about. The notes give you two points you have to write about, and you must add a third point of your own. This third idea must be different from the other two, and cannot simply be your conclusion at the end of the essay. Write a brief plan so you know what to include in each paragraph.

▶ The register should be neutral or semi-formal. Try to consider both sides of the argument objectively and write a balanced essay. It is a good idea to wait until the concluding paragraph to express your personal opinion.

▶▶ Model answer

Introduce the topic in the first paragraph.

Many people believe that sitting down to eat together regularly is vitally important for families and friends. Others, however, think that this is an old-fashioned idea in our modern, busy world.

In this paragraph, the arguments in favour of eating together are presented, using the points given in the question.

It is certainly true that many people take the time to prepare and eat food together at least once a day. We all have to eat, so why not also take the opportunity to catch up on everybody's news? And throughout history all over the world, on special occasions such as birthdays or national holidays, eating a meal with family and friends has been a good way of getting together and relaxing.

Remember to add your own idea. Here, the third point states that there are other ways to communicate regularly with family and friends, and is used to argue against the necessity of eating together regularly.

On the other hand, many people are so busy nowadays that sitting down to eat with others regularly is impossible. Nevertheless, this does not mean that they no longer communicate with their family or friends. For example, people can text, email, or talk on the phone whenever they want to.

Use linking words or expressions to list the main points (advantages or disadvantages) in your paragraph.

Sum up by giving your personal opinion.

Overall, my personal opinion is that there are a number of different ways of maintaining good relations with those we care about. Eating together regularly is one of them, but is not a necessity.

2 Informal letter / email

▸▸ **Exam task – Part 2**

You have received this letter from your English-speaking friend, Sara.

> My class is doing a project about special events that have been held in different countries, such as international sports competitions, festivals or celebrations of historical events. Can you tell me about an event that has taken place in your country? What was the event? What did people do? Why was the event important for your country?
>
> Write soon!
>
> Sara

Write your **letter**.

Useful phrases

Introduction
Thanks for your letter / email.
It's really nice to hear from you.
I hope you are well.
I'd love to help you with / tell you more about ...

Body of email
I thought you might be interested to hear ...
I'm going to tell you about ...
Did you know ...?
As far as I know ...
I think / believe ...

Conclusion
I hope this information is useful.
Write soon and tell me (about) ...
I hope to hear from you soon.
Take care.
Best wishes / regards.

▸▸ **Model answer**

Dear Sara,

Greet your friend in the introduction.	Thanks for your letter. I hope you're well. Your project sounds really interesting and I'd love to tell you about a special event that took place in my country.
Refer to your reason for writing.	I'm going to tell you about the Olympic Games, which took place in my country a few years ago. As you can imagine, it was a really special event for my country.
The exam question requires you to describe the event and say what people did.	The main parts of the Olympic Games took place in my city, which was great for me. But everyone in my country was able to enjoy the event in one way or another. Some people were volunteers and helped visitors to find their way to the different sports events in the city. Other people bought tickets to watch the events, but even those who couldn't get tickets were able to enjoy the atmosphere.
You also have to say why the event was important for your country.	The Olympic Games were really important for my country because they created jobs, and also helped to promote tourism and bring people of all nationalities together.
	I hope this information is useful for you. Write soon and tell me about other events you've found out about.
Finish your letter in an informal way.	Best wishes,
	David

Divide your letter into short paragraphs. Write about a different idea in each paragraph.

Ask your friend to write back.

3 Review

▶▶ **Exam task – Part 2**

You see this announcement in an English-language magazine called *Book Reviews*.

The book that changed my life.

Have you ever read a book that changed your life in some way? What was the book about? How did it change your life?

Write a review of the book and tell us all about it. The best reviews will be published next month.

Write your **review**.

Useful phrases

Adjectives
life-changing, exciting, funny, entertaining, emotional, thoughtful, powerful, informative

Adverbs
especially, particularly, unexpectedly, brilliantly, amazingly, dramatically, extraordinarily

Book-related vocabulary
The book is set …
The main character(s) …
It is written by …
The plot / story / topic is …
It is about …
The message of the book is …
The main event in the book is …
The ending of the book is …
I would recommend this book to …
action, romance, historical, mystery, novel, fiction, non-fiction, (auto)biography

▶▶ **Model answer**

A review is a piece of writing where you give your opinion about a film, book, website, play, TV programme, exhibition or place you have visited.

Decide how formal the language should be. This review is for a magazine, so you can use neutral or semi-formal language.

In this review you need to say how the book changed your life. Make your review as interesting as possible by using descriptive language.

Book review: Sunsets

The book that changed my life is called *Sunsets* and it is an autobiography about an artist who paints sunsets. But it's about much more than that, too.

The book is written by a painter called Maria, and it's about her working life as an artist. Maria describes how she travels all over her country painting sunsets, and talks about the people she meets along the way. Each person teaches her something interesting about life.

The book is emotionally powerful and it's a real page-turner. Maria learns about herself and shares what she has learned with her readers. For example, she learns to live life in the moment and worry less about the future, which she can't control. As a reader, I felt as if I was learning about life along with Maria and some of the lessons have helped me to see things and approach things that happen to me in a different way. It has made me a much more positive person.

Sunsets is a fascinating read and I would recommend this book to anyone who wants to improve their life through positive thinking.

Make your introduction interesting, so that people who read the review will want to know more. Avoid giving details about the book at this point.

Provide a brief summary of what happens in the book and say something about the main character(s).

In your conclusion, briefly summarise why the book is worth reading. You could also say to whom you would recommend the book.

---

4 Article

▶▶ **Exam task – Part 2**

You have seen this announcement on an English-language website.

> ### Articles wanted
>
> ## Learning to do something new
>
> Tell us about something new you have recently learned to do. What was it? Who taught you? Why did you learn it? How useful do you think your new skill will be in the future?
>
> We'll publish the best articles in our magazine next month.

Write your **article**.

Useful phrases

Ordering language
To start / begin with, …
First of all, …
Next, …
Additionally, …
Finally, …

Involving the reader
Have you ever …?
As you can imagine …
You may not believe it, but …
Strange as it may seem, …
I'm sure you will agree that …
What would you do if …?

Giving your opinion
I personally think that …
I really do believe that …
It appears to me that …
To my mind …
As far as I'm concerned …

▶▶ **Model answer**

Learning to ride a bike – at the age of 22!

You can speak directly to the reader by using 'you' from time to time.

You may not believe it, but until a few weeks ago, I'd never been able to ride a bicycle. I grew up in a small city-centre flat, and my parents never had time to teach me, so I just never learned.

An article is a piece of writing on a particular topic for a newspaper, magazine, newsletter, website or other publication.

Gain the reader's interest in the title and introduction.

Make your article lively and interesting. Use descriptive language.

Then one day a friend of mine asked me to go on a long-distance bike ride with her. When I said I'd love to, but didn't know how to, she couldn't believe her ears. She took me straight out to the park near her house, and spent several hours running along behind me as I slowly learned to balance. As you can probably imagine, I looked rather silly to start with, and a few small children stopped and stared, but I didn't care because I was so excited to be learning to ride a bike at last!

You can end your article by referring back to something you mentioned at the beginning.

My friend was a patient teacher, and although she was absolutely exhausted by the time we'd finished, she never once complained. I'm delighted and yes, I'm going on a 50 km bike ride with my friend next month. I can't wait!

Make sure you have answered all the questions you are asked.

5 Report *(for FIRST candidates only)*

▶▶ **Exam task – Part 2**

A new sports centre has recently been built in your town. Your English teacher has asked you to write a report about it, in order to encourage students to use the centre to get fit. In your report you should include a description of the sports centre, say what people can do there, and make recommendations for improvements to the centre.

Write your **report**.

Useful phrases

Introduction

The purpose / aim of this report is to …

This report will consider …
… and make suggestions / recommendations about …

Making suggestions / recommendations

I suggest that …

Improvements could be made by …

I think / believe that …

In my opinion / view …

Conclusion

In conclusion, …

To sum up, …

In summary, …

▶▶ **Model answer**

Date: 12th May
Subject: Greenway Sports

> You could begin with the date and the subject of the report.

> In the introduction you should state the purpose of the report.

The purpose of this report is to consider Greenway Sports and explain what is available for its visitors, as well as to make recommendations for improvements.

Greenway Sports

The Greenway Sports is a brand new sports facility in the centre of the town. Its central location makes it easy to visit. The centre is modern, bright and spacious, and there is a large car park where visitors can leave their cars for free while they exercise.

> Organise the information in your report in a clear way. Use headings, numbering or bullet points.

What people can do at the centre

> Keep the language neutral and impersonal. Use passive forms and write in the third person, rather than using 'you'.

Visitors to the new sports centre can take advantage of a full range of facilities, including a swimming pool, gym, tennis courts and an outdoor football field. Classes for all ages and abilities are offered, from aerobics to weights. There is also a café on the first floor where healthy meals are served.

Recommendations

> Finish your report by making a recommendation or concluding with your opinion, depending on the wording of the exam question.

Although the sports centre provides a good variety of sports and exercise facilities and activities, I think the prices are quite high. In order to encourage more people, including students, to use the centre, I would recommend that the centre offers discounts and special promotions.

> You should not write your name at the end of the report.

6 Letter of application (*for FIRST candidates only*)

▶▷ **Exam task – Part 2**

You see this advertisement in an English-language film magazine.

International film making course

Would you like to learn how to make films?

We have ten free places to give away on our two-month film-making course this summer.

No previous experience is required, but applicants should speak English, have plenty of enthusiasm and work well with other people.

Apply in writing to the course director, Mrs Keller.

Write your letter of **application**.

Useful phrases

Introduction

I have seen your advertisement in …

I am writing about …

I am writing to apply for a (free) place on …

I am writing in connection with …

Body of letter

I am … years old and I …

I have a good command of …

I have a good knowledge of …

I have experience of …

I think I should be given a place on the course because …

I would be grateful for the opportunity to …

Conclusion

I hope you will consider my application …

I look forward to hearing from you / to your reply.

▶▷ **Model answer**

In a formal letter start with *Dear Mr / Mrs …* if you know the person's name. If you do not know the person's name, start with *Dear Sir / Madam*.

Dear Mrs Keller,

I am writing in connection with the film-making course you have advertised. I would like to apply for one of the free places you are offering, as this would be a fantastic opportunity for me and would help me to prepare for the work I hope to do in the future.

In the introduction say briefly why you are writing.

Give relevant information about yourself if you are writing to apply for a job or a place on a course.

I am 18 years old and have just finished school. My dream is to become a film director one day. Although I have never had the chance to go on a film-making course before, I have made a number of short videos on my own and with friends.

I speak good English, having studied it for five years at school. Furthermore, I get on well with other people, and have always enjoyed working as part of a team, for instance when doing project work or giving group presentations. I am very keen indeed to learn as much as I possibly can about how to make films.

Make sure you provide all the information asked for in the question, using your own words as far as possible and giving brief examples where appropriate.

If you know the person's name, end with *Yours sincerely*. If you do not know the person's name, end with *Yours faithfully*.

I hope you will consider me for one of the free places on your course.

Yours sincerely,
Louise Garcia

Finish your letter by saying that you hope you will be considered for the place on the course / job.

7 Story (for FIRST FOR SCHOOLS candidates only)

▶▶ **Exam task – Part 2**

You have seen this announcement in an English-language magazine.

We want your stories!

We are looking for new stories to publish in our monthly magazine. Your story must begin with this sentence:

The sun shone brightly on the lake as someone walked out of the water towards me.

Your story must include:

- a boat journey
- an animal

The best stories will be published in the magazine.

Write your **story**.

Useful phrases

Setting the scene
While I was walking along the path one day …
It was a beautiful morning …
The rain was pouring down …
We had been waiting for this moment …

Sequencing events
First, …
Suddenly / All of a sudden …
Without warning …
As soon as …
In no time at all …
Then, / Next, …
Before long …
Finally / In the end …
Afterwards, …

Feelings and reactions to events
I'd never felt so embarrassed …
I was so surprised that …
I was speechless …
I felt extremely nervous …
I couldn't help laughing …
I was terrified …

▶▶ **Model answer**

You must begin your story with the sentence given. Don't change the sentence or use it in a different position.

Use dialogue to bring the characters to life.

Make sure your story has a beginning, middle and an end. Put the events into chronological order. Use narrative tenses (past simple, past continuous, etc.) and sequencing words (*then, suddenly, before long, etc.*).

The sun shone brightly on the lake as someone walked out of the water towards me. As I watched the figure approach me, I suddenly recognised who it was.

It was my neighbour, Martin. 'Hi, Martin,' I said. 'Have you been for a swim in the lake?' Martin shook his head and it was then that I realised he looked worried. 'What's wrong?' I asked. 'I've lost my dog, Pep,' he replied sadly. 'We came for a walk along the lake and he suddenly ran off. I saw him in the water and went into the lake after him, but now he's disappeared.'

Suddenly, I saw Pep in the water. He was far away from the edge of the lake, splashing around. He seemed frightened. 'There he is!' I shouted. Martin looked around hurriedly and spotted an old rowing boat on the shore. 'Come on, let's rescue him!' he said.

Before long, Martin and I were rowing quickly out onto the lake. We soon reached Pep and pulled him on board. Martin and Pep had a happy reunion and I was really glad to have helped!

Continue after the opening sentence in an interesting way that will make the reader want to know what happens next.

Describe events and people's feelings. Try to use interesting language including similes, metaphors and a range of adjectives and adverbs.

End the story in an interesting way.

TEST 1

▶▶ PART 1

1

A: So, what are you going to study at university, then?

B: History. I wasn't sure whether it'd be useful for a career at first, but you can't overlook the way history helps us gain an understanding of the world around us – and why it is the way it is today. I mean, if we understand how people have lived through the ages, we can make informed decisions about the present. That doesn't mean I'm thinking of a career as a world leader, but <u>I'm sure I'll learn how to make reasoned arguments and other things like that – which is bound to help me, whatever field I work in later.</u>

A: Definitely!

2

As a poet, I'm often asked what the value of poetry is. In my experience, <u>quite a few people think it's limiting and that ideas can be expressed much more easily in prose</u> – you know, ordinary written language. <u>Yet you can convey just as much feeling in poetry and address any subject in as much depth as a work of fiction.</u> It makes no more sense to ask what the point of poetry is than to ask what the point of a story is. It's simply another form of expression and I love the fact that I can say a lot in just a few words.

3

I studied abroad and when it came to job interviews, it appeared to give me an advantage over other candidates. Employers seemed to be convinced I must be more confident and self-reliant than if I hadn't done it. I suppose everyone imagines you're bound to be sure of yourself if you've done something many people wouldn't do. Actually, I was as nervous as anyone else would have been, but <u>I survived on my own for a year in a foreign country with all its challenges.</u> I feel a sense of achievement about that, so perhaps the interviewers were right. I still need to find my perfect career, though!

4

A: <u>What a fascinating lecture! The importance of choosing the right colours for a global website never crossed my mind.</u>

B: I already knew different colours mean different things in different cultures – so it makes sense to think about how choice of colour affects how successful a website is. <u>I was totally absorbed in the lecturer's arguments, though.</u>

A: I thought the approach some companies take was a good solution – you know, changing the colours of their site according to the country they're marketing products in.

B: Well, I'd use a universally-safe colour, like blue. It maintains a uniform appearance for the company.

5

A: <u>Have you had chance to read through the comments I made on your latest essay?</u>

B: Yes. I thought what you said was fair, though I wasn't sure what you meant by working on justifying my arguments.

A: <u>Well, it's never enough to make broad statements without backing up what you're saying – with references to reading you've done on a subject.</u>

B: <u>You mean, providing more evidence for why I think what I'm saying is right?</u>

A: <u>Precisely.</u> You're not the only student in the class who needs to work on this a little more, so I'm going to spend a bit of time this week on helping you get your head around it.

6

A: How's that drumming workshop you've been going to?

B: Well, I'm not that musical as you know – though I've always wanted to learn an instrument. <u>I thought learning the drums would be easy</u> enough because there's no melody to follow and I don't have to read music. You know what, though? <u>I have trouble keeping up with some of the rhythms</u> the teacher shows us. It isn't necessarily the speed – <u>it's remembering the beat patterns that I struggle with. I hadn't realised there'd be so much effort involved,</u> but the end result is awesome – when the whole group's in time with each other and we get it right.

A: I can imagine.

7

A: What did you think of that film adaptation of *The Silver Birds*? <u>It's so frustrating when they take a great story and alter the ending so it's nothing like the original.</u>

B: They make the film because the book's been a bestseller. <u>Surely that would make you question the idea of changing things.</u> If I was the author I'd be pretty annoyed …

A: Wasn't he involved in writing the screenplay, though? Anyway, I don't think the message of the book was interpreted correctly.

B: That's one thing I wasn't disappointed with, actually. Anyway, I guess they change stuff to appeal to the widest audience possible.

8

When we were told we had to give a presentation as part of a course I was doing, <u>my immediate reaction was that I'd be way too nervous to make a decent job of it.</u> But I couldn't back out of it – not because I needed to prove anything to myself – but because the teacher gave us no option! People advise you to do all kinds of stuff like practising delivering your speech in front of a mirror and all that – some of it sounds a bit strange. I didn't want to overwhelm myself getting ready for the presentation, so I just visualised myself making a success of it – which I did.

TEST 1

▶▶ PART 2

I'm a weather forecaster, which means I study what happens in the atmosphere and the weather conditions that this causes on Earth. People are always surprised to learn that <u>forecasters aren't just involved in weather reporting on TV – although that's what I do on a local station</u> – but you could work at a radio station, too, or as an advisor to transport services and so on.

On a daily basis, there's a lot of data collection and observation involved, as well as detailed study of what are known in the field as <u>weather models. These are sophisticated computer programs – without them, forecasters would find it much more difficult to predict the weather. After looking at these and doing a bit of maths, I'm eventually ready to make short and longer-term forecasts.</u>

Things can get hectic on 'big weather days' when there's more serious weather about. Forecasters spend most of their time putting together reports for TV or radio stations and other customers. When there's something major going on, though, we have to be extra vigilant – I know the public will be checking the weather maps on the station's website – and it's vital that I issue warnings for heavy snow, or whatever, as quickly as possible.

I often get asked how I got interested in weather. Believe it or not, as a teenager I became nervous of thunderstorms and I'd often check the forecasts to see if any were coming. However, where we lived was more prone to flooding and strong winds than thunderstorms, so I should have been more nervous about those! Anyway, from there my interest developed.

If you are thinking of going into weather forecasting there are some important skills you'll need. You have to be good at science, of course, though the key thing is having an ability to interpret patterns. You won't go too far wrong with that. Another useful skill is being able to translate a forecast into something people at home can understand.

Most weather experts study physics and maths before going on to do a more specialised course in forecasting. My own way in was somewhat different as I did a business degree before getting into television as a researcher. I moved around quite a lot at the station and eventually ended up in the weather department, where I did my training.

People often complain that weather reports aren't totally accurate – but we aren't usually too far out on short-term forecasts. Longer-term ones are trickier and that's where we get criticism. We can only make predictions based on the data available. And no one complains when the weather is better than we predicted!

Besides being reporters, some weather experts carve out a career in research – something I'd like to get involved in later. There are lots of possibilities, such as ocean forecasting, climate change – which is an area I'd like to focus on – investigating specific types of weather and so on.

It's tough getting a position without experience. If you're lucky you might get a work experience placement at a weather organisation. The central weather office tends to offer placements in their membership department. Even doing basic administration for them will improve your chances.

I love my work and have been lucky enough to do some interesting things. My team's often asked to advise on likely weather conditions for things like major sports competitions such as golf or sailing. Twelve months ago I presented the weather forecast during a tennis tournament! The weather's different every day, so it's a rewarding job.

Any questions?

FIRST TEST 1

▸▸ **PART 3**

1

I used to volunteer at a community theatre, where I helped out making costumes and preparing scenery. I'd been into sewing all my life and spent most of my spare time making cool clothes for myself and my friends. It's important to keep your skills up to date and working at the theatre helped me do more of what I already loved. I guess what I didn't expect was the chance that arose out of it to set myself up as a theatre costume designer. Simply through talking to other

professionals in the team, it came to light that there was a real need for someone with my talents in the region.

2

Volunteering at an animal sanctuary during my student holidays was unforgettable. Not only did I love spending time caring for the animals, which I'd never done before, but I also met people from all walks of life. Sharing tasks and responsibility for the animals made me suddenly grasp the value of pulling together with my new friends to reach a common goal – I hadn't considered that before. It's something that I'll take with me into the professional community after I finish my studies. I'm unlikely to take up an animal-related career or see those people again, but it was a fabulous experience.

3

It was a childhood friend who got me into volunteering. She loves children and asked me to go and help out at a day nursery with a small team of other volunteers in our town. Although I wouldn't have said dealing with kids was where my own skills lay, I found that I seemed to instinctively know what they wanted. I wouldn't say I felt confident enough to do anything professionally in that field, like teaching or whatever, but it got me thinking about what else I could try that I might be good at, and it was a good life skill to learn.

4

I've always thought of myself as a good team player and I enjoy working with others. Since studying psychology at university, I've become interested in how different personalities complement and inspire each other within a group. I suppose that's what made me take on a role guiding others when I volunteered at a sports charity. I can't say I was a natural and I'd always thought you needed to be a really confident person to direct other people, but I think I chose to do it so I could get involved in something I truly cared about. I'm glad I did, 'cause I'm pretty good at it now!

5

I have strong maths skills and when I heard about a student mentoring scheme I had to give it a go. I helped school students in my town who were struggling with the subject. It was fantastic to see how they gained confidence in something they weren't enjoying. I identified with them because I felt the same about foreign languages. I'd always wanted to work abroad but without a language I knew it'd be difficult. On the back of volunteering I got a French tutor. I'm still not that sure of myself when I speak in French but I thought, if I can help other people, I can help myself, too.

FIRST TEST 1

▸▸ **PART 4**

Interviewer: Rod, you work in the field of saving endangered languages. What does that mean and how did you become involved in it?

Rod Chambers: An endangered language is one at risk of disappearing – nobody's learning it as a first language. I did a degree in communication – though decided against doing a course on the theme of endangered languages at that point. The issue had actually been staring me in the face my whole life – my grandparents speak a language with a limited population of speakers. Yet it was only when

I visited an isolated community while I was travelling the world after university that I realised the importance of the matter. I could see that the younger people had moved away for work, so who would the language be passed on to?

Interviewer: Why *do* languages stop being spoken?

Rod Chambers: As technology's spread, communication across the world has improved, and schools have focused on teaching international languages like English – rather than minority languages. It's a pity but it's understandable. People, such as those in the business world, are aware that they have to be able to speak to others in the global society, and parents may just stop using the minority language at home because they want their children to succeed in communicating in an international language.

Interviewer: Is it possible to save a language?

Rod Chambers: Yes – with a lot of determination from the whole community – including those who speak the majority language. Some simple measures can be taken. For example, putting up road signs or launching a local TV station in the minority language, or printing official literature in that language can help people recognise it as a part of their community. These options aren't without their challenges – but there's plenty that can be done, provided communities are willing.

Interviewer: Is it really worth all that effort, though?

Rod Chambers: Of course! It's tempting to think there are greater concerns, such as saving our rainforests or protecting endangered animal species. In a way, though, these are quite similar to a minority language! A lot of identity and culture is bound up in a language – so if you lose a language, you risk losing what may be thousands of years' worth of tradition and knowledge along with it.

Interviewer: And you're currently recording a language that's becoming extinct?

Rod Chambers: Right – there're only a handful of speakers left and I've been recording some of them speaking the language. I focus on capturing as much natural language as possible, so I might get the person to talk about their childhood, for example. Questions about grammar can be difficult for interviewees to answer and not particularly helpful for me. Later, I listen carefully to the recordings and analyse the structures and vocabulary.

Interviewer: What happens with the data you've collected?

Rod Chambers: The material can be used as an important teaching tool. This means that current and future generations of children can listen to and learn about their ancestors' language. In some cases languages are revived – brought back to life in other words – and taught as a second language in schools, which is an attempt to maintain that connection with the past.

Interviewer: What can listeners do if they're interested in language-saving projects?

Rod Chambers: Several things. If your relatives or people in your local community speak an endangered language, persuade them to talk to you in it, so you can learn it and pass it on to your own children. Being surrounded by it will be enough without the need to ask for lessons. Or you can make your own recordings of people speaking and upload them onto an online database – don't worry about doing any analysis – the experts will do that. That's it really.

▶▶ **PART 1**

1

A: So, what do you think about our new boss then?

B: Kelly? She seems alright.

A: She didn't look as if she was enjoying it much, though, did she? You have to love your work if you're going to do it well, don't you think?

B: I don't think she wasn't enjoying it, I think she was just getting to grips with everything, you know. It isn't easy, taking over a new team, and she did appear a bit shy, I suppose.

A: I think that was it. We'll soon find out what she's really like, won't we?

B: Yeah, we will.

2

Yes, I'm very pleased with the course! The teaching is excellent, as we'd been promised when I applied, and I've learned so much. I still have two years to go – I'm pleased about that, because I'm enjoying it so much. I'm also aware that there's a lot more to cover – by the time we leave, we'll all have specialised in one or two sports, but we'll still officially be allowed to coach people in quite a range of others, too. I hadn't expected to see people on the course who aren't particularly sporty, but in fact what we study really is appropriate for everybody.

3

I'd been looking forward to it for weeks. I love Shakespeare, you know. And this production had been given fantastic reviews. I thought I might regret going on this particular trip, though, because the woman next to me coughed all the way there on the bus, poor thing, and I thought she'd be doing that all the way through the play. But she must have had some very good throat sweets – I wish I'd found out what brand they were, actually – because she never coughed once when we were in the theatre. I must say I hope she was alright when she got home, because it was a rotten cold.

4

A: So how do you think the experiment went? Have you got plenty of results to work on?

B: Yes, but some of them were a bit surprising so I think I'd better repeat it.

A: Fair enough. In fact that's exactly what I wanted to talk to you about. It's a good idea to do that anyway, just to satisfy yourself that you've recorded everything properly.

B: I think I have, but I'll have another go. It won't take long.

A: Great – if the equipment isn't set up exactly right, that can cause problems of course, but it all looks fine to me. I'll come back when you've finished.

5

It's not a bad book, I suppose. It's about some people living in a fairly conventional community in the countryside – you know the sort of thing, it's been done before. I did start to care what happened to them, though – the author really brought some quite complex personalities to life. The trouble is, I just knew what was going to happen all the way through the book, and I always find that a little disappointing in a novel. Having said that, it is quite entertaining, and I can recommend it as an enjoyable, relaxing read.

6

A: So how was your geography trip, then?

B: Not too bad in the end, actually. I was happy to get home, but I also felt it had lived up to my expectations – certainly as far as the coursework we covered was concerned. I really feel I know what I'm doing now. The weather was disappointing, but it didn't matter because they'd organised loads of things for us to do. And spending all that time with my classmates turned out to be a real bonus, too. I've made quite a few new friends – I needn't have worried about that side of things at all.

7

A: This is a good exhibition, isn't it? It's great to see so much all in one place like this.

B: Yes, and the reviews I read said there was a lot to take in, so I knew there'd be plenty to look at. And they were right about another thing, too.

A: What's that?

B: There's a lot here that all sorts of people will enjoy, I think. This kind of thing is very fashionable at the moment.

A: Yeah, I suppose you're right.

B: I haven't seen anything like this myself, though, so it's great to be able to come here and see what they mean.

8

I didn't have to learn a new language as well as everything else I have to do on my course, but I thought it would be worth it. I'll definitely need it at some stage, so I might as well get on with it now. I'm enjoying the challenge, actually. I've always found languages fairly straightforward, but this is a bit more complicated, what with all the different tenses and everything. I think people should always be able to choose, you know, whether they do something like this or not, because you really do have to be motivated if you're going to make a success of it.

 2

▶▶ **PART 2**

Hello and thank you for inviting me to talk to you this evening about how to get into the music industry.

So, the first thing to note is that the music industry is constantly changing and evolving. You need to make sure you stay up to date and keep up with trends affecting the business. Check out specialist music websites for news and insight into the industry, and also trade magazines, which are produced for industry insiders, unlike other music magazines.

Obviously you'll need a CV when you apply, whether it's for an unpaid internship or for a paid job. And you need it to make an instant impression if you want to have a chance of getting an interview. It doesn't have to be very long, but it really does need to be memorable – as you know, there's a huge amount of competition for places.

The person looking at your CV needs to see that you are enthusiastic and can use your own initiative. Unpaid interns are often expected to do administrative work, so if you have any experience in that area, do include it. You are unlikely to be involved in PR work or dealing directly with the stars.

Lots of people who are now high up in the industry did low-paid jobs when they first started. You might be surprised to

know that one top executive started out as an office cleaner. My first job was as what's known as a 'teaboy', and I'm happy with the way my career has progressed. I'm glad I didn't turn that first work offer down – it was a great way to get in.

So I suppose my main piece of advice to anyone considering applying for an internship is: don't limit yourself. People need to remind themselves that life is full of surprises and unexpected developments. You just never know what something relatively unexciting may lead to.

And if you have any experience at all in the music industry itself, that will help too. I'd worked as a volunteer before applying for paid work: I'd spent three summers helping out at music festivals, and what started off as a desire to have a bit of fun turned into a passion for me. So I'd definitely recommend volunteering. All experience is useful, but having this kind of experience on your CV shows that you don't just know about theoretical aspects of the industry, but practical ones too.

You should also try to get out and meet people who work in the music business. Go to as many different networking events as possible – check industry websites to find out about these, and there are also plenty of experts giving talks that you'll find useful. Conferences are also worth going to if you can, because you'll meet all sorts of helpful people there.

One big music organisation also holds a series of informal music career talks in different parts of the country. You can meet people doing things from marketing to digital music production, a reminder that there are more roles in the music industry than just being a singer! If you're interested, come and see me after the talk and I'll give you the details.

Finally, don't forget that like all other businesses, creative industries like the music industry also need lawyers and accountants, and people to do all those other 'back-room' jobs. So if you're already training for or doing a job like that, it could be a great way of combining a love of music with your chosen profession.

 2

▶▶ **PART 3**

1

I always loved music as a child. I can remember singing and playing the piano with my mother. She was a musician – very talented and incredibly energetic. One of the many things she did while we were growing up was to make sure that all her children learned to play an instrument. I didn't inherit her talent as a player, unfortunately, but as a music critic I get to attend – in fact I have to attend – some of the best classical concerts in the world. Funnily enough, I rarely listen to music in my spare time these days. I find silence more relaxing!

2

I have a very busy job in the music industry. I don't actually ever have to listen to music as part of my job, because I work in the accounts department, but I do listen to it a lot in my spare time. Apart from the fact that I love it, especially jazz and blues, it really helps me forget about all the stress at work. In the office, where I'm surrounded by people, I have to be extremely focused, and I wouldn't have the energy to carry on sometimes if I didn't have a way of getting away from it all from time to time.

3

I work in a busy office. I've discovered that <u>the best way to block out the noise around me, and get on with what I'm supposed to be doing, is to put on a pair of headphones and play some music.</u> Classical works best, although I enjoy rock and folk too. Of course if I want to chat to other people – my work colleagues, I mean – then the headphones come off and I end up shouting to make myself heard like the rest of them! Those breaks with other people do mean that I usually return to my work feeling more relaxed and inspired!

4

I can't imagine my life without music. It's just always been there in the background, for as long as I can remember. I wouldn't say I really focus on it that often, <u>but I do listen, and when I go out running with music on, the run often feels as if it's over before it's even started!</u> I think lots of other people are the same – they might not sit down and listen to it carefully, but they do enjoy it. And miss it when it isn't there! I have my favourites, of course, but everything's on my player and I just have it on shuffle.

5

I'm quite fussy about what I listen to, I suppose. When I'm feeling energetic, I play something with a faster beat, and when I'm feeling more chilled, then I like to have something quieter on. And music is vital for me when I'm painting, which is my hobby. Somehow <u>new ideas seem to come to me more easily when I'm listening to music</u> – it's always been that way for me. I know a lot of other people say the same thing, too. I suppose music has always been important for human beings, in all kinds of different ways.

 TEST 2

▸▸ **PART 4**

Interviewer: I'm delighted to be interviewing Gail Koch, a biology student, via satellite link to the rainforest in South America. Hello Gail.

Gail Koch: Hi!

Interviewer: So, after nearly a year studying in the rainforest, what's it like being a field scientist?

Gail Koch: Well, people often imagine scientists being in laboratories wearing white coats. But they don't all work that way – field scientists work outside, exploring and investigating, then trying to understand what they observe. That's what I'm doing here, though I wouldn't say I'm a real one yet, even though I've been out here for almost a year. But <u>although I still lack experience and have a lot to learn, I hope my enthusiasm more than makes up for that.</u>

Interviewer: And what do you enjoy most about living out there?

Gail Koch: I'm living in a typical tropical rainforest, at a small scientific research station. It's very hot and humid, the trees grow tall and very close together, and it's absolutely full of life – both plants and animals. <u>But at the end of the day, before it gets dark, it finally cools down a little and the trees look stunning in the light of the setting sun. That's what I'll really miss when I have to go home.</u>

Interviewer: And what does your research involve?

Gail Koch: <u>I'm studying lizards, trying to find out exactly which species are here. I explore the area around the research station,</u>

helped by a local guide, or I'd soon get lost. It's incredibly exciting when I actually see a lizard. I have to catch it, of course, and then check whether or not I've already found an example of this particular species. <u>I spend most of the time, though, walking extremely slowly</u> – and all I can see are leaves! That's very much what it's like for most field researchers.

Interviewer: So what inspires you most about your work?

Gail Koch: It's demanding and often repetitive, but it's rewarding too. It's not that I want be the first person ever to discover a new species, or gain academic glory – though of course I'd like that – but that <u>I could really add to what scientists know about the world. That's what motivates me.</u>

Interviewer: That's wonderful! How easy is it to become a field scientist?

Gail Koch: It's quite a hard world to break into, because <u>so many people want to do it,</u> even though it's poorly paid compared to many other graduate jobs. In many cases you have to work for no salary at the beginning of your career and even pay your own expenses! That's tough when there seem to be endless opportunities for science graduates in other careers.

Interviewer: So would you recommend working at this research station to other biology students?

Gail Koch: Yes, absolutely! I could be an assistant in a lab going through endless pages of numbers and results, day after day. But luckily I'm here. And <u>I'm sure the countless skills I've learned over the past year will be an advantage when I apply to do further study.</u> I can choose my own research, and it's entirely up to me how I organise my day.

Interviewer: That all sounds very positive. There must be some disadvantages to being there, though!

Gail Koch: Well, sometimes I've got no idea what I'm supposed to do next, or how to do something, and it can be hard to get myself organised. I had all sorts of plans to improve my little living space when I arrived, but somehow I've never got round to it. Also, the technology I use here is fairly basic, and <u>there is always the possibility that I'm missing out on the latest advances in zoology while I'm here.</u> But I personally wouldn't be anywhere else for the world!

TEST 3

▸▸ **PART 1**

1

A: What does 'beat deafness' mean?

B: It's when people can't hear the beat in music. They can't move in time to even the strongest beat – I'm not saying they don't know what rhythm is, though.

A: I've seen those people in my exercise class, when I do aerobics, or whatever, to music – they step to the left when everyone else is moving to the right.

B: Well, it's possible that the people *you're* talking about just have a problem with learning a new routine at speed. <u>It's pretty rare to find people who are genuinely beat deaf – though lots of people tend to think they are, when actually they're just poor dancers!</u>

2

A: So, we have to make a map of our local area for our next geography lesson.

B: Where do we start? Our teacher told us to look at that online map-making tool, but she didn't give too many details about it. <u>Using it might be easier said than done, judging by how complex it looks.</u>

A: <u>The teacher said it looked harder than it actually is to use but I'm not convinced, either.</u> We need to become really familiar with the area before we start doing anything, I'd say.

B: Walking around and sketching stuff? I'd rather just get on with it.

A: OK. Well, I'll meet you after class.

3

A: Did you see that programme about new food technology?

B: Yeah. Those hollow salt crystals they can make were amazing – they look like real grains of salt, but aren't solid. Apparently your mind gets tricked into thinking it's traditional salt, so you can eat more healthily but don't notice the difference!

A: <u>I question whether it can really be as nice as the real thing.</u> And it must be complicated to process …

B: … so it's unlikely to make it into supermarkets any time soon. It would be pretty expensive, anyway.

A: But it might be worth it for the sake of being healthier.

4

I know you'd rather bury your heads in the latest popular novels than read anything that sounds a bit serious, but I must recommend *Chortown*. It's not something I'd normally pick up in a bookshop, and I wouldn't have read it if someone hadn't passed it on to me. It's set 200 years ago, and follows the story of a family living in our town at that time. I won't spoil it by saying any more, but <u>you'll love recognising the places that are mentioned. Lots of things have changed since then, but the characters' lives are strikingly similar to our own.</u>

5

I'm blind, so I rely on my other senses a lot, especially when I travel. It's all very well asking your companions to describe a scene but I was eager to find my own way of experiencing all the new places I visit. So I decided to focus on smelling them instead. It wasn't easy focusing my attention this way at first, but now I can recall a place instantly when I smell certain things. Sea spray reminds me of South Africa, and fresh coffee of Colombia. <u>I'm convinced this method makes my travel experiences more intense than if I could see where I was.</u>

6

A: Are you settling into your new cycling routine?

B: I love it but it's tough. I feel hungry all the time, though I've put loads of effort into making sure I eat the right things – slow-release carbohydrates and so on. But I keep waking up in the middle of the night starving!

A: Well, you're enjoying the training, and you're on track food-wise, but <u>you *have* significantly increased the amount of training you're doing – your body's bound to want more food.</u> Eating straightaway after training will help to avoid feelings of hunger later in the day when you might be tempted to snack on the wrong things.

7

A: Hey! Congratulations on getting your book published! Are you going to have a launch party?

B: Well, I've been so relieved the writing's finally finished I haven't given it much thought – it isn't really my kind of thing. It'd be nice if the publisher organised something but they don't do that unless you're an established author …

A: … yes, who's making them lots of money! Have you got a decent budget for the party?

B: It's not bad. Maybe I could have the party at the Condor Hotel. <u>What I'm concerned about is how to attract publicity.</u> I don't suppose you have any ideas about who to invite?

A: Let's have a think.

8

Today's session is about navigation – finding your way on the ocean. This is a complex science and even highly experienced sailors who've spent years perfecting their navigation skills can still make errors of judgement. <u>It boils down to just two things – knowing where you are and knowing how to get where you want to go. Safely.</u> It's easy to spend enormous amounts of time poring over maps – this is better done before you set off than during the voyage – that's when you should be concentrating on what's happening right now.

 TEST 3

▶▶ **PART 2**

Thanks for inviting me to talk to you about my experiences of olive farming. I'm aware you're thinking of doing this yourselves, so I'll tell you about the oil production process as I've experienced it this year for the first time.

Growing the olives went pretty smoothly, but every crop farmer falls victim to the weather at some point. I'd been lucky to get away with a generally mild winter, and fortunately the farm wasn't damaged in the one violent storm there was. <u>A sudden frost did claim a number of our trees</u>, though, so their olives didn't mature.

I also found out that humans aren't the only creatures which like olives! There are a few insects, such as the olive fly, which can hang around the fruit. <u>I wasn't bothered by them but I was by a certain species of worm.</u> Fortunately these aren't harmful to the olives, though.

I picked the olives with help from my wife in autumn, and it was as challenging as you'd expect. Some methods are more efficient than others – I was tempted to pick them by using an electric-powered tool. <u>In the end I opted to collect them by hand</u> in order to maintain quality – though they can also be collected by machine – the trees are shaken and the olives fall.

Traditionally, olives are collected straight from the tree into a basket. This keeps them in the best condition and they say it produces the best oil. <u>Not having any, I used a bucket instead</u> – and hoped it wouldn't affect the olives too much!

Once they were picked, the next step was cleaning the olives. I knew I'd have to select only the best ones for pressing – that's the process where they're squeezed to produce oil. Any with bruises I threw on the fire, and <u>picking out leaves was possibly the most uninteresting job I've ever done</u> – I was glad I didn't need to take the olive stones out as well.

I remember standing there after I'd finished sorting the olives. It was as though the kitchen had turned into a kind of temporary factory. There were boxes and trays everywhere. <u>Everything was covered in stains</u> – not just the tables but our clothes and skin, too.

The next step was getting the olives to the busy press outside the village. I'd booked the first time slot, so we loaded up at dawn. I arrived on time but then <u>confusingly had to sit in a line</u> while trucks got waved in ahead of me. Whatever the system was, I clearly didn't understand it.

After only half an hour the oil was bottled. The taste was disappointing to say the least. Olive oil is often used to pour over salads, but you wouldn't have wanted to put my oil on anything! I knew it would be OK to use for cooking and my wife laughingly said we'd be able to burn it in lamps. My first attempt at oil production had not been the great success I'd imagined!

What had gone wrong? I concluded that it must have been choosing the wrong time to pick the olives. We say that fruit becomes ripe when it's ready to be picked, and this word is used to describe olives, too. But many of the olives in our first batch had gone past that point. We'd been waiting for them to grow bigger, and so picked them too late. That's why there was so little flavour to my first oil.

Hopefully next year, I'll be much more successful! I'd like my oil to have that delicious pepper taste it should have. If that works, then the following year I might even try making some flavoured oils – chilli, garlic and herbs are great ingredients. I can't wait!

Now, are there any questions?

▶▶ PART 3

1

When I was six, my granddad bought me a telescope. It was only a kids' one and wasn't particularly powerful but it sparked my fascination with space. I'd spend hours gazing up at the dark night sky. As I grew up and became interested in other stuff, I forgot about the stars for a while, but when I did a postgraduate degree I ended up doing astronomy so I could put my maths and physics degree to use in an interesting way. My parents didn't think there'd be many well-paid job opportunities in the field and they were right – but I only studied it because I liked it.

2

As a kid I used to visit my dad at the observatory where he worked. I remember looking through fancy telescopes there. He was so enthusiastic about his work that he wanted me to follow in his footsteps. That was his dream – I wanted to be a racing driver. I only got as far as working as a mechanic on a team, though, which I didn't want to do forever. In order to get ahead I knew I'd have to have a certificate or two. I turned to astronomy simply because I already knew so much about it. Dad still thinks I did it for him!

3

My family moved around a lot when I was a child, and even when I felt a bit unsettled being in yet another country, the one thing I could rely on was the stars above me. They made me feel safe. So, from being a kid, studying astronomy was the only way forward for me. I can't imagine what I'd have done if I hadn't become an astronomer. I had to work pretty hard at the theoretical side of things – my knowledge of physics and maths was weak. But I was determined, and now I'm doing a job I love.

4

I didn't go to university straight after school. Instead, I worked for an organisation which developed computer software for interpreting satellite images. It was specialist work and although I started off as the office junior, I picked up quite a lot of knowledge in a very specific field. I did occasionally get to do a bit of practical stuff, which got me interested in astronomy. If I'm honest, I just wanted to play with the big new telescopes I knew were available to students at the university I chose to study at. I passed the course and now travel around the world making observations.

5

As a teenager I wanted to travel all over the world studying volcanoes – something exciting that very few people knew about. That idea didn't last long as I realised it would be more satisfying to do what generations of my relatives had done before me and study the universe. Now I'm involved in theoretical astronomy – making observations and testing theories. It's as fascinating as I'd hoped, though the salary could be better – maybe it will be when I make a major discovery about space.

▶▶ PART 4

Interviewer: Mel, you're a life coach, which means you help people improve the way they live their lives. You specialise in achieving a work-life balance, don't you?

Mel Candy: Right. The most frequent complaint from clients is that they're 'too busy'. Some high-powered managers love that, and they're successful at making free time too, but for others, no matter what their position, it's a problem. They recognise there must be something they can do about it – that's why they approach me. I think they expect me to pick a number and say 'you should only be spending X number of hours at work,' but it depends what's best for the individual.

Interviewer: Do people who work from home find it more difficult to switch off?

Mel Candy: Definitely – especially those who live alone, because it's tempting to work late. For these people it's essential to get out and have some contact with others every day. The more time you spend on your own, the harder it becomes to hold a conversation when you *do* see someone. You can spend too much time inside your own head without realising it, and that isn't healthy.

Interviewer: What's your opinion of multi-tasking?

Mel Candy: Trying to do more than one thing at a time? Sounds great, doesn't it, saving time by making a business call while you're eating your lunch at your desk? I used to think I was really good at this, but when I read some ground-breaking research I realised it was actually counter-productive – my brain couldn't cope with constant switching between activities. It's better to do one task at a time.

Interviewer: So, what's the expert solution to achieving work-life balance?

Mel Candy: Work can become all-important. I get clients to turn that around – let life become the important thing. I know you can't necessarily get work done faster, but those who successfully achieve a work-life balance put family occasions and important dates in a diary and stick to them. That's where I come in, sitting down and getting people to consider not just what they've got to do today, but in the next few weeks or months.

Interviewer: What do people find most difficult when they're trying to achieve a balance?

Mel Candy: Putting the fear of losing out to one side – thinking exciting things are happening and they aren't there to experience them. And people feel guilty if they don't respond to an email straightaway, even though people don't usually expect you to answer immediately.

Interviewer: Have you picked up any good tips from clients?

Mel Candy: Yes, I have. I never used to leave the house if everything wasn't in its rightful place. Then a client I was helping told me she'd realised it wasn't a sign of failure if she left the house a little untidy when she went out to work. She said she'd rather spend her free time on the golf course than tidying up. I adopted her approach – and although I can't exactly advise other people not to do their cleaning, it saved me half an hour a day.

Interviewer: How do you know when you've achieved work-life balance?

Mel Candy: I feel energetic and I want to get out there and do things – both personally and professionally. I don't sit there at my desk wishing I was in front of the TV chilling out. As long as I don't feel overwhelmed by work and am comfortable with the amount I have to do, that's balance for me.

Interviewer: Thanks, Mel.

FIRST
TEST 4

▶▶ PART 1

1

My driving instructor has always said I was very motivated, and I am. He says that's why I've made such rapid progress, but in fact I've always been quite a fast learner, and pretty sure of myself whatever I do. Driving isn't easy, though, and there's a lot to take in when you start. My instructor puts across new concepts very clearly, which has helped me enormously. He repeats things a lot sometimes and that makes things stick in my head better – I find it very helpful. When I'm driving on my own in the future, I'm sure I'll hear his voice in my head!

2

A: I've heard that most university courses will soon be held online. People won't sit together in large lecture halls any more – they'll just watch recorded lectures online.

B: Yeah, I've heard that too, but do you really believe that's what people want? I think there's no substitute for actually being in a lecture hall with other people. You really miss out, otherwise.

A: Well a lot of people wouldn't agree with that – though I do. And you must admit there are some people for whom it's the perfect solution!

B: I'd say everyone benefits from being able to attend traditional lectures in person.

3

A: I'm interviewing candidates for the office manager position tomorrow. I'm going to watch their body language carefully – it can tell you so much!

B: Really? After all, there are so many other more relevant things to consider – like their qualifications and experience.

A: I think the way people sit and speak can give away important clues, without them even realising it.

B: I can't say I'm convinced. There are people who just present themselves well – that doesn't mean they're actually competent. You need to listen to their answers and think about what they're saying, not how they're saying it.

4

Flyerdale Chess Club was set up 35 years ago, and it's still going strong. In fact there's a waiting list now for some evening sessions. Our teams take part in national tournaments, and we've won our fair share of cups over the years. You may wonder if you'll be made welcome if you come along never having played chess before, but I can guarantee you will. We've met in a number of places in the past, but now our regular meetings are held in a pleasant room in the central library building. It's very easy to find.

5

A: I've been reading some interesting stuff about recycling. Apparently some things, like aluminium drinks cans, are a lot cheaper to produce from recycled materials than from raw materials.

B: Is that so? I thought it was relatively expensive to recycle things.

A: Apparently not. I always try to recycle as much as I can, and so do most people I know – glass, paper, textiles, that sort of thing – though I sometimes wonder …

B: What?

A: Well, we're putting all this time and energy into recycling, but maybe we'd be doing more for the planet if we focused on something else.

B: Yeah, maybe.

6

A: How are your courses this year?

B: My English literature course has turned out to be really good. Initially, I wasn't sure it would be, because I'd put my name down for something else instead. I'd not got on that one, and at first I was pretty disappointed. Anyway, it's all fine now because my tutors are fantastic, though apparently very demanding – I wrote my best essay ever for the first assignment and they said there was room for improvement! The seminars are fascinating, and though the other students there seemed a bit unfriendly at first, I've got to know them and actually they're great.

7

We're very excited about this new fabric, and think it'll be very popular with sportspeople. We've been concentrating on sportswear rather than promoting a range of uses for it because it's the obvious thing to do. Like similar fabrics that have come onto the market in recent years, it keeps the wearer cool and dry as the fabric absorbs moisture from the skin and then allows it to evaporate off the surface. What will give our fabric a particular advantage is that it's amazingly competitive on price. And all this has happened so rapidly, giving us great hopes for the future!

8

A: That talk was interesting, wasn't it? I didn't realise that bringing in plants from other parts of the world could cause so many problems for native species when they spread.

B: I didn't either.

A: And the way people think birds are responsible, moving seeds from place to place, but they aren't – it's humans letting them grow in gardens and parks – we just don't think, do we?

B: No, we don't!

A: And I know some people think we'll never sort it out, but I don't believe it's actually as bad as some people say it is. I think now we're more aware of the issues, we can do something about it.

▶▶ PART 2

Hello, my name's Lukas Royle, and I'm a glass artist. Essentially, I make pictures in glass, often very large ones. I must say that it wasn't the career my parents had hoped I'd follow. According to them, a much more suitable thing to do was to work as a mechanic. My father was a farmer, and he thought I should do something conventional, even if I didn't follow in his footsteps.

I've always been artistic, though, and loved drawing in particular. I'd never thought of working with glass until one day I saw a beautiful glass window and knew that I wanted to make that sort of thing too. We were driving to a new shopping centre in town, and the window was in a conference centre we passed. I'll never forget that moment.

I wouldn't have gone to art school, though, unless I'd been encouraged to do so. My older brother and cousin used to tease me a bit when I preferred painting to climbing trees, but my sister was kinder. She said I was so good at art that I should definitely study it, and that gave me the confidence to apply.

I was lucky enough to find a job while I was still at art school. There was a furniture shop nearby, and I went in and told them I was specialising as a glass artist. I offered to produce some lamps for them, because they sold designer furniture like tables and sofas. What I made sold well, and the shop's owner was delighted, so that turned out to be very successful.

By the time I graduated from art school, I'd managed to save up a bit of money, so I could get all of the equipment I needed. I rented a small studio and started my life as an independent artist. It was a bit scary, because it can be hard work to make a living as an artist, but it was also a very exciting time!

I took part in various exhibitions with other artists, and one day, at an exhibition in a small gallery, a few pieces of mine were sold to a well-known sportsman. He showed them to some of his famous friends – a dancer, for example, and a designer. They then started dropping in to my studio to see how I worked, which I thought was amazing.

Reviews are very important for an artist, I think, and another boost to my career came when an arts reviewer said a lot of complimentary things about my work in the magazine he wrote for. After that, loads more people visited my website, and I was even interviewed for a national newspaper.

I began to concentrate on one particular thing, though for the first few years my subject matter had been broad: people, animals, still lives – you name it. I decided that landscapes were really my thing, and I've mostly stuck to those ever since.

I've designed windows for hotels and restaurants over the years, and recently I've been designing windows for factories. I've done one for a tractor factory – this time the one I'm working on is for one belonging to a truck manufacturer. I like the idea that people can look at my art while they're at work.

I do work a lot, especially when I'm trying to complete a commission, but of course I have time off too. A lot of my friends are into hill walking. I'm not so keen on that and prefer cycling, which a bunch of us often do at the weekend. I used to go jogging with a couple of neighbours, but I've given that up because I don't have that much time, unfortunately. I wouldn't change anything about my life, though, I love what I do!

▶▶ PART 3

1
Being a tennis coach is a great job, and every day brings fresh challenges, which I find energising. There's never a dull moment, and to be honest, even the mistakes you make can teach you valuable lessons. Because I'm so enthusiastic, I have to be careful to go easy on my players. I know they're doing their best, and if I ask for more than they can actually give, that won't get us anywhere. If there's anything I wish I didn't have to do, it's travel long distances to tournaments. Luckily there isn't too much of that – most of the time we're here at the tennis centre.

2
I think the best thing about being a tennis coach is getting to know the people I work with extremely well. It's a requirement of the job in fact, as unless I do, I won't know how to respond when things are going badly. That's one reason why I'm glad it's up to me who I take on. There are some sports people I'd struggle to get on with, and I think very carefully before agreeing to work with anybody. I'm a hard worker, which is a good thing, because the people I coach are very determined. They have to be, of course, since it's such a competitive world.

3
When you have young children, as I do, it's good to have a job that allows you to be with them as much as possible. Because all the coaches live and work at the tennis centre, within minutes of finishing work, I'm back at home. There are tough times, of course, and players can be hard to handle when they're doing badly. I'm always careful what I say, because past experience has taught me to consider what message I want to put across, whatever I might actually feel like saying at the time. I've never regretted my choice of career – it's great to work with people who really want to succeed.

4
I realised I'd never be a top tennis player, but knew I had a lot to offer, so I trained as a coach instead. I'm still relatively junior at this tennis centre, so my bosses decide who I'll work with. What I've found, though, is that the players other coaches have a bit of trouble with are actually my favourites. That's probably because I'm not the easiest at times myself, and have a tendency to say exactly what I'm thinking. That works with some players, but with others, it's definitely a mistake! I love waking up and knowing I'm going to work hard at something I enjoy all day.

5
I'm a tennis coach for my children, as well as other people's, which isn't always easy. Children don't miss anything, so when I get something wrong, I always tell them. It's no good

trying to cover it up, though I must admit I'm tempted to sometimes. I work at a large tennis centre, and I didn't ask to have my own children in the group. It just happened, and I didn't complain. The good thing is that when in the future we start going to tournaments abroad, I'll be right there with them. I demand commitment and hard work from them all, but it gets results.

▶▶ **PART 4**

Interviewer: I'd like to welcome Barry Green, the successful concert violinist, to our studio today.

Barry Green: Hello. It's good to be here.

Interviewer: Barry, why did you decide to be a violinist?

Barry Green: It was something I'd been desperate to do since I was about six years old. My parents weren't musicians, but they let my brother and I to do whatever we liked as hobbies, as long as it didn't interfere with our education, so we could get what they called a 'proper job' if necessary. My brother's a good footballer, but sport's never really been my thing. I watched a concert on TV, and after that I was hooked.

Interviewer: Was it hard to combine this passion with ordinary school life?

Barry Green: Well we certainly got plenty of homework, and I wasn't treated any differently just because I had grand ambitions – though I must say my teachers were always very supportive. It probably helped that my marks were always pretty good, without my ever having to make too much of an effort. Not fair, I know! But I always had to get my school work done before any music lessons or practice.

Interviewer: So what did you do when you left school?

Barry Green: I thought about studying maths or physics, but then I heard about a youth orchestra that was doing a world tour. They offered me a scholarship so I could afford to go, which was brilliant. When I got back, as I already knew what I wanted to do, it seemed pointless to delay going to music college, so that's where I went.

Interviewer: And did you like music college?

Barry Green: Well, I'd really looked forward to being there, but some of the teachers were far stricter than the ones I had before, and it wasn't easy at first. I had to learn to play the piano, too, which I felt was a waste of time, as the violin was the only thing I cared about. It did help develop me as a musician, though, which was what I needed – some of the people there had been at special music schools from an early age and I had a lot of catching up to do.

Interviewer: When did you start playing in professional concerts?

Barry Green: I didn't for a long time. I played solo violin in competitions – I had to do a lot of those, and didn't get anywhere for ages. After I won my first prize, though, the city orchestra invited me to play with them sometimes, though not as a soloist of course. That came later, after I'd won a few more competitions. The other musicians were very kind to me, and playing in the violin section with them was a huge chance to learn – some of them became good friends of mine.

Interviewer: How would you describe your life these days, Barry?

Barry Green: Hours and hours of practising, travelling a lot to give concerts but being stuck in hotels that all seem to look the same, rarely having time off to see the sights. ... Huge amounts of pressure when I'm on stage, knowing the audience is out there and being afraid I'll completely forget the notes I've spent so long memorising – not that I've ever actually done that in a concert. And worrying that I'll leave my violin on a seat at an airport!

Interviewer: Is your life as a musician really that tough?

Barry Green: No, I just like to complain sometimes. I know I'm very lucky to be able to do what I love, and to have achieved what I set out to do as a young child. Not many people get the chance to do that. And bringing something to life that was written two hundred years ago is really something extraordinary and fascinating. I hope I'll be able to do it until I'm too old to hold a violin any more.

Interviewer: Thank you very much for talking to us, Barry.

▶▶ **PART 1**

1
A: This is going to be the most challenging climb we've ever done. What do you know about hiking at altitude?
B: I know we're likely to get short of breath because there's less oxygen in the air. It's nothing to be concerned about, though. It'll slow us down a bit, that's all.
A: I can cope with that. At least we've invested in decent gear. We ought to have done a bit more training, though. I'm not sure how confident I am that we'll reach the summit.
B: I'm sure we will. And the views are said to be spectacular. You can look down over the whole of the island from up there.

2
A: Why preserve traditions? I mean, a lot of them are old-fashioned and they're just not relevant to today's culture.
B: Well, I see it slightly differently, though. Customs do get adapted to suit modern circumstances as they pass through the generations. Not that I'm saying we should respect traditions that promote inequality or damage the environment …
A: … which is my precise argument.
B: But don't forget that knowing about our past is vital to making progress in the future. Old traditions can teach us something about the way we used to be.
A: So, it isn't wasted knowledge. You've got a point.

3
A: Have you logged on to that website our tutor recommended?
B: The philosophy one you mean? Yeah, I hadn't expected much from it. There's a bunch of useful articles and resources on there, though – could be worth checking out when we do our next assignment. I've never been a great fan of forums – you know, everyone having a say about any old thing. I must admit this one's changed my mind, though. I'm quite impressed with the way it promotes the exchange of ideas for anyone interested in philosophy – and there are some big names sharing their ideas. I wouldn't dare argue with any of their comments, though!

4

A: How's business at your cookery school?

B: Good, thanks. We've attracted a great deal of interest in classes since we opened in the autumn. What sets us apart is our focus on the experimental side of cooking.

A: It's the 'in' thing, isn't it? Well done! Investing in your test laboratory is really paying off.

B: Fortunately. Though I admit I wasn't enormously confident about the technical elements before – if it weren't for our new head of training, I'm not sure that side of things would've taken off.

A: And you're branching out into catering now?

B: Yes, though we don't expect to make much money for a while with that.

5

A: You're a zoo-keeper. Tell us about the role of modern zoos.

B: Well, zoos were given a bad press for a long time for keeping wild animals in captivity. I agree that roaming animals need space to satisfy their natural instincts, but there's also a convincing argument in favour of zoos. Some species would've died out completely if they hadn't been kept and helped to reproduce. The modern zoo is quite different to that of the past – there's a strong emphasis on the health, nutrition and well-being of the animals that live there. By buying a ticket to a zoo, the public plays an important role in animal conservation and welfare.

6

OK, guys. Before we kick off today's training session, I want to say a few words about winning and losing. You're bound to be upset when the side loses a match. But there's a way to lose gracefully and I haven't seen much evidence of this from you lately. As far as winning is concerned, I've no criticism. I've seen the way you handle it, congratulating the other side and none of that leaping about and shouting which can be irritating for the losing team – be proud of that. There haven't been many occasions to celebrate so far this year, but keep positive and don't let your disappointment show.

7

A: Hosting this year's regional games is going to be a fantastic source of income for the town.

B: I know. Tickets have already sold out for the main athletics events, like the 100-metre sprint. Clearly we got the pricing policy right.

A: The advertising programme's certainly been doing the job – we ought to turn our thoughts to coming up with ways to get rid of tickets for some of the less popular events, now.

B: That's our agenda. Before we do that, I'll you a quick update about the facilities. I had a chat with the project manager and it looks like everything will be completed on time.

8

A: Did you read that article by that physics teacher in the weekend paper – the one about the point of studying it?

B: Yeah, it summed things up well.

A: I really couldn't get my head round some of the laws of physics when I was at school. Getting a teacher's perspective was fascinating. I mean, it's not that everything suddenly became clear – I didn't get half of what the article was saying. No, it was his passion for teaching the subject. It made me think I could do anything if I put my mind to it.

I'm still not keen on physics itself, but I wish he'd been my teacher!

 TEST 5

▶▶ **PART 2**

Hi everyone, and thanks for listening to my talk about restoring old furniture. My name's Thomas Booth and here are a few of my top tips for furniture restoration.

Firstly, make sure you've got enough time to devote to your project. I learned in my first project that trying to restore a beautiful old four-poster bed while doing my day job was a bit too much to take on. I spent days cleaning up the decorations – these were cut deeply into the wood. Sorting out things like rusty metal legs can take ages, too.

Find out the value of your piece before deciding whether it's worth restoring it. Old items of furniture are often covered in scratches, but do check your item for marks. What I mean by this is anything scraped into the wood that might identify whose workshop it originated from. This can give you an idea of a piece's age. If you think it's worth something, seek advice from professionals.

If your piece *does* happen to be of value, you need to decide how much you're willing to spend on its restoration. I always establish a budget before I do anything – then I can decide whether to progress or not. Think about how much of a challenge it's going to be as well. Be realistic.

Once you've decided to go for it, look at how the piece has been constructed, and how you'll put it back together again. Take a photo of it from every angle before you take it apart to begin work. And don't forget to attach a label to the individual pieces – that'll save time later.

If it's your first attempt at restoration, you're likely to have lots of questions. Keep yourself as well-informed as possible. Why not borrow a DVD from the library to do a bit of research in advance? And keep a manual to hand during the restoration process so you can quickly look up the answer to a query.

Safety is, of course, very important. Wear protective clothing, as some of the materials you'll be working with – such as chemicals used in wood-strippers – can be harmful to the skin. I always put on a long-sleeved T-shirt and protect my eyes with a pair of safety glasses – and a mask helps me to avoid breathing in dust or fumes.

The chances are if you're having to restore the item, it won't have been well looked after and will need a good clean. Give larger surfaces a scrub with something like a cloth or sponge to remove the build-up of dirt. To get into any finely-detailed areas I use a toothbrush. It works surprisingly well.

Next, you need to think about repairing or replacing any broken or missing parts. It's always worth looking in antique shops – I couldn't believe my good fortune when I found a handle that was identical to one that was lost from a drawer on a chest I was restoring. Otherwise, you might need an expert to make a substitute.

The final coat on a piece is called a finish. Finishing can be demanding and messy work, so make sure you're ready to put in some muscle power! Old finishes can be what I call 'stubborn'. What I mean is that they're really tough to remove. Be patient and don't rush – you might end up having to do more repair work otherwise.

And last but not least – the tools you'll need. Get some rough sandpaper, wood glue, and a screwdriver. There'll be nails to knock back into place as well. Work with a rubber hammer so you don't harm the wood, and invest in some plastic gloves for the finishing work, too, so the chemicals don't cause problems for your skin.

Well, now you're ready to go! Good luck!

▶▶ PART 3

1
I don't think I've ever felt as happy as the day I left school. It wasn't that I didn't enjoy it, I just wanted to get on with life. I'd done pretty well on the whole and my teachers said some really positive things about my work, so I knew I'd cope with the literature degree I was going on to do. I was looking forward to being able to focus on a single subject. In fact, I was so keen to get going I didn't even want to take my well-earned summer break. I felt strange leaving the place I'd made so many memories in with my friends, though.

2
School was OK, but I wouldn't say it was the best time of my life. I kept my head down and managed to get all the certificates I needed – even in chemistry, which was my weakest subject, so I was pleased about that one. On my last day it was like my friends and I were never going to see each other again. We were going to the same college though, so I think we were just upset about moving on. It was a bit scary going from somewhere your teachers kept an eye on you to somewhere where you were responsible for your own study.

3
I made the most of my time at school and worked hard. My friends were going on to college, but I was happy with my decision to go into employment instead. In fact I couldn't wait for the independence I knew it would provide me with – not that I wouldn't have gone on to do more study if I'd known what to do – I didn't really mind doing it! I was sad to say goodbye to some of my teachers at our leaving ceremony, especially those who'd been particularly encouraging, but I'd got the qualifications I needed and I was off to get on with my future!

4
I remember my last day at school very clearly. I arrived late and was really worried about missing part of our awards ceremony. That was where, at my school anyway, they handed out prizes for people who'd done particularly well at school. I was amazed when my history teacher called out my name for the history prize. I hadn't come top of the year or anything like that but my teacher said she wanted to give me recognition for having put in so much effort in class. It was a proud moment and it made me think twice about my decision not to study history on my university course.

5
I'd decided to have a break from studying after school, even though I was looking forward to eventually going to university. I'd hoped to go travelling for a while before I started my degree course, but even though we'd planned everything carefully, the friend I was supposed to go with backed out at the last minute

and I was left wondering what else I could do. It ruined my last day at school as I was so disappointed when he told me. You can imagine that I was less than thrilled when I later realised I'd have to get a job for a year, though I did save some money.

▶▶ PART 4

Interviewer: Today we're talking to mathematician Ben Chadwick about a possible connection between maths and music. First Ben, tell us what it's like being a professional mathematician.

Ben Chadwick: Well, it's a bit of a conversation stopper! People tend not to know what a professional mathematician does on a daily basis, and they rarely know how to respond. Inevitably, they assume that I must be a teacher, which has never been the case. What I *do* do, is research, testing theories. When I say this, some people look uneasy, as if they're worried I'm about to ask them some complex mathematical question.

Interviewer: Now, could you explain the theory that maths and music are linked?

Ben Chadwick: The idea is that if you play classical music to young children, they'll become good not only at music, but at maths, too. I guess the theory came about because of the idea that you have to be able to count in order to play a rhythm. Unfortunately, some people are scared of maths because they think it's hard. If they can help their children succeed without them having to put in too much effort, they'll go along with anything they think might work – and who can blame them, really?

Interviewer: What's your personal opinion about the maths–music theory?

Ben Chadwick: Well, I don't think it can be as simple as just listening to music to improve your marks in maths. Both maths and music deal with abstract structures, so I believe that what connects the two is being good at dealing with abstract structures. This is where the connection comes in – but it isn't the one many people believe it to be.

Interviewer: Can you prove, for example, that mathematicians are better than other people at music?

Ben Chadwick: I'm going to do a study on this! If you look at someone who becomes a professional mathematician, they probably come from a family who believe in academic study – which includes learning music. There seems little point comparing mathematicians to everyone else as not much would be proved. If you've studied both subjects seriously, you're bound to be better at them than people who haven't.

Interviewer: I've read that mathematicians who *are* musicians are attracted to the piano more than other instruments. Why's that do you think?

Ben Chadwick: I'm writing a paper about that and my personal belief is that they like listening to music that appears to have a particular set of patterns in it. What remains to be seen is whether they are collectively likely to prefer playing the music of particular composers. I'll look forward to that discovery.

Interviewer: Is there a connection between maths and languages?

Ben Chadwick: Languages deal with abstract structures, too – such as grammar. Grammar seems a bit like maths – building up blocks of meaning – which is why no one's surprised that a mathematician might also be a good linguist.

Because music is more emotional, and anyone can enjoy it, it appears to have less in common with maths – so a connection between them seems fascinating, unlike the connection between maths and other subjects, like science.

Interviewer: And finally, what is it that you love so much about maths?

Ben Chadwick: Good question. It was the one subject I could get a 100 per cent in – and I didn't have to work too hard at it! By the time I realised that wasn't always the case, I'd invested years of study in maths and had developed a love for the theoretical aspects of the subject. It isn't so much that I want to prove people wrong – I just want to prove a theory right!

TEST 6

▶▶ PART 1

1
A: It's interesting to see what holidays people choose, isn't it?
B: Yes – they tend to love all the coach tours and trips where they can be with lots of other people all the time.
A: You've been finding that, maybe, but I can't say I have.
B: Well they certainly appreciate staying in nice hotels at a reasonable price.
A: Can't argue with that, but you can do that travelling alone, can't you? I've noticed more people are looking for trips to major cities.
B: I've been dealing with people looking for something a bit different – usually involving beaches!

2
People often assume that being a novelist is something you do because that's what you've always dreamt of doing, and in many cases that's absolutely true. In mine, though, it was more of a process of trying out a few different things first, then finding myself having a go at writing something. And I knew almost immediately it was exactly the right thing for me as a career. The books I've written so far are by no means perfect, but that's hardly surprising. When people say it must be tough to be a writer, I tell them they're wrong: it's a whole lot worse than tough!

3
A: Did you watch that programme on Channel 4 last night?
B: Yeah! And those shots of penguins in Antarctica – weren't they funny!
A: Yeah, when they were speeding through the water, then leaping out when they got to the edge of the ice – it was brilliant!
B: And then they slid down those icy slopes, or just fell over!
A: That really made me laugh. They're so fit and fast when they're swimming – they'd easily beat the best Olympic swimmers – and then so clumsy on land! But that was the point, wasn't it? To show how world-class swimmers can learn from animals – in the water, at least.

4
I can't say my first day went very well. I know it wasn't my fault at all, and I did my best. And I don't blame anyone else in the kitchen, in fact. We were all working as fast as we could and the restaurant was absolutely full. There were also some staff off sick and we just couldn't keep up with the orders. Of course I'm a bit concerned about that, even though the manager told me not to be and that it was just bad luck. But I

can't help it because after all, chefs are supposed to be able to deal with things like that.

5
A: Have you read that report on Chester Park?
B: I have, lots of people say it's a great place for a walk after work.
A: That's good.
B: One thing they mention is that it's all a bit overgrown, so people who like their parks neat and tidy aren't keen! But as a result, it's full of birds that you wouldn't find elsewhere in the city.
A: It sounds perfect, sitting under a tree on a park bench …
B: Well there were lots of complaints about the benches being old and broken, I'm afraid.
A: Oh well, we can easily sort that out!

6
I'm going to decorate the living room today, and if I need your help, I'll ask, of course, but I think I can manage to move most of the furniture out on my own. It shouldn't take long and none of it's that heavy. If I were thirty years younger, like you, it would be even easier, but I'll be fine. But I will take your advice on one thing, and it's nice of you to think of it – I'll leave the piano where it is, as it's so heavy, and just cover it while I do the decorating. You've got plenty to do yourself, I know.

7
A: So what do you think about the course so far, then?
B: Not bad at all. It's a bit dull at times, but it's all pretty useful, I think.
A: Absolutely.
B: I mean, once we've qualified, and we're employed in a lab, or wherever, what we've been taught here will mean we really do know what we're doing.
A: Right. There are some things, though, which I'd hoped we might look at in a bit more depth.
B: Yeah, but I suppose they have to make sure we have all the basics, and then we can specialise later on, in the final part of the course.
A: That's true.

8
The good thing about the room I rent is that it's only ten minutes away on foot from the university campus, so I always get to lectures on time. The downside is that during the day there's lots of traffic in the street below, so I have to have the window closed so that it's quiet enough for me to work. But it's fine in the evenings. It's certainly not spacious, though, so I've had to leave some of the stuff I wanted to bring at my parents'. There's plenty of room there. And of course, I wish the rent was a bit lower – but it's manageable.

TEST 6

▶▶ PART 2

Hi everybody! I'm delighted to see so many of you here today for my introductory talk about the university music society. The society was originally set up fifty years ago by a group of tutors in the music department, and is open to anyone at the university who'd like to join. They ran it themselves for the first ten years, and then handed over the organisation of the society to students, and it has stayed that way ever since.

We're extremely proud of all our different groups, from the small chamber ensembles to the swing band. If you want to join the orchestra, there are auditions at the beginning of every term, and everyone's welcome to come along and try out for a place. And if you're interested in being part of the choir, our largest group, all you need do is come along when we're practising and if you like what we're doing, then you're in!

We invite experts from all over the world to give talks on various different subjects throughout the year – we've had speakers telling us about pianos through the ages, and how to make trumpets. The first one of term is this evening, and it's all about violins. It promises to be very interesting, so I hope you can come along, even if flutes are really more your thing!

And next Wednesday, you'll have a chance to hear our jazz group playing in a concert. Do you remember where the Kings Hall is, where you had your first-year welcome talk yesterday? Well, the concert will be in the slightly smaller Union Hall, just opposite. It's where a lot of our concerts take place.

We also have an active social programme, with events sometimes only loosely connected to music. They're a great way of getting to know other members in an informal, relaxed setting. We have a quiz every couple of months, which is very popular, but coming up this month before the next one, there's a dinner, so you can get to know both new and more long-standing members of the society.

We have a competition every year for aspiring composers. It took us a bit of time choosing a theme this year – in the past we've covered topics from nature to dance – the committee finally agreed it would be poetry, so we'll see how that goes!

There is a small annual charge for membership: fifteen pounds. But thanks to generous additional funding from the University Music Department, that not only includes free tickets to concerts here at the university, but also transport to concerts all over the country, offering members the chance to see some great performances. We always get good discounts on tickets to those.

The music department also funded work restoring the music practice rooms. The floors were all redone last year. You'll see how great they look now – they were in quite a state before. And they've made a start on the ceilings, but we hope this work will be finished very soon.

The society doesn't only do things that benefit the students here. We also promote music in the local community. Some of the things we do include going to local schools to give talks – which have led to schoolchildren then coming to attend concerts here at the university – as well as actually giving concerts, which is what we've done in local hospitals, and had lots of positive feedback, so we'll be doing that again!

Keep up to date with all our goings-on by looking at our website. There's a blog by a cellist that's particularly funny and popular – check it out! And every week we upload a newsletter with all the information about what we're doing and where.

Now, does anyone have any questions?

▶▶ PART 3

1
I don't expect to win the young engineers' competition, but it's been an interesting experience so far. I've always liked making things, and I'd had this idea for a while for a new type of battery charger. When I saw the advertisement for the competition, I'd actually been wondering what to do with myself during the summer holidays. All my friends were away and I couldn't find a summer job so I thought: right, time to get on with it and stop just lazing around. I knew that if I didn't do something that got me thinking and was a bit of an effort, I'd have just wasted the summer.

2
I've entered other young engineers' competitions in the past, and haven't come anywhere near getting a prize. But it's good fun and this time, a guy on my course who I get on well with said he was entering and that he hoped I would too. Our entries are very different – he's got an idea for a navigation system and mine's just a new kind of drinks bottle – so we'll see how it goes! Our lecturer thinks it's a great idea and has offered lots of advice and encouragement. I think all engineering students should enter a competition if they can – it really is an opportunity to develop your skills.

3
I know a few people who've entered young engineers' competitions, and some of them have even won prizes. One of my friends was even interviewed for a national newspaper when he won. I'm sure I won't win anything myself, but I still think that doing something like this will impress potential employers. I'm trying to do all the right things to get my career off the ground. It's also fun putting an idea into practice that so far I've only carried around in my head. I've only recently graduated from university, and it feels quite relaxing to do something fun like this after all the demanding work for my course.

4
When I told one of my lecturers I'd entered the competition, he said it sounded very time-consuming but he'd back me. He also said he'd tell the other students on the course about it in case they wanted to enter as well. If there are a whole load of us there, it'll be fun! I'm actually quite confident I might have a chance of getting a prize, which is why I entered, even though I've never done anything like this before. I've got this great idea for a new type of compact and easy-to-use ice cream maker, and I've really enjoyed working on it over the past few weeks.

5
I saw an ad in the paper for the competition, and I contacted them straight away. I'd never heard of anything like that in our area before, and no one I know is into engineering. I'm hoping it will give me the chance to talk to people I have something in common with. I'm applying for university at the moment, so any practical experience I can get before going will help. Having to design something and develop it on my own is proving very interesting, and though I had a few doubts before, I'm absolutely sure that that engineering is the right course for me.

▶▶ PART 4

Interviewer: Today, we have in our studio Matt Brown, who recently trained as a sailing instructor.

Matt Brown: Hi!

Interviewer: First of all, what made you want to be a sailing instructor, Matt?

Matt Brown: Well I've always loved the sea – we lived miles from the coast when I was a child, but had fantastic summer holidays by the seaside every year. I learned to sail with my brothers, but it never occurred to me when I was younger that I might actually teach anyone else to do it. Then a good mate of mine suggested I should consider becoming an instructor. While I was busy working in a restaurant last summer to finish paying my university fees, he'd been having a much better time doing just that.

Interviewer: Was it hard for you to find somewhere to train?

Matt Brown: Yes, harder than I'd expected. I searched for courses on the internet, though people advised me not to take the online course reviews too seriously. And although there was a wide range of courses at reasonable prices, a lot of the ones I liked the look of were full, so it took a while for me to sort it out.

Interviewer: And did you like the other people on the course?

Matt Brown: I'd been a bit nervous about meeting them, I suppose, but maybe that's not particularly surprising! What was, though, was the different types of people doing the course with me, and how much they already knew. I'd realised they would mostly be older than me, and of course we were all very eager to learn, but I was very lucky to be in a group like that.

Interviewer: How did the first day go?

Matt Brown: It was fantastic: we saw a group of five dolphins hunting together. We were all in one boat, and suddenly they were coming straight towards us! Some people thought they might turn the boat over or something – I wasn't concerned about that – I was just so amazed, and I don't know why, but I did my best to look cool about it, as if it was the sort of thing I saw every day. Everyone else rushed for their cameras. I got mine out too but then just stood there, staring.

Interviewer: What about the rest of the course?

Matt Brown: It was very hard work indeed, but I learnt so much. After the course was over the thing I missed most wasn't, I have to admit, the early mornings, though there were some memorable sunrises. It was never reaching the end of a day without acquiring at least one different skill. That was a tremendous feeling. Now I'm qualified, which is very satisfying. The school have even said I can come back and sail there whenever I want, which is great.

Interviewer: What do you think you'll enjoy about being a sailing instructor, Matt?

Matt Brown: It will be great to teach very young children to sail – it gives kids so much confidence, I think. Then when they're teenagers, you know, they'll be able to do what I'm doing if they want. And also, it'll be cool to have a job working alongside colleagues who like the same things as I do – not everyone can do their hobby as a job! Some people want to train other instructors, but I'm not sure that's for me, really.

Interviewer: And what's next?

Matt Brown: Well, I'd love to go on a sailing holiday now, but before I can afford that I need to put what I've learned into practice, and be paid for it this time! So that's the plan and I've got a place in mind on the Mediterranean. They run the kind of courses I'd love to teach, so I'm going to contact them …

Interviewer: Well good luck with it all, Matt.

Matt Brown: Thanks!

TEST 7

▶▶ **PART 1**

One of the most frequent complaints I hear from air passengers is lack of leg-room. No one wants to sit scrunched up in a ball for hours on end. Checking the seating plan of the plane you're taking will help you identify areas where there's space to stretch out – usually at the back, though there's increased engine noise there. Passengers tend to stand and move around in the aisles – I won't advise against this as it keeps blood moving round the body – though we do need to keep asking them to sit down while we're serving refreshments.

2
A: What do you think about taking vitamin pills?
B: I've always believed that if you eat a balanced diet, there's little reason to. It depends how much effort you put into preparing healthy meals, which is what I'd encourage. It's tempting not to bother if you're taking vitamin supplements – you rely on them instead.
A: So, you're against the idea?
B: I wouldn't say that exactly. Occasionally your doctor might prescribe you a particular vitamin if your body's lacking in something. Anyway, it's up to you. Vitamin pills tend to be more affordable than they used to be – but check the recommended daily amounts carefully.

3
A: I hadn't expected yoga to be that hard!
B: Don't you feel energised now, though?
A: Come to think of it, I suppose I do. I can see how it builds strength – some of the positions are pretty difficult to hold. I thought I was going to fall asleep when we did the meditation, though – closing your eyes, breathing deeply …
B: Mm. I haven't come across the techniques the teacher used before, and I guess it was like a trip to a foreign land for you …
A: … as a complete newcomer, you mean? True. Whether I'll go again remains to be seen …

4
Hello, my name's Carla Flanders. I'm enrolled on the finance course. I couldn't attend today's lecture I'm afraid – my tutor excused me. The thing is, he was meant to be giving back our latest essays today. Obviously without being there I couldn't pick mine up from him. I need his comments on it – there are no classes now until after the break but I really want to do some work on preparing my presentation in the meantime. Is there any chance of coming in for a chat with him over the holiday? Can you ask him to ring me to set it up? Sorry to cause any inconvenience.

5
A: I hear you've resigned! Are you moving on to better things?
B: I wouldn't put it like that! I've loved my job here – and I wouldn't have got the new one without the experience I've acquired at this company.
A: How so?
B: By polishing my management skills – they're much improved. The toughest lesson I've learned here is not trying to be everyone's friend. I don't mean not being approachable or kind, I just mean maintaining a professional distance – give people direction, then back off and let them get on with the task – being available if needed.
A: Pity you're going!

6

A: So, you've chosen a topic for your French project?

B: Yes, I was thinking about doing something on social greetings – what people say in different situations.

A: That sounds achievable within the word limit. Do you have any access to native French speakers to collect the data? Remember you're doing original research. Relying on relevant literature isn't sufficient for this project.

B: I've got some French friends, actually. I'm thinking of recording them speaking.

A: Will that work, given that you need to compare both informal and formal settings? Have you overlooked that?

B: Ah … I have, haven't I?

7

A: Do you like painting people's walls for a living?

B: Of course! People always compare painting people's rooms with being an artist and think it's what would-be artists do when they discover they have no talent! I haven't done a drawing since I left school. I could draw quite well but I never had any intention of being an artist. People often overlook what a skilled job painting and decorating is. It probably doesn't seem like it requires any imagination – but I'm often asked for advice about colour schemes when clients can't make up their minds.

8

For the uninformed, it's easy to think horses behave in unpredictable ways. Yes, they're highly sensitive creatures, and yes, you do need to put some real work into training – but you'll find they respond positively on the whole. You don't have to be a qualified trainer to understand how horses react to humans. Horses are aware of subtle movements and eye contact, so if you're nervous, your horse is nervous – guaranteed. Get to know your horse – and your horse will get to know you.

TEST 7

▶▶ PART 2

Thanks for coming along to the workshop today to learn about candles! Before we get to work making our own, here's a bit about their history.

The outside part of a candle is made from wax. Many ingredients have gone into making wax over the centuries. I was amazed to find out that wax could be made from not only nuts and olive oil, but spices, too. The earliest candles we know of originated in China and were made from a kind of fat.

Of course, candles were used for the purpose of providing light, but another early use was for time-keeping. I've tried to reproduce some of these 'candle clocks' myself. I tried to make my own version of a kind of stick that was used – while it was burning, it gave out a new perfume each hour. My version – which I made in a lovely red colour – didn't really work, but I was more successful with the method of drawing lines around candles to mark the hours.

Candles were also used to time shorter periods. Like me, I bet you didn't know that by inserting a nail – or other small, heavy object – into a candle, you would hear the noise of it dropping onto a plate, for example, when the wax around it melted – telling you time was up!

By the thirteenth century, candle making had become a profession in Europe. 'Chandlers', as candle makers were known, sold home-made candles in their shops. I found out that, despite the fact that it was such a useful item, candle production was prohibited in many factories at this time because the process released a terrible smell.

Candle makers continued to improve their products, making them burn with a brighter flame, using wax that wouldn't melt in the summer heat, and – something that was particularly useful – reducing the amount of smoke they generated. Cheaper ingredients were also used which lowered the cost of production.

In the 1830s, the manufacture of candles became industrialised. This meant they could be produced continuously and were more affordable. If you go to the Museum of Industry you can see a machine from the period built for this purpose. They occasionally set it working and I've watched it in action – fascinating! While we're talking about the museum, I bought an excellent book on candle making in the gift shop there – worth a visit.

In the mid-nineteenth century, other types of wax became available and the quality of candles improved. I've researched this thoroughly and I even had a piece published in a magazine about how these new waxes were created. I focused on petrol, though there were other new waxes, too – coal can be used, for example.

Also around this time, candle makers started to make wicks out of new materials, too. The wick is the bit that runs through the centre of a candle and burns the wax as fuel. Experiments with early wicks included using rolled tubes of paper, though cotton became the most effective material. It was tightly woven so it would curl over when it burned, safely maintaining the height of the flame.

In the later part of the nineteenth century, candle making declined rapidly as lamps and eventually light bulbs were introduced to the home. After this point, candles became used simply as a decorative item. After getting home from work I love nothing better than the relaxation provided by lighting a candle, sitting down and just chilling out for the evening!

And there's such a variety of candles nowadays. I'm forever trying out new methods of production, new waxes and different patterns. This afternoon, however, we're going to concentrate on my current area of development which is different colour combinations. I hope you'll enjoy the day!

TEST 7

▶▶ PART 3

1

I'm a frequent traveller and hardly a week goes by when I don't find myself in an airport lounge. I used to think jetting off abroad was glamorous, but that wore off when I realised how much time I'd be spending alone in hotel rooms. It took me ages to work out that I could save packing time by keeping a separate bag of toothpaste and other necessities I could pick up at a moment's notice. Those free items hotels provide are the perfect size. Don't forget to collect the free newspaper on board the plane – you can catch up on business news while you travel and it passes the time.

2

If you're anything like me, you'd forget your head if it wasn't fastened on. That doesn't combine well with travel – losing your passport is a no-no. I guess I could make copies just in case. I've got the usual stuff down to a fine art now – checking in online so you don't have to queue … I've never found it all that useful trying to communicate in the local language like people say you should – I can never understand the reply! Researching how things are done in the workplace in the country you're visiting is vital, and helps avoid making mistakes when you're in an unfamiliar office – there's plenty about this online.

3

I'm always off somewhere around the world for work, and I'm lucky enough to have been to some exotic places. I must have coins from at least half the countries in the world. OK, I'm exaggerating, but I do travel a lot and I love every minute of it, even though it's for business rather than pleasure. I love trying out my language skills on local people, but I wouldn't say this is essential to survival. One tip I picked up along the way was to repeatedly book a seat with a company you trust – you'll get to know flight staff when they see you frequently and they'll look after you.

4

I have a reputation for being a worrier when it comes to travelling. I'm confident in my business role – I just feel disorientated when I land in a new place. There's no way I'd ever drive in an unfamiliar city, so I've found that knowing some polite expressions and the address of your hotel in the local language is worth doing for when you take a cab, for example. I usually check up on how much things cost before I go away. I write down the currency exchange which helps me work local prices out and I use a money belt – they're light to wear and keep your documents safe, too.

5

I tend to travel to the same countries, and I've always got leftover currency hanging around in my jacket pockets. It comes in useful if you need a taxi from the airport or something. A note on that by the way – ask around for the best price – some taxi companies don't use meters and charge a fortune! Anyway, I prepare myself well for flying. I just take a small bag which fits easily into the lockers on board. I don't take many clothes – I have my shirts and things laundered on a daily basis instead. It's the easiest way to travel – you don't have to drag your stuff along behind you.

TEST 7

▶▶ **PART 4**

Interviewer: Sheena, you're a behavioural psychologist, which means you study the way people behave. What's so interesting about human behaviour for you?

Sheena Smith: Everyone's a psychologist really, aren't they? I mean, we're all fascinated by what other people do, especially when it isn't what we do ourselves. I guess that's the heart of the matter for me these days. I've always been pretty good at reading people's faces and understanding how they really feel and that's what first got me interested in psychology.

Interviewer: One of your earliest experiences of observing behaviour was seeing what your father did when he answered the phone. Tell us about that.

Sheena Smith: Well, he had quite a strong local accent but whenever he picked up the phone he'd speak in what I used

to call his 'telephone voice' – he sort of became a bit more posh. My mum and I would exchange secret smiles when we heard him. What sticks in my mind is the thrill of realising that once he knew who was calling he'd either carry on with the posh voice or relax into his normal way of speaking, if he felt comfortable with them.

Interviewer: What kind of things did you study during your psychology degree?

Sheena Smith: I enjoyed writing about how we're affected by social norms. We like to think we're complex and individual – and yet we all tend to behave in similar ways when faced with the same situation! It isn't that we couldn't do something differently if we felt like it, but we do what's expected of us – people rarely challenge fixed ideas, even if they like to think of themselves as different. Sooner or later, we realise it's easier to go with the crowd.

Interviewer: One of your first projects was studying how people behave in lifts, wasn't it?

Sheena Smith: Yes! At the beginning of the project I assumed that if I started a conversation in a lift, people would join in. But they just nodded politely and went back to staring at their phones – I couldn't believe it! It's the lack of space in lifts that makes people worry about appearing strange or threatening. So people do nothing at all!

Interviewer: What are you working on at the moment?

Sheena Smith: I'm looking at behaviour that seems irrational – that appears to make little sense – like waiting in a long queue, because we think there must be something worth waiting for. But if we see an empty restaurant we won't go in! It's not difficult to understand why. I thought I could put an original slant on the work, but I've realised this research isn't going to change the world of psychology – that doesn't make it any less interesting than other research, though.

Interviewer: What's been your favourite project so far?

Sheena Smith: I did some research about the psychology of giving gifts. People are as happy to receive small gifts as larger ones – except when they learn the cost of the item. Then they start judging it. That was news to me – I'd imagined people wouldn't be bothered. That was the first article I had published in my professional career, so it was a very satisfying piece of research

Interviewer: What would you like to study that you haven't yet?

Sheena Smith: I'm interested in people's behaviour 'behind closed doors'. The way we behave publicly and in private can be enormously different. You can't observe people without their knowledge, so studies like this require careful setting up. It isn't that it can't be done – you have to observe people for long enough until they forget they're being observed – video cameras are the best way to do this. It's easy to find participants for this kind of study – though people don't always like what they see of themselves!

TEST 8

▶▶ **PART 1**

1

Now Jim, in my team at work, you know – now he's an interesting character. Whenever he thinks something looks as if it's going to be rather demanding, he just doesn't want to know about it. And yet what he actually does is always really good – it's top quality in fact. And you know how some people are always asking for help – not that I mind giving it, of course – but I do like the way he just gets on with the things he *does* feel are within his capabilities. I'll just have to think of ways to encourage him to be a bit more willing to stretch himself, I suppose.

2
A: That was a tough training session, wasn't it?
B: Yes, I'm glad it's over! It's always worse when they're picking people for competitions, the coaches push us to the limit.
A: How do you think you did?
B: I don't know if I'll be in Saturday's competition, but I think I did pretty well today, to be honest.
A: I'm not sure I did. I doubt I'll be selected this time. We should train a bit longer every day. That would do us good, I think.
B: I really don't think I could manage any more training than we're already doing. It's the effort we put in during the training that counts, I reckon.

3
It's always an amazing feeling whenever there's a scientific breakthrough, and the excitement about the new drug a few months ago was huge. What often happens immediately after something like that is that the news media report on it without getting all the details right. And then the general public imagine that the benefits of the research will become available far sooner than they actually will. This is what seems to have happened in this case: people are disappointed that things haven't moved faster. In fact it usually takes a few years to be sure that a new drug or treatment is safe for everyone to use.

4
A: I'm doing some research on celebrity lifestyles for my project.
B: Sounds interesting!
A: Yeah, though I kind of know what I'm going to find … I mean they get sick of all the luxury after a while, don't they? It's all the same, day after day …
B: Really? Lots of them can't have enough of it, I think! But I'd say they do get tired of never being able to leave home without people pointing at them and staring.
A: I can't disagree with you there. And I'm sure that's why they tend to mix with other famous people in their free time.
B: They probably like that less than we think.

5
The customer came in and asked to look at the watches. He asked a few questions, but spent most of the time looking at the ones I showed him in silence. He wasn't exactly rude, but I wouldn't say his manners were the best, either. Saying hello when you come up to the counter, and goodbye when you leave, is what most people do and he didn't bother with any of that. The impression I got was that compared to the average customer he knew a fair amount – more like someone in the business themselves, actually. Anyway, he eventually left without buying anything.

6
A: What do you think about the new university football kit? I like the way the men's and women's versions are so similar, and I love the orange they chose. I think it's cool!
B: Well, apart from the colour, I'm not particularly impressed.
A: Really? What's wrong with it?

B: Well for one thing, the material. There are so many better ones that weigh next to nothing, and still keep the wind out. Why couldn't we have had something like that?
A: Yes, that's true. But I suppose they didn't want it to be too expensive.
B: Yes, you're probably right, but I wouldn't have minded paying just a bit more for something better.

7
Like any job, teaching maths has downsides as well as upsides. But what job doesn't? For every morning I wake up and feel it might be preferable just to stay in bed, there are at least ten when I don't. I know maths isn't everyone's favourite subject, and lots of my pupils can't wait for the lesson to be over. But the atmosphere at the school's good, partly because the kids are OK really, and also because I couldn't have more supportive workmates. The school's hardly the best-equipped as far as smart whiteboards and things like that are concerned, but I don't really mind about that.

8
A: Have you read the report on increasing numbers at the amusement park?
B: Yes, it makes some good points. How can we persuade tourists to stay there all day if there are only two small cafés? People have to eat!
A: Yeah – lots of people take their own food, but many don't.
B: It also says the park should be better advertised, though you see posters up about it all over the place.
A: Maybe TV ads about all the new rides this year would help?
B: Possibly. TV advertising seems a little out-of-date now. But visitors always say they love the new rides, don't they?
A: Well, some like to stick with the old favourites.

 TEST 8

▶▶ **PART 2**

Hello, I'm going to tell you about my geography field trip, so you know what to expect when you go on yours.

The field centre we went to is in Wales, in a rural area where a lot of the old buildings are protected and can't be modernised – called a conservation area, and the building really was lovely but rather old.

We arrived in time for lunch, then straight after that, we were taken out by Bill, a staff member there, for a walk and a talk. Bill's an expert on the local area and knows all about the native woodlands there. He told us about the deer that they provide a good habitat for – it was fascinating. I knew people had sometimes seen eagles around there too, but we didn't see any.

I spotted a number of interesting things on the walk, and took a lot of photos. There were beautiful traditional stone walls and lots of hedges. There was also a lovely little wooden bridge over a stream, and also a modern aluminium gate into a field, which was rather a contrast. I saw an iron one later and Bill said it was 100 years old. My picture of that gate is now one of my favourites.

The next morning we got up early, and after breakfast, we had to make a few decisions about what we were going to do during the week. We could choose what projects to work on while we were there, and the plan was that when we got back to university, we'd write up our notes and produce reports on what we'd done.

Then we went outside and it was incredibly wet and windy! I held onto my hat, but the wind got my map. I ran after it, but it ended up in some muddy water and was completely ruined!

I was working with two classmates on water quality in the local area. I needed to collect some samples to analyse. There was plenty of water around, what with the lake, a small pond behind the field centre, and where I got mine from, the river. I was interested to know if there'd be any pollutants in it.

The field centre has a small lab, and we did work there in the evenings. I was glad that at school I'd paid attention in some classes, because it turned out to be handy to know some chemistry. Luckily it didn't require any knowledge of biology, because that's all a distant memory!

On the last day it was time for us to give presentations about what we'd done during the week. Nobody wanted to go first, of course, so somebody suggested that we should do it according to height, tallest first. I was glad it wasn't done by age, because I was the oldest!

All the presentations were good, and there were several about farming. It was interesting to learn the methods they use, combining the traditional and the modern. The best one, to my mind, was the one on the difficulties involved in dairy farming. Sheep farming is important round there too, and someone gave a talk on that as well.

We decided to get the field centre staff a present before we left. But the village shop had little to offer apart from a few chocolate bars and some cake that looked a little past it. Then I saw they had some local honey, so that was our goodbye present.

I'm sure you'll all have a great time when you go yourselves.

TEST 8

▶▶ PART 3

1

Digital, or ebooks, are all I read these days. My parents have shelves of old-fashioned paper books, and I do love turning the pages, and the whole look of the words on the page, and the lovely pictures. It's not a matter of taste, however, but of convenience. I read a lot, especially when I'm travelling, which I often have to do for my job. I love knowing that as soon as I've finished one novel, there's another one there for me to start. It's something I always make sure of, and of course, it's much easier to do that with digital books. I can't imagine my life without them!

2

I grew up with paper books, and my parents don't like digital books very much. But what they don't understand is that there are so many things you can do with digital books that of course you couldn't do with paper books. I love following the links to relevant internet sites, for example if I want to see more about something I'm reading about. Also the way I can make notes if I want to without feeling I'm somehow damaging the book – I could never do that in one of my parents'! And I've never had any trouble getting hold of what I want to read in digital format.

3

I read digital books a lot, but the only reason is that I can enlarge the print easily. I find that very useful, but I don't take advantage of the other stuff you can do, like following links to photos and things. I just can't be bothered. I suppose I'm a

bit old-fashioned. I don't think I'd read that much if it weren't for the convenience they offer, but now I always seem to be absorbed in one book or another, whether I'm at home or on the train to work. So as far as I'm concerned, if paper books disappeared tomorrow, I wouldn't really mind.

4

I know everyone goes on about how incredibly practical digital books are. But I don't really see it like that, because I'm the kind of person who's always forgetting their phone charger when they go abroad, so all this digital stuff doesn't really work for me. I'm often in remote places with no connection to the internet, so if I were relying on downloading a new book as and when I felt like it, I simply couldn't. I'm not against them though – in fact, if I had a different lifestyle, I might well get rid of all my paper books, and just have digital books instead.

5

Everybody's reading digital books now, and I can see why, though I must say I don't read them much. Maybe it's because I don't travel around a lot, though the e-reader I was given by my brother is very useful when I do, and I do sit and read it at home sometimes. The thing is, I read a lot of old books that just aren't available as digital books, so the kind of things I buy tend to be old-fashioned paper books. Otherwise, I'd happily clear my bookcases and use the space for something else! Maybe one day, if all the books in the world are digitalised, I will!

TEST 8

▶▶ PART 4

Interviewer: I'm talking to Claire Hirst today, a student architect. Hi Claire.

Claire Hirst: Hi.

Interviewer: Claire, first of all, are you enjoying your course?

Claire Hirst: Yes, I am. I chose architecture because it is such a creative, yet practical, profession, and I've certainly learnt loads. We've done technical drawing and construction skills, to know what's going on at the sites, and I've loved that. We've had to design buildings, and present our ideas to the other students on the course. So presentation skills are essential – both through speaking and drawing – that's been quite stressful.

Interviewer: You're now in your last year of studies, and architecture is a long course. Does this final year feel different?

Claire Hirst: It's definitely more intense. Some of the people who started on the course have dropped out, and everyone who's still left knows they're in it for the long haul – they know this is the career for them. You have to be self-motivated – there are no tutors telling you what to do and how to do it. They just give you tasks to complete – often several at once – and a set of deadlines, then check on you every week or so, so you really have to be well-organised.

Interviewer: You've done work placements as part of your course. Was this useful?

Claire Hirst: It's the only way of really finding out what life is like as a professional architect. Of course, there's some design involved, but you soon realise that your time is mainly spent doing things like talking to people on the phone and having meetings. A work placement means that at the end of it, you're much more likely to know whether or not you want to carry on with your course – that was the case for me, anyway.

Interviewer: Can you tell me about a project you're working on at the moment?

Claire Hirst: Yes, at the moment I'm designing a city apartment block. I've done a lot of research into the materials I could use. Some of them are expensive, and I have to work out if the block would be economical to build, and how long the construction would take. It would be great if it could be built, because I think it's looking good, but of course it's just a student project.

Interviewer: What do you think about architects' approach to designing people's homes?

Claire Hirst: Most typical families in the local area aren't looking for anything very unusual. Architects can sometimes forget that ordinary people, not necessarily other architects, are going to live in the homes they design, so the design should suit the people, not the other way round! If you're sitting in an office and looking at perfect images on a computer all day, you can lose sight of that if you aren't careful.

Interviewer: And how will you go about finding a job once you've graduated?

Claire Hirst: You can ring all the local architecture practices, which is what some of my friends who graduated last year did. I must say it took ages and none of them was offered an interview, so I don't think I'll do that. The tutors are contacted by practices, too, and asked about good students they think might be suitable for a particular vacancy. The students still have to go through the application process, of course, but at least they have a chance of getting an interview that way.

Interviewer: And finally, Claire, do you have any advice for people thinking of studying architecture?

Claire Hirst: Don't go into it for the money! Often the hours can be very long and the income relatively low. Find out as much about it as you can – read books and magazines, check out websites, visit buildings. Also, be prepared to work hard and play hard. You get to know your course mates extremely well because you spend so much time together.

TEST 1

PAPER 1 Reading and
Use of English

▶▶ **PART 1**

1 C 2 B 3 A 4 D 5 C 6 B 7 A 8 D

▶▶ **PART 2**

9 so
10 only
11 at
12 the
13 of
14 are
15 who / that
16 to

▶▶ **PART 3**

17 darkness (adjective to noun)
18 activity / activities (adjective to noun, singular or plural form)
19 Scientists (noun to plural noun)
20 energetic (noun to adjective)
21 relaxation (verb to noun)
22 recordings (verb to noun, plural form)
23 uploaded (verb to verb, past participle)
24 depressing (verb to adjective)

▶▶ **PART 4**

25 reminded me I to buy
26 had difficulty I (in) choosing
27 wish I I hadn't / had not left
28 can't / cannot have I been
29 won't / will not call I you unless
30 is I good at

▶▶ **PART 5**

31 A: Incorrect: She wants to do something different from traditional nature documentaries.
31 B: Correct: 'she's taking advantage of the power of the internet to reach a new audience'
31 C: Incorrect: Although she is using the internet, she is also using films (not necessarily online) and TV programmes effectively.
31 D: Incorrect: She has a sense of humour, but she uses it to reinforce her serious message.
32 A: Incorrect: Cooke doesn't say people either feel embarrassed or have a lack of knowledge.
32 B: Correct: 'conservation messages ... make people feel guilty'
32 C: Incorrect: Cooke says people find it a hard subject to think about, and she makes them laugh to make them more willing to do so.
32 D: Incorrect: Cooke says people may not want to hear about it because it's so serious, not because they have heard a lot about it before.
33 A: Correct: 'Weird, freaky creatures fascinate me because they tell an amazing evolutionary story. I'm interested in all of nature, not just the shiny, fluffy bits'

33 B: Incorrect: Cooke doesn't say that too much research is being done. She says that while a lot of research is being done into some endangered species, not enough is being done into others.
33 C: Incorrect: She doesn't say that any of the scientists' studies are unnecessary – just that they get more money to study certain types of animals.
33 D: Incorrect: She says that there are lots of TV programmes about sweet (cute) animals, but this is only supporting her main point.
34 A: Incorrect: She didn't start the blog in order to make money.
34 B: Incorrect: She started the blog, not a search for a new species.
34 C: Correct: 'it's the worst extinction crisis since the dinosaurs were wiped off the planet. Yet I couldn't convince anyone to commission a film about it. That motivated me to start my Amphibian Avenger blog.'
34 D: Incorrect: The statement is true, but it isn't the reason why she started the blog.
35 A: Incorrect: Everything else does worse: birds and snakes disappear.
35 B: Incorrect: Birds and snakes disappear, so they don't carry on as usual.
35 C: Incorrect: She doesn't say they can deal with the situation. On the contrary, she gives examples of other animals disappearing.
35 D: Correct: 'Amphibians also occupy a crucial spot in the middle of the food chain. "If you remove them, ... birds and snakes that eat them also disappear ..."'
36 A: Incorrect: Sloths are just another type of animal Cooke is trying to help – she doesn't say they are more important than others.
36 B: Incorrect: Cooke does not connect sloths with scientists, or suggest that scientists don't tell people about their work.
36 C: Correct: 'sloths, animals that she insists are unfairly laughed at and misunderstood ... "My video showed the world how interesting they are," Cooke says'
36 D: Incorrect: On the contrary, Cooke says sloths do not deserve their bad reputation.

▶▶ **PART 6**

37 C: Link between 'weeds' and 'This was to reflect the character in the movie ...' also between 'replace [her garden]' and 'would be temporary'.
38 G: Link between 'looking at houses' and 'Of the 50 being considered'.
39 A: Link between 'they'd repaint them ... they'd fix' and 'And very importantly, her garden would also be replanted'.
40 E: Link between 'Fleischmann agreed to be out of her house' and 'But she visited every day'.
41 B: Link between 'she ended up painting it again herself' and 'That was a bit annoying'. Also between 'overall, ... it was a good experience' and the positive things described after the gap.
42 F: Link between 'When I saw the film for the first time, I was mostly watching the house' and 'She felt like a proud parent'.

43 D: 'I'd imagined I might not actually do much, but I was asked to look for some photographs of animals to go with an article my boss was writing. I found several suitable ones, and went home at the end of a long day feeling pretty pleased with myself!'

44 B: 'I didn't want to look as if I had nothing to do, though, so I typed it out three times.'

45 A: 'I decided I'd bring in some pictures and a plant for my desk, just to make it feel more mine.'

46 B: 'They all introduced themselves and were very friendly, but I immediately got everyone muddled up'

47 D: 'when I got there, nobody seemed to know who I was or what I should be doing. That was a little odd, I thought'

48 C: 'I was a little taken aback when she told me most people went home fairly late and I'd have to do the same if I wanted to be considered for promotion in the future.'

49 A: 'I wasn't familiar with the computer system, but I thought if I told anyone I needed help with it, they might just laugh at me.'

50 C: 'It was a nice surprise to be greeted by someone I was at school with … That was great as I'd been a little worried about not knowing anyone there at all.'

51 B: '… it was soon clear to me that there were huge gaps in my knowledge.'

52 D: 'I wished I'd listened to a friend who'd worked there the previous summer and had told me not to wear a suit.'

> Questions **1–24** = 1 mark each
> Questions **25–42** = 2 marks each
> Questions **43–52** = 1 mark each

PAPER 2 Writing

▶▶ **PART 1** (*suggested answers*)

Question 1
Style: Neutral or semi-formal.
Content: 1 In your introduction, say if you agree, partially agree or disagree with the statement.
2 Consider each of the three points in turn (remember to include a third idea of your own). Say whether you think the internet is the best way of learning about these three things, or whether you can learn them better from teachers / family / friends, etc. Give reasons for your opinion, and brief examples.
3 In your conclusion summarise your opinion.

▶▶ **PART 2** (*suggested answers*)

Question 2
Style: Neutral or informal.
Content: 1 Start with 'Dear Dan' or 'Hi Dan'.
2 Express sympathy for Dan's situation and say you are happy to give him some advice.
3 Give Dan some ideas about how to get fitter. Should he take up a sport? If so, what exactly, and why? Or should he try exercising on his own?

What do you think he should do, and why should he do it? How often should he do this? Have you or someone you know had any experience of this that you can tell him about briefly?
4 Finish by saying you hope your advice is useful and maybe asking him to let you know how he gets on.
5 Close with *Best wishes* or *Write soon*.

Question 3
Style: Neutral or semi-formal.
Content: 1 Think of a title, or use the title in the question: 'A great place to live!'
2 In your introduction, give some information about the place: What's it called? Which country is it in (remember that you are writing for an international audience)? Is it on the coast or inland? Is it a village, town or city?
3 In the second paragraph, say why it is such a good place to live, in your opinion. Give three or four reasons, if possible.
4 Think of one or two things that would make the place even better. You could end your article by encouraging readers to visit the place.

Question 4
Style: Neutral or semi-formal.
Content: 1 Give your report a title. Think about what areas you are going to cover, e.g. saving electricity, using less water, recycling, etc.
2 In your first paragraph, explain what you are going to do in your report.
3 Give each of the following paragraphs a separate heading, e.g. 'Electricity', etc. and in each paragraph, address the three points: suggested changes, how they would help, and what you yourself can do to help.
4 In your final paragraph, you could give your opinion on how much difference these changes would make.

Question 5 (*FIRST FOR SCHOOLS only*)
Style: Neutral or semi-formal.
Content: 1 Decide which character you are going to write about, and in your introduction, briefly describe the character and their role in the plot.
2 In the main part of your essay, which could be one or two paragraphs, explain what you admire about them and why. Is it their personality or their actions, or both?
3 In your conclusion, summarise your views briefly.

The two parts of the Writing Paper have equal marks.

PAPER 3 Listening

▶▶ **PART 1**

1 A   **2** C   **3** B   **4** C   **5** B   **6** B   **7** A   **8** C

PART 2

9 (local) television / TV
10 models
11 warnings
12 thunderstorms / thunder storms
13 patterns
14 business
15 accurate
16 climate change
17 membership
18 tennis

PART 3

19 D
20 H
21 B
22 A
23 F

PART 4

24 B **25** B **26** C **27** A **28** B **29** C **30** A

Questions **1–30** = **1** mark each

TEST 2

PAPER 1 Reading and
Use of English

PART 1

1 B **2** C **3** A **4** D **5** A **6** B **7** C **8** D

PART 2

9 in
10 for
11 which
12 has
13 it
14 them
15 be
16 a

PART 3

17 height (adjective to noun)
18 active (verb to adjective)
19 swimmers (verb to plural noun)
20 depths (adjective to plural noun)
21 circular (noun to adjective)
22 disappear (verb to negative verb)
23 natural (noun to adjective)
24 pollution (verb to noun)

PART 4

25 succeeded in **I** solving / doing
26 as long **I** as
27 though **I** there were so
28 didn't / did not **I** turn up
29 in case **I** it gets
30 aren't / are not **I** allowed to eat

PART 5

31 A: Incorrect: The writer mentions throughout the paragraph all the things that need to be arranged, so we know that travelling in the desert is not straightforward.
31 B: Incorrect: The writer refers to the high temperatures when she says 'people who like to fry themselves', but she doesn't say this causes problems.
31 C: Correct: 'No one travels alone to the hottest place on earth'
31 D: Incorrect: The writer makes the point that it is expensive to travel in the desert, but she doesn't say this stops people from doing it.
32 A: Correct: 'I've inherited both tendencies ... for stalking the edges of maps'
32 B: Incorrect: The writer's father likes to travel to places where no one goes on holiday but the text doesn't say that he misses people's company.
32 C: Incorrect: The writer says she doesn't have to mention what she knows about the desert to her father, but this is because he already knows, not that he doesn't want her to discuss it with him.
32 D: Incorrect: The text mentions maps, but this is in the context of finding places to visit – not for planning the details of a trip.
33 A: Incorrect: The writer says that the travelers have 'nothing in common' but she doesn't mention getting to know them better.
33 B: Correct: 'The heat is, of course, brutal' and 'The real heat won't strike until ...'. These phrases tell us that the most difficult part of the journey is yet to come.
33 C: Incorrect: Although the writer mentions the distance below sea level they will reach, this is not connected with what she reminds herself about.
33 D: Incorrect: The writer talks about the vehicles traveling through the desert, but she doesn't suggest that the drivers aren't sure of where they are going.
34 A: Incorrect: The writer mentions sand, but she is talking about traveling over salt, and doesn't suggest this is similar to a beach.
34 B: Incorrect: The writer mentions a 'huge brown mound' and a 'lumpy brown mountain' but she doesn't say it is like mud.
34 C: Correct: 'white crystals' and 'like a ... frozen lake'.
34 D: Incorrect: The writer talks about fine sand, but does not compare this to dust.
35 A: Incorrect: The writer describes the different colours of the landscape but doesn't suggest the travellers can't look at them.
35 B: Incorrect: The travellers are very quiet but they are carefully looking around them. There is no suggestion that they are disappointed by what they see.
35 C: Incorrect: The text doesn't suggest that the travellers don't understand what they see, but it does suggest they can't believe what they are seeing.
35 D: Correct: 'Astonished ...' and 'heads down, staring at the ground and shaking their heads'. The fact that they are staring at the ground suggests they can't believe what they are seeing.
36 A: Incorrect: The ground 'breaks and splinters' but this suggests that the earth is hard, not soft.

36 B: Incorrect: The writer expresses an element of fear or nervousness when she talks about 'working up the nerve' to step with force, but this is not connected to feeling lost.

36 C: Incorrect: The writer does say that the human body wasn't built to handle the desert, but she doesn't express worry, or that her own body won't be able to cope.

36 D: Correct: 'You start to think: we really shouldn't *be* here'

▶▶ **PART 6**

37 C: Links between 'getting used to …' and 'while eating' with 'A tenth bite …'

38 A: Link between 'A lot of people … try to avoid thinking about the foods they really want,' and '… may not be the best strategy'

39 E: Link between '… the technique only works with the specific food you've imagined' and 'For instance, visualising yourself eating chocolate wouldn't prevent you from eating lots of cheese.'

40 G: Link between '… inserting 30 coins into a laundry washing machine …' and 'This requires the same motor skills …'

41 B: 'bowls containing the same amount of chocolate each' and '… these were taken away and weighed'

42 F: Link between '… Physical digestive clues … are only part of what tells us …' and '… psychological factors … also influence how much a person eats.'

▶▶ **PART 7**

43 A: 'I stare blankly, then ask what it is I'm meant to be looking out for.'

44 D: 'I watch in awe as they ride the waves, expertly zigzagging their way towards the beach …'

45 B: 'Warming to his role of teacher, Danny launches into an enthusiastic account of things I've never heard of … There's no stopping him …'

46 C: 'Rather than looking in the direction the waves are travelling – as I would have expected – they appear to be looking out to sea.'

47 A: 'That's easy for him to say, having spent his youth with a surfboard glued to his feet, while I haven't even pulled on a wetsuit before.'

48 D: 'It's thrilling to watch … I'm full of inspiration. "Ready to give it a go?" asks Danny. I nod readily …'

49 B: '… I desperately will my already-overwhelmed brain to hold on to this vital information.'

50 C: '"Dropping in", or attempting to ride a wave before it's your turn, is, I become aware, to be avoided at all costs.'

51 A: 'In a bid to produce an article for the sports magazine I work on, I'm learning to surf …'

52 B: 'I watch surfers limbering up in preparation, stretching and jumping from their stomachs to their feet on their boards.'

PAPER 2 Writing

▶▶ **PART 1** (*suggested answers*)

Question 1

Style: Neutral or semi-formal.

Content: 1 In your introduction, repeat the statement in your own words and say why you think people hold this opinion. Your essay should answer the question 'Do you agree?', so make sure your opinion is clearly stated and give reasons for why you think this.
  2 The main body of the essay can be divided into three separate paragraphs, focusing on each of the three points in turn. Remember that the third point is your own idea. In the second paragraph, talk about the people you might meet doing a shared activity and why talking to different people might be important to you or to other people. In the third paragraph, discuss whether you think learning new skills or improving existing skills is important or not, and why. In the fourth paragraph, discuss your own idea. Give reasons for your opinions in each paragraph, and brief examples.
  3 In your conclusion summarise your opinion.

▶▶ **PART 2** (*suggested answers*)

Question 2

Style: Neutral or informal.

Content: 1 Give your article a title if you wish. Your title can be the same as the one in the question, or you can use your own idea.
  2 In your introduction, you could say what you think having a good imagination means.
  3 In the main body of your article, you should answer the three questions. You could divide the ideas into three separate paragraphs. In the first paragraph you should say why you think it is important to have a good imagination (or not) and give some examples. In the second paragraph, you should say how having ideas can help us in life, for example, in order to find solutions to problems, or invent something useful. In the third paragraphs say when it might be less important to have a good imagination, for example, when you have to write a factual essay. To finish, briefly summarise your ideas.

Question 3

Style: Neutral.

Content: 1 Say which computer game you have played. You could also briefly say why you liked it.
  2 In the second paragraph, write a description of the game. What do you have to do in the game? Who are the characters in the game? Where does the game take place?
  3 In the third paragraph, write about what you learned from playing the game. For example, did you learn something about the world that you didn't know before? Or did you improve your physical or mental skills, such as hand-eye coordination or decision making? You could also say what other people might learn from playing the game.
  4 In the final paragraph, say whether or not you would recommend the game to other people your age, and say why.

Question 4
Report (FIRST only)
    Style: Neutral or semi-formal.
  Content: 1 Provide a title for your report. Decide how the information will be organised.
           2 In your first paragraph, explain what you are going to talk about in your report.
           3 Give each paragraph its own heading, for example, 'Description of the event', 'How the event brought people together', 'Recommendations for future events'. Under each heading, discuss these different points.
           4 In your final paragraph, you could say that you hope your recommendations are helpful and that you hope they might help to improve similar future events in the future.

Story (FIRST FOR SCHOOLS only)
    Style: Neutral or semi-formal.
  Content: 1 Decide who the characters are in the story and what the basic plot will be.
           2 You must include the two elements: a letter which is or has been lost and a celebration of some kind.
           3 Remember that your story must follow on from the prompt sentence. It should have a logical development and have a clear beginning, middle and end.

Question 5 (FIRST FOR SCHOOLS only)
    Style: Neutral or semi-formal.
  Content: 1 In your introduction, give the title of the set book and say what kind of book it is (e.g. fact / fiction / adventure / historical novel, etc.) and introduce the main theme (e.g. hope, overcoming problems, discovering yourself, good versus bad).
           2 In the main body of the essay discuss the main theme in the book. Explain how the theme develops throughout the book and talk about other events or ideas in the book that relate to this theme. Then write a paragraph about what you already knew about the theme and what you have learned about the theme from reading the book, for example, a better way to approach a problem, or some interesting facts about a period of history. You could say how your opinion or attitude towards a theme or idea has changed because of reading the book.

PAPER 3 Listening

▶▶ **PART 1**
1 A 2 C 3 A 4 B 5 B 6 B 7 A 8 B

▶▶ **PART 2**
 9 trade
10 memorable
11 administrative
12 teaboy / tea boy
13 limit

14 festivals
15 practical
16 conferences
17 marketing
18 accountants

▶▶ **PART 3**
19 E 20 C 21 A 22 G 23 D

▶▶ **PART 4**
24 B 25 A 26 C 27 B 28 A 29 B 30 C

 TEST 3

PAPER 1 Reading and
          Use of English

▶▶ **PART 1**
1 B 2 C 3 A 4 C 5 D 6 A 7 B 8 D

▶▶ **PART 2**
 9 being
10 all
11 well
12 could
13 it
14 no
15 in
16 where

▶▶ **PART 3**
17 unusual (adjective to negative adjective)
18 threatened (noun to verb, to past participle)
19 similarities (adjective to plural noun)
20 location (verb to noun)
21 madness (adjective to noun)
22 physically (adjective to adverb)
23 softly (adjective to adverb)
24 greeting (verb to noun)

▶▶ **PART 4**
25 feel like **I** going
26 told him **I** to do
27 if I had / I'd **I** known (that) **OR** had I **I** known (that)
28 looking forward to **I** starting (at)
29 asked me **I** not to
30 looks **I** as if

▶▶ **PART 5**
31 C: 'But if 10,000 other people weren't put off, I wouldn't be either.'
32 C: The writer didn't have much time to try out her new wetsuit because it had only arrived two days before the swim – so she gave it 'a quick try out'.
33 A: 'There seemed to be a mix of open-water enthusiasts alongside complete novices'
34 B: What he suggested is easy for an experienced swimmer to do, but not for her.

35 D: 'We'd been warned that the first 100 m would be really rough, but that it would feel much calmer after that. Somewhere near the 750 m mark I was still waiting for the calm'

36 B: 'I'm hooked, and want to give it another go. I've already signed up for my next open-water swim.'

▶▶ **PART 6**

37 D: Link between 'We have few clues as to who created it' and 'Nor do we know …'

38 A: The cavern train takes visitors past marvellous sights. 'However, the trip's highlight is the Great Ceiling.' There is then a link with 'It is a stunning experience'.

39 G: Link between 'coloured paintings' and 'Many of these …'

40 E: Link between 'an exact replica, Lascaux II' and 'its vivid modern reproductions'.

41 F: Link between 'our ancestors camped at cave entrances and enjoyed diets mainly made up of reindeer meat' and 'Deep inside these caves, however, their minds moved to different matters'

42 C: Link between 'The reason why they were created is obscure, however. Some scientists believe they may have had a spiritual significance' and 'Whatever the case, it is clear that …'

▶▶ **PART 7**

43 C: 'Then they use that angle as a lens that sets them on a path.'

44 E: 'Looking back at my travel biography, I realize I've subconsciously used trips to do things I dreamt of being able to do as a child.'

45 A: 'I'm likely to remember the local people I meet more vividly than the history museums I breeze through'

46 F: 'You might not want to 'travel like a travel writer' on every trip you take'

47 D: 'those old keepsakes you keep in a box under your bed. That chunk of volcano lava your dad got you when you were six? That old video tape or DVD of a band you still enjoy? Anything can turn into a makeshift guidebook …'

48 B: 'a subtle, but fundamental, difference'

49 D: 'The goal isn't being 'different' in what you do, it's being personal. Seriously, what do you like?'

50 C: 'They do as much research as they can, devouring novels, articles, TV shows, and films about where they'll be going …'

51 E: 'I'll never hear those songs the same way again.'

52 B: 'I would have never found unexcavated ruins … if I had passively relied on advice I got from locals on the ground. … doing so often means being steered toward shopping malls, and cafés that are part of global chains.'

PAPER 2 Writing

▶▶ **PART 1** (*suggested answers*)

Question 1

Style: Neutral or semi-formal.
Content: 1 In your introduction, you could say that clothes are part of the way we present ourselves to the world, and that some people think that they say a great deal about our characters, but others disagree.

2 In the body of your essay, you could consider each of the three points in turn in a separate paragraph (remember to include a third idea of your own). In the second paragraph, say whether or not you think people's appearance matters. In the third, discuss how people wear different clothes depending on the situation – for example for work, at home, or when they visit friends. In the fourth paragraph, discuss your own idea. Give reasons for your opinions in each paragraph, and brief examples.

3 In your conclusion summarise your opinion.

▶▶ **PART 2** (*suggested answers*)

Question 2

Style: Neutral.
Content: 1 Think of a title, or use the title in the question: 'An interesting person.'

2 In your introduction, name the person you are going to write about, and say who they are (or were, if you have chosen a historical figure). You could write about someone in your family, a friend, a sports personality or other celebrity, or someone from history.

3 In the second paragraph, give information about the person, and why you think this person is interesting. Give examples.

4 You could end your article by briefly summarising what you think people can learn from this person.

Question 3

Style: Neutral.
Content: 1 Say which shopping centre you are going to write about and where it is.

2 In the second paragraph, write about the different types of shops you can find there.

3 In the third paragraph, write about the different places to eat and say what you think about the range available.

4 In the fourth paragraph, write about the different things you can do there. Can you go bowling, or are there places to sit and chat to friends – by a fountain, for example? Is there a cinema? Say what you think about them and use plenty of adjectives.

5 In the final paragraph, say whether or not you would recommend it to people your age, and give reasons.

Question 4
Report (*FIRST only*)

Style: Neutral or semi-formal.
Content: 1 Give your report a title. It will probably be the name of the place you visited. You could also use headings to introduce each of the following paragraphs.

2 In the first paragraph, describe the place you visited. You could also say why your class

went there. Maybe it was somewhere where you could find out more about something you were studying in class.

3 In the second paragraph, say what you and your class did there.

4 In the third paragraph, describe the transport you used to get there and back. Was it comfortable? Did you get to the place on time?

5 In the final paragraph, think about what was not very good about the trip. Make recommendations for improving future trips.

Story *(FIRST FOR SCHOOLS only)*

Style: Neutral or semi-formal.

Content: 1 Decide what is in the box. Remember it is a large box. This could be the surprise that you must include in your story, or the surprise could come later.

2 You must include the two elements: What is the surprise? What are the instructions? Has somebody written instructions telling Maria what to do, or is there an instruction manual for the contents of the box?

3 Ensure your story follows on from the prompt sentence, and that it develops logically and has a clear beginning, middle and end.

Question 5 *(FIRST FOR SCHOOLS only)*

Style: Neutral or semi-formal.

Content: 1 Decide which event you are going to write about, and in your introduction, briefly say what leads up to this event in the story. Don't summarise the whole plot, just make sure the reader knows what is happening around the time of the event, or briefly introduce the characters involved.

2 In the second paragraph, summarise the event.

3 In the third paragraph, explain the consequences of the event. What happens in the story or to the main characters as a result of the event?

4 In your conclusion, explain why you think the event is so important.

PAPER 3 Listening

▶▶ **PART 1**

1 A 2 A 3 C 4 A 5 C 6 B 7 B 8 C

▶▶ **PART 2**

 9 frost
10 worm
11 hand
12 bucket
13 leaves
14 stains
15 line / queue
16 lamps
17 ripe
18 pepper

▶▶ **PART 3**

19 F 20 D 21 H 22 A 23 B

▶▶ **PART 4**

24 B 25 C 26 B 27 C 28 B 29 A 30 A

TEST 4

PAPER 1 Reading and Use of English

▶▶ **PART 1**

1 D 2 A 3 C 4 B 5 D 6 C 7 A 8 B

▶▶ **PART 2**

 9 from
10 as
11 have
12 will / should
13 through
14 are
15 which
16 its / the

▶▶ **PART 3**

17 original (noun to adjective)
18 Archaeologists (noun to noun, plural)
19 rebuilt (verb to past participle with a prefix)
20 construction (verb to noun)
21 Surprisingly (verb to adjective to adverb)
22 appearance (verb to noun)
23 actually (adjective to adverb)
24 evidence (adjective to noun)

▶▶ **PART 4**

25 was **I** far more
26 spent the whole journey **I** watching
27 going to be made **I** into
28 apologised for **I** not having
29 of roses **I** reminds me of
30 brought a / their camera **I** apart from

▶▶ **PART 5**

31 D: '... like the similarly endangered qualities of solitude and quiet, the true value of darkness is something we are barely aware of.'

32 B: 'Our night sky continues to shape us, but now it is the absence of the universe around us that influences our beliefs, our myths, our impulse to create.'

33 B: 'A sky wiped clear of stars encourages us to exaggerate our importance, to imagine humanity as the center of all things.'

34 A: '"Everyone needs beauty as well as bread," ... and varied degrees of darkness are rich with this.'

35 C: The paragraph focuses on the beauty found in darkness and it concludes by saying, 'natural darkness has many offerings of its own'.

36 C: 'Artificial light at night is a miracle ... but the same has always been true of darkness and can be again.'

37 F: Link between 'various scenes' and 'achieving a goal', with 'These included things like stretching to get an object ...'

38 C: Link between the act of children helping and the chimps demonstrating similar motivation. The chimps' motivation was 'less strong' which links with the fact that they didn't help in some of the situations.

39 G: Link between 'related chimps rarely help one another' and 'chimpanzee mothers did not assist their infants'

40 B: Link between the chimps letting a partner into the room when they couldn't manage the task alone and the chimps having to go out and get help.

41 E: Link between 'chose them equally' and the fact that there are two chimps to approach for help. Also a contrast between 'at first' and 'but once'.

42 A: Link between the negative structures 'no evidence' and 'neither can they'. Also a link between there being no evidence for communication and the studies 'just' suggesting understanding.

▶▶ **PART 7**

43 D: 'If often makes use of gymnastic elements ... which are not the easiest skills to acquire.'

44 C: 'When I'm dancing, I use my body to express my deepest emotions, from sadness to joy.'

45 B: 'It also concentrates the mind when you're involved in performing challenging routines, which is certainly a welcome release from the pressures of daily life.'

46 A: '... wearing beautiful costumes faded into insignificance, as love for the art form itself took over from the desire to look pretty.'

47 C: '... nothing is more satisfying than exploring movement and making up my own dance sequences.'

48 D: '... it therefore comes under close examination from the critics in its field. But I would argue that there are elements of techniques and styles from all kinds of older disciplines wrapped up in street dance.'

49 B: 'As a tap dancer I consider myself a musician, as essentially I'm making music with my feet.'

50 A: 'And far from skipping about pretending to be a butterfly, I discovered to my disappointment that ballet requires an enormous amount of self-discipline in order to meet its physical demands and mental challenges.'

51 D: '... what first appealed to me was its 'street cred'. In other words, it's current, and it looks cool.'

52 A: 'But the effort paid off, and I wouldn't have had it any other way, because now I truly appreciate where I am today as a principal dancer in the company.'

PAPER 2 Writing

▶▶ **PART 1** (*suggested answers*)

Question 1
Style: Neutral or semi-formal.
Content: 1 In your introduction re-state the idea using your own words. Briefly say why people might say this, for example, they think some subjects aren't relevant to life. You could say whether

you agree or disagree with the statement, or you could say what you think in your conclusion. You could say that you are going to discuss the arguments for and against the idea given in the statement.

2 You could divide the main body of the essay into two paragraphs. The second paragraph of the essay could give reasons why people might think studying subjects they aren't interested in is a waste of time. The third paragraph could give the opposite point of view and discuss why it is important to study a range of subjects, even if you don't find them interesting. In each paragraph, you could talk about each of the three points, including your own idea. You could use your idea to support your overall viewpoint, so it could go into the 'for' or 'against' paragraph. Give reasons for your opinions, and brief examples.

3 In your conclusion summarise your opinion.

▶▶ **PART 2** (*suggested answers*)

Question 2
Style: Neutral or informal.
Content: 1 Start your reply with an appropriate greeting, for example, *Hello Sara* or *Dear Sara*.

2 Say that you would be happy to tell Sara about the differences between your grandparents' lives and your own. You could briefly say whether you think your grandparents' lives were very different or not so different from your own.

3 Make comparisons between the way life was when your grandparents were growing up, and how that was similar or different to the way you grew up. For example, was their school day the same? Did they eat the same kinds of food? How did they spend their free time?

4 Say whether you think life was better when your grandparents were growing up compared to what life is like now for children growing up. You could say something about people having a better quality of life now: more money, healthier food, better communications; or you could say how life was more relaxed in the past because there wasn't so much fast technology. You could say that some things were better before, and some things are better now.

5 Finish by saying you hope that you the information you've provided is useful and use an appropriate closing formula such as *Best wishes* or *Bye for now*.

Question 3
Style: Neutral or informal.
Content: 1 Give your article a title if you wish. It can be the same or different from the one given.

2 In your introduction, you could briefly say whether you think the world would be more boring if people were the same.

3 In the main body of your article, go into more detail about what makes people different from each other (such as physical appearance, opinions, likes and dislikes, personality) and how you think this might make life more interesting, for example, being able to have interesting discussions, or learning things from other people. You could also argue that if people were more alike, it might be easier to solve problems or get on with each other. You could end your article by briefly summing up your ideas.

Question 4
  Style: Neutral or semi-formal.
  Content: 1 Give your report a title. Think about what areas you are going to cover, for example, playing games in the park, walking in the countryside, sightseeing in the city, meeting with friends, or other free activities available in your town.
  2 In your first paragraph, explain what you are going to do in your report.
  3 Give each of the following paragraphs a separate heading, for example 'Places to visit', 'Things to do', 'People to see' and so on.
  4 In your final paragraph, you should give your opinion on which activities you think are most suitable for families.

Question 5 *(FIRST FOR SCHOOLS only)*
  Style: Neutral or semi-formal.
  Content: 1 In your introduction, say which two characters you are going to talk about and why.
  2 In the main body of your essay, describe the two characters. You could write a description of each character before you compare them, or you could compare them throughout the essay. You could talk about their personalities, how they react to events which happen, what their opinions are, how they behave and so on.
  3 Decide which character you are most like and say why. You could say which things are similar and which are different. You could also write about the elements of both characters which are most like you.

▶▶ **PART 1**
1 C   2 C   3 B   4 A   5 C   6 B   7 A   8 B

▶▶ **PART 2**
 9 mechanic
10 conference
11 sister
12 lamps
13 equipment
14 sportsman
15 magazine

16 landscapes
17 truck
18 cycling

▶▶ **PART 3**
19 F   20 B   21 E   22 H   23 A

▶▶ **PART 4**
24 A   25 B   26 C   27 C   28 B   29 C   30 A

 TEST 5

PAPER 1 Reading and
          Use of English

▶▶ **PART 1**
1 C   2 D   3 B   4 B   5 C   6 A   7 A   8 C

▶▶ **PART 2**
 9 Although
10 it
11 no / little
12 if / though
13 To
14 What
15 how
16 on

▶▶ **PART 3**
17 particularly (adjective to adverb)
18 powerful (noun / verb to adjective)
19 knowledge (verb to noun)
20 survival (verb to noun)
21 warning (verb to noun)
22 experienced (verb / noun to adjective)
23 ensure (adjective to verb)
24 considerable (verb to adjective)

▶▶ **PART 4**
25 was **I** put off (by officials)
26 the best essay **I** he had / he'd
27 only did **I** Naoko arrive
28 far as **I** I'm / I am concerned
29 last time **I** (that / when) I did
30 impossible for me **I** to meet

▶▶ **PART 5**
31 B: 'Procrastinating … is in our genetic make-up.'
32 A: Dr Steel claims that people who don't procrastinate have more money, have better relationships and are happier, and the writer gives examples of people who don't procrastinate and who do well.
33 C: 'We've evolved to respond to the moment' … 'now is the time to unlearn your time-wasting techniques and work-avoidance tactics'
34 B: The dissertations seem like endless tasks.
35 D: The difficult tasks become 'something concrete with easily measured progress' when the technique of making pre-commitments is used.

36 B: 'Overcoming procrastination ultimately comes down to planning, which, if you're not careful, becomes procrastination in itself.'

▶▶ PART 6

37 E: Link between 'people who understood what that meant … and had offered encouragement and support' and 'Not because …'

38 B: Link between 'Some people …' and 'Others …'

39 G: Link between 'Non-runners struggle to comprehend …' and 'Similarly, it's difficult for people …'

40 A: Link between 'Of course, there's money to be made from blogging' and 'But for all the bloggers I've met, the motivation …'

41 C: Link between 'We had a panel of expert speakers … as well as a bag full of free stuff for them all' and 'But what mattered most to everyone was …'.

42 F: Link between 'Running and blogging can be solitary pursuits' and 'So we invited bloggers across the UK to … meet up in real life'

▶▶ PART 7

43 C: 'I hadn't really got a clue what was going on.'

44 D: 'Then the manager asked me if I'd like to work at a week-long film festival in a neighbouring town. I met all sorts of amazing people with similar interests to mine, and a group of us ended up running our own independent film festival a few years later.'

45 A: 'I saw something just recently I wanted to walk out of, but had to sit through it to the end as a good friend of mine had talked me into going'

46 D: 'Sadly, I'll never make up for losing out on the magic of seeing things on the big screen as a young child'

47 B: 'I'd decided to learn about the cinema industry in depth'

48 C: 'I'd like to make a living as a film critic one day.'

49 A: 'My family went to the cinema every Saturday when I was a child. My parents both worked long hours … and going to the local Picture Palace meant a great deal to all of us.'

50 C: 'It also turned out that one of the actors lived in the next street to us … I'd never had a clue who he was before then and was very impressed.'

51 B: 'There used to be three cinemas in the town I grew up in, and I suppose I just thought they'd always be there. They're long gone, of course, … and now I wish I'd been more often.'

52 A: '… although I'm a great reader, and a fan of the arts in general, nothing comes close to the feeling I get when I'm fully absorbed in a film.'

PAPER 2 Writing

▶▶ PART 1 (*suggested answers*)

Question 1
Style: Neutral or semi-formal.
Content: 1 In your introduction, repeat the idea in the statement, using slightly different words, and giving one or two reasons why people might say this – information on the internet, TV documentaries about other countries. You could

say at this stage whether you tend to agree or disagree with the statement, or wait until the conclusion to do this. You could say that you are going to consider the arguments in favour and against the view expressed in the statement.

2 You could organise the body of the essay in two paragraphs: a second paragraph giving reasons for travelling to a country and a third paragraph giving reasons why it is unnecessary. Within each paragraph, you could address the points in the notes and your own idea. Your own idea does not have to go in both paragraphs, however: you could have 'going on holiday' as your own idea, in which case you would probably use it as an argument against the statement. Give reasons for your opinions, and brief examples.

3 In your conclusion summarise your opinion.

▶▶ PART 2 (*suggested answers*)

Question 2
Style: Neutral or informal.
Content: 1 You could give your article a title, which could be exactly the same or different from the one in the question.

2 In your introduction, you could mention a few things that you find funny.

3 In the body of your article, go into more detail about what makes you laugh, and say whether your friends and family laugh at the same things as you. State why you think this is the case. Say what sort of things are, in your opinion, probably considered funny all over the world. Explain what it is about these things that might make people laugh about them in many different cultures.

Question 3
Style: Semi-formal to formal.
Content: 1 Think about what points you need to address in your letter of application: your ability to work in a busy place, your level of English (particularly spoken English), and your knowledge of sport. You might also want to say you have experience of working in a shop, or that you have experience working with people / get on well with different types of people.

2 Start with *Dear Mrs Jones,*.

3 In your introduction, say that you are writing in response to the advertisement and that you would like to apply for the job.

4 In the body of your letter, address all the points, writing a paragraph for each point. Try to think of good reasons why you should be given this job.

5 In your final paragraph, say that you hope you will be considered for the job and say that you are available for interview at any time.

6 Finish your letter with 'Yours sincerely, ... [your name]'.

Question 4
Report *(FIRST only)*
   Style: Neutral or semi-formal.
 Content: 1 Give your report a title. Think about what areas
          you are going to cover, e.g. parts of the college
          the English students should visit, classes they
          could attend, what they could do in the evenings.
         2 In your first paragraph, explain what you are
          going to do in your report.
         3 Give each of the following paragraphs a
          separate heading, e.g. 'Places to visit in the
          college', etc. and in each paragraph, address
          the points you have decided to include.
         4 In your final paragraph, you could say that you
          hope your suggestions are helpful and that
          you hope the English students enjoy their visit.

Story *(FIRST FOR SCHOOLS only)*
   Style: Neutral or semi-formal.
 Content: 1 Decide who the person on the bus next to
          the narrator is. Is it somebody famous? Is it a
          friend the narrator hasn't seen for a long time?
          Or someone else?
         2 You must include the two elements: Who
          makes the phone call: the narrator, the person
          next to them, or somebody else (ringing the
          narrator, for example)? What happens as a
          result of the call? What is the party for? Does
          the narrator invite the person on the bus to the
          party, or is it the other way round?
         3 Make sure your story follows on from the
          prompt sentence, and that it develops logically
          and has a clear beginning, middle and end.

Question 5 *(FIRST FOR SCHOOLS only)*
   Style: Neutral or semi-formal
 Content: 1 In your introduction, give the title of the set
          book and say what kind of book it is (e.g. fact /
          fiction / adventure / historical novel, etc.)
         2 In the main part of your essay, write a
          paragraph explaining briefly what the book
          is about (don't go into too much detail) and
          a paragraph about the main characters. Then
          write a paragraph saying what you personally
          thought of the book: Did you enjoy it? Say why /
          why not: Was it an interesting story? Did you
          care what happened to the characters? Was the
          time / place the book was set in well described?
          Depending on your answers to some of these
          questions, recommend the book to other people
          or advise them against reading it!

PAPER 3 Listening

▶▶ PART 1
1 A   **2** B   **3** B   **4** C   **5** A   **6** C   **7** A   **8** B

▶▶ PART 2
 9 decoration(s)
10 marks
11 budget

12 label
13 manual
14 mask
15 toothbrush
16 handle
17 stubborn
18 rubber

▶▶ PART 3
19 F   **20** B   **21** D   **22** A   **23** G

▶▶ PART 4
24 B   **25** B   **26** C   **27** A   **28** C   **29** A   **30** A

TEST 6

PAPER 1 Reading and Use of English

▶▶ PART 1
1 A   **2** D   **3** B   **4** C   **5** A   **6** C   **7** D   **8** B

▶▶ PART 2
 9 a
10 has
11 the
12 to
13 that / which
14 of
15 What
16 whether

▶▶ PART 3
17 length (adjective to noun)
18 atmospheric (noun to adjective)
19 initially (adjective to adverb)
20 impossible (adjective to adjective with negative prefix)
21 courageous (noun to adjective)
22 unfortunately (adjective to adverb with negative prefix)
23 evidence (adjective to noun)
24 excitement (adjective to noun)

▶▶ PART 4
25 to have **l** my car fixed
26 would not / wouldn't have come **l** if
27 to **l** take advantage of
28 run out **l** of
29 giving me **l** a lift
30 as soon as **l** she had / she'd

▶▶ PART 5
31 A: 'limits our appetite for extreme risk'
32 C: 'tests what you are made of and how far you can take yourself'
33 B: 'it seems like the stupidest thing in the world'
34 B: 'says he is struck by' and 'But the climbers took every precaution they could think of'
35 C: The conditions are referred to as 'the flow' which includes becoming absorbed and focussing the

mind. Also 'Something that makes you try doing a tougher climb than usual, perhaps, is that your adrenaline flows and you become very concentrated on what you're doing'.

36 D: The article says that enjoying taking risks is a personality trait and that some people feel compelled to take risks. Therefore, we understand that wanting to take risks is a desire we are born with.

▶▶ **PART 6**

37 C: Link between 'fastest long-distance, nonstop fight … in as little as two days' and '6.760 kilometres at an average speed of 97 kilometres an hour'.

38 E: Link between 'don't look especially speedy or well equipped' and 'That's because …' and also between 'the birds become rather well rounded' and 'it's these plentiful fat reserves that …'.

39 D: Link between 'the Artic Tern clocks up … 80,000 kilometres' and 'However, the bird spreads the flight out … and stops … along the way'.

40 F: Link between 'Godwits … have no opportunity to stop' and 'For this reason, their amazing flights are not their choice' and also between 'their amazing flights are not their choice' and 'By constrast, Snipes have several rest-stop options … but choose not to take advantage of them'.

41 A: Link between 'it's unclear how Great Snipes can apparently fly for such long periods with little or no sleep' and 'This is one of the unsolved mysteries …'

42 G: Link between 'many surprises in the near future' and 'these will be due to the recent development of tiny recording devices'.

▶▶ **PART 7**

43 C: 'All you have to do is enter keywords on the topic of your choice and in a moment you'll gain access to hundreds of articles and papers'

44 D: 'Also lacking is any focus on why being able to do a presentation may be useful beyond the classroom'

45 A: 'finding your way around the site isn't straightforward'

46 B: 'One thing many reading websites fail to do is provide a comprehensive portfolio of an author's work and biographical information, something Readwell does with style.'

47 A: 'I haven't come across any similar site with such a wide range of charts, graphs and graphics to choose from.'

48 D: '… expert advisors can give detailed feedback on their performance.'

49 E: 'This is one for the independent-minded out there'

50 C: 'In my opinion, there's no better site for first-time researchers.'

51 B: 'Some of the comprehension quizzes aren't as challenging as I'd have liked to see for the intended audience, but at least they get users to carefully consider what they've read.'

52 E: '… without examples of how to apply the information to a particular piece of writing, the site is less successful. … users don't have the opportunity to communicate with others or seek answers to any questions they might have.'

PAPER 2 Writing

▶▶ **PART 1** (*suggested answers*)

Question 1

Style: Neutral or semi-formal.

Content: 1 In your introduction, rewrite the statement in your own words. Say briefly why people might think this. In your essay, you have to say whether you agree or not with this statement and why.

2 You could divide the main body of your essay into three paragraphs, each focussing on one of the three points. The third point should be your own idea. In the second paragraph, talk about why people care about the way they look, and why others might think some people care too much about their appearance. In the third paragraph, discuss the idea of spending money on your appearance. Is this a positive or a negative thing? Why? Does it depend how much money you spend? Should people spend their money on other things instead? In the fourth paragraph discuss your own idea.

3 In your conclusion summarise your opinion.

▶▶ **PART 2** (*suggested answers*)

Question 2

Style: Neutral or informal.

Content: 1 Give your article a title. This can be the same as the one in the question, or you can invent your own.

2 In your introduction, you could say what the best game or match you've ever seen was. This could be a match you've seen on TV, or a game you've been to watch at a stadium. Briefly say what the game or match was, who was playing and why it was a good match.

3 In the main body of your article, answer the questions. You could divide your ideas into two paragraphs. In the second paragraph you should describe the game or match you watched and why you thought it was so good, for example, did the team you support win? In the third paragraph, you should say what you think makes a game or match exciting, for example, do lots of goals need to be scored? Does there need to a big crowd watching? Does it need to be an important competition? You could finish your article at this point, or you could briefly summarise your ideas.

Question 3

Style: Neutral or informal.

Content: 1 Start with an appropriate greeting, for example, *Hi Robert* or *Dear Robert*.

2 Say you're happy to help Robert by giving him some ideas.

3 Explain your ideas. Think about ways in which people can communicate with each other even

when they don't speak each others' language, for example, using hand gestures, drawing things, using facial expressions to communicate feelings and so on. You could give some examples of what gesture might be appropriate in a particular situation, for example miming drinking to ask if someone would like a drink. Have you had any experiences yourself that you could tell Robert about?

4 Finish by saying you hope your ideas will be useful or that you hope his project goes well. You could ask him to let you know what other ideas he thought of.

5 Use a closing formula such as *Best wishes* or *Write soon.*

Question 4

Style: Neutral or semi-formal.

Content: 1 Include a title for your report and decide how to organise the information you want to include.

2 In your first paragraph, explain what you are going to talk about in your report.

3 Provide a heading for each paragraph, for example, 'Description of the building / monument', 'Importance of the building / monument', 'Visiting the monument' and 'Recommendations for improving visits to the building / monument'. Under each heading write about these different points.

4 In your final paragraph, you could say that you hope your recommendations are helpful and that you hope they might help to improve visitors' experiences in the future.

Question 5 *(FIRST FOR SCHOOLS only)*

Style: Neutral or semi-formal.

Content: 1 Introduce the character that you have decided to talk about and give a brief description of the part the character plays in the book.

2 In the main body of the article describe the character in more detail. You could talk about their personality, reactions towards events, their behaviour and opinions. Then explain how you think people might identify with this character. Does the character react to an event in the same way that most people would? Is the character an ordinary person with an ordinary job like many people? You could also say whether the character is likeable and why / why not, and whether the character is realistic. You should also say whether or not you have anything in common with the character yourself.

PAPER 3 Listening

▶▶ PART 1

1 B   2 A   3 C   4 A   5 C   6 B   7 C   8 A

▶▶ PART 2

9 tutors
10 choir

11 violins
12 Union
13 dinner
14 poetry
15 transport
16 ceilings
17 hospitals
18 newsletter

▶▶ PART 3

19 C   20 F   21 H   22 B   23 E

▶▶ PART 4

24 C   25 A   26 B   27 C   28 A   29 B   30 B

TEST 7

PAPER 1 Reading and Use of English

▶▶ PART 1

1 A   2 C   3 B   4 C   5 A   6 D   7 B   8 B

▶▶ PART 2

9 long
10 that / which
11 your
12 an
13 like
14 it
15 How
16 on

▶▶ PART 3

17 appearance (verb to noun)
18 truly (adjective to adverb)
19 functional (noun to adjective)
20 development (verb to noun)
21 rearranging (verb to gerund form and addition of a prefix)
22 living (verb to gerund form)
23 necessarily (adjective to adverb)
24 thought (verb to past form of verb)

▶▶ PART 4

25 insisted on I driving / taking Tim
26 might have I taken
27 would not / wouldn't / did not / didn't I let me
28 made up I your mind
29 in favour of I making
30 make sense I to me

▶▶ PART 5

31 A: 'I also want the subject to like that shot of themselves. I won't go: "That's great, it doesn't matter what you think, it's going in."'
32 B: 'I wanted to know all about what she'd done.'
33 A: 'I imagine she's quite done – she'd probably arrive camera-ready'

34 C: 'he likes to make it interesting for himself, he doesn't just want to do a straight portrait' and 'you may get that one unexpected shot'

35 D: The contrast is made between Mary's professional life mainly involving photographing women and her family: a husband and four sons.

36 C: '… there's not very much difference between the pictures' and 'It's the same gruelling schedule and time commitments. You couldn't necessarily tell them apart.'

▸▸ **PART 6**

37 E: Link between 'what style of bike I wanted to build' and 'Personally I felt …'. Also between 'a relaxed one' and 'contrasted with the stiff geometry …'

38 B: Link between 'the precise list of body measurements requested from me had already been transferred onto a personalised diagram of my frame' and 'This was the plan that I would follow'.

39 F: Link between 'finding pieces that were the colour I wanted' and 'Some people like the frame to be consistent, others like a mix of light, dark or speckled'.

40 A: Link between 'a problem … threatened to make my frame useless' and 'Luckily … Ian confirmed that it was alright'.

41 C: Link between 'most things can be fixed' and 'If all else fails'.

42 G: Link between 'soaked in a special glue' and 'to dry' as well as between 'All that was left now' and 'In a few hours I would be …'.

▸▸ **PART 7**

43 C: 'My course has been very interesting so far, and I'm sure it will become even more so when we are sent out to get work experience in a company in our second year. We'll report back to our college tutors on how our project is progressing'

44 A: 'We're all part of a community, and it's a great feeling to walk into the building every morning and see lots of people I know and like'

45 D: 'I've also found that the fashion side of things appeals to me, though I'd never thought about that very much before.'

46 A: '… they give us a topic, and then let us go wherever we like with it … which is ideal.'

47 B: 'There's no limit to the amount of fabric we can use'

48 D: 'I've been doing a project with a famous sportswear company this term, and the designers there have been very friendly and helpful. They add a different perspective to that of the college tutors, and I really appreciate that.'

49 A: 'the focus is on actually making things'

50 C: 'the skills we're acquiring can be adapted to any area of fashion'

51 D: 'I spent a year working in a sportswear shop, which is where I became interested in the way sports clothes are designed, and all the different materials available. I realised it was an area I wanted to explore further'

52 B: 'No two weeks are the same, which is what I love about this course. There are so many different things to do that it never feels dull.'

PAPER 2 Writing

▸▸ **PART 1** (*suggested answers*)

Question 1

Style: Neutral or semi-formal.

Content: 1 Decide how you are going to approach the essay. You could decide to organise it so you first present arguments saying the only good reason for working **is** to earn money. The following paragraph would then consist of **other** good reasons for working. Also think about what your own idea will be – it could be liking the work itself, for example, or free time, or something else.

  2 In your introduction, say what you are going to talk about (why people work) and say that there are different points of view.

  3 The body of your essay could be divided into two paragraphs. The first could argue that money is the only good reason for working (people have studied or trained a long time / paid for their studies and they should be financially rewarded for this when they get a job, people sometimes have to put up with difficult colleagues. Your own idea could come in here too.

  4 The next paragraph could argue the other point of view: people have worked hard at their studies / training and find it rewarding to put what they have learned to good use, people enjoy the sociable aspect of work – spending time with colleagues for example.

  5 In your conclusion say what your own opinion is.

▸▸ **PART 2** (*suggested answers*)

Question 2

Style: Neutral or informal.

Content: 1 Start with *Dear Alex* or *Hi Alex* and thank Alex for the email.

  2 **Don't** say that you don't read at all, even if this is true: you won't have enough to say to answer the question adequately, and should choose a different Part 2 question instead.

  Do say what type of things you read: if you read books, what sort of books do you read (fact / fiction, books / articles / websites for college / work / in your free time, etc.)? Give details, and say why (do you enjoy them or not, do you have to read them or not, etc.). Explain how important reading is in your life – is it something you spend a lot of time doing and look forward to, or is it something you just do from time to time?

  3 Answer Alex's question about people your age. Do you think they read more or less than older people? Why do you think this is the case?

  4 Use a closing formula such as *Best wishes* or *Write soon*.

Question 3

Style: Neutral.

Content: 1 Think of a title, or use the title in the question.

  2 In your introduction, say you are going to tell the reader about something unexpected that

happened to you. Use adjectives like *amazing*, *extraordinary*, *exciting*, and *incredible* to capture the reader's interest.

    3 In your second paragraph, describe the event, making your account as interesting and lively as possible. Don't forget to say why you found it so surprising.

    4 In your third paragraph, explain what happened as a result of the event. For example, did it change your life, even in just a small way, or did it make you feel differently about something or someone?

Question 4
Report *(FIRST only)*
   Style: Neutral or semi-formal.
Content: 1 Give your report a title. In this question, the three areas you should cover are given to you as bullet points.

    2 In your first paragraph, explain what you are going to do in your report.

    3 Give each of the following three paragraphs a heading, e.g. 'Places to eat' (e.g. restaurants, cafés, fast food outlets, street stalls, markets, etc.), 'Different types of food' (e.g. Italian, Chinese, etc., vegetarian, fast food and so on), 'Suggested improvements' (e.g. What do you think is missing in your area as far as places to eat are concerned? Is there enough variety? Are there places for young people to go? Could some of the places already there be made better in some way?).

    4 In your final paragraph, you could give your overall opinion on the options available to people in your area when they want to eat out.

Story *(FIRST FOR SCHOOLS only)*
   Style: Neutral or semi-formal.
Content: 1 Decide where James is. One of the elements you must include is a river. Is James by a river at the beginning of the story, or does he go to one later? Or does the river come into your story in another way?

    2 Where is the light? Does James know what the light is, or does he find out during the story?

    3 Remember you must include both elements: a river and a happy ending. As you plan your story, make sure it leads to a happy ending.

    4 Make sure your story follows on from the prompt sentence, and that it develops logically and has a clear beginning, middle and (happy) end.

Question 5 *(FIRST FOR SCHOOLS only)*
   Style: Neutral or semi-formal.
Content: 1 Decide which characters you are going to write about, and in your introduction, briefly say who the characters are, and whether each one is a main character or someone who plays a less important role in the story.

    2 In the main part of your essay, describe the two characters. If the two characters are closely connected throughout the book, you could organise this part of your essay into two

paragraphs: one describing the characters and the relationship between them, and another explaining their roles in the story. If, on the other hand, the two characters not very closely connected, then you could write about one character in one paragraph (their character and their role) and the other character in another paragraph. Remember to include how the two characters are connected in the story, even if it is not a very direct connection. You could do this in a separate paragraph.

    3 In your conclusion, you could give your opinion on the characters you have described.

PAPER 3 Listening

▶▶ **PART 1**

1 B   2 B   3 A   4 C   5 B   6 B   7 A   8 C

▶▶ **PART 2**

 9 spice(s)
10 perfume
11 nail
12 (terrible) smell
13 (amount of) smoke
14 machine
15 petrol
16 cotton
17 relaxation
18 colour(s)

▶▶ **PART 3**

19 H   20 E   21 D   22 F   23 C

▶▶ **PART 4**

24 A   25 A   26 B   27 A   28 B   29 A   30 C

FIRST TEST 8

PAPER 1 Reading and Use of English

▶▶ **PART 1**

1 B   2 C   3 D   4 A   5 B   6 D   7 C   8 A

▶▶ **PART 2**

 9 if
10 Why
11 at
12 a
13 or
14 the
15 to
16 There

▶▶ **PART 3**

17 intention (verb to noun)
18 life (verb / adjective to noun)
19 historical (noun to adjective)

20 disappeared (verb to past participle with a prefix)
21 surroundings (verb to plural noun)
22 social (noun to adjective)
23 majority (adjective to noun)
24 principally (adjective to adverb)

▶▶ **PART 4**

25 has never / has not / hasn't been cleaned **I** since
26 he would / he'd **I** rather eat
27 even though **I** we've / we have invested
28 has no **I** intention of
29 to go outside **I** when it
30 should have **I** taken

▶▶ **PART 5**

31 C: 'There are some with no musical ability (me) …' and 'My niece … Emma, however, is at the top of the musical league'.
32 D: 'Even the most inexperienced can sit alongside those with a drumming track record.'
33 C: 'Steve is fine with this, and the whole group smile supportively at us, so with renewed energy I join in as we start again.'
34 A: 'I listen to what I'm playing and realise it is out of time'
35 B: 'I feel as if I've done a tough work-out session.'
36 B: At the end of the article, the writer is feeling more confident and says 'we have enjoyed ourselves'. They agree that 'drumming rocks' and indicate that they can't stop drumming. The writer also says 'I can't wait to go back'.

▶▶ **PART 6**

37 B: Link between 'who wanted to see …' and 'In particular, they wanted …' and also 'they wanted to know … or whether' and 'But how to find out?'.
38 G: Link between 'very hard for a researcher …' and 'What Tracy and Matsumoto needed was …' and also between 'a large group of people' and 'some of these subjects … Where could such a group of people be found?'.
39 A: Link between 'athletes who were born blind' and 'Therefore, they could not possibly have witnessed …'
40 C: Link between 'the researchers painstakingly recorded the positions of their head, arms and bodies' and 'After analysing this data' and also between 'sighed and sightless athletes behaved in exactly the same ways' and 'The winners tilted their heads up … while slumped shoulders … were the hallmarks of losers'.
41 F: Link between 'Men and women who have never seen other people behave in these ways still make exactly the same movements' and 'parents may have taught their blind children some of these behaviours'.
42 D: Link between 'remarkably consistent between … contestants from every part of the world' and 'athletes' culture was found to have only a very small effect …'.

▶▶ **PART 7**

43 B: 'Each type of paint has a different quality and texture, and I think it adds to the visual richness to apply colours using different paint media.'

44 D: 'The way I make paintings reflects the way I experience the world, and what I'm like as a person. I think this is unavoidable.'
45 E: 'Just because I'm able to do lots of different things in paint, it doesn't mean I don't mean it' and 'they're a sincere attempt to make sense of the world'.
46 A: 'What I love about painting is that it embodies a series of thought and feeling processes. It's all there on the canvas as a record.'
47 C: 'I used to think I could only use something once, but I'm now realising that some of the ways I use paint … develops the theme further.'
48 B: 'oil paint is so flexible that I can adjust what I'm doing almost endlessly … oil paint remains wet long enough for countless changes of mind'
49 D: 'I have never wanted to limit myself to one or two kinds of mark-making – I find it exciting and challenging to find different ways of using paint'
50 C: 'I'm still hooked on 15th-century German artist Dürer's woodcuts for the way he uses line so inventively to describe everything from patches of grass to cloudbursts.'
51 E: 'I don't want to make paintings that sit quietly in the corner of the room'
52 A: 'I tend to make up what I do on the canvas as I go along. I have a vague idea in mind, but usually abandon it pretty quickly.'

PAPER 2 Writing

▶▶ **PART 1** (*suggested answers*)
Question 1
   Style: Neutral or semi-formal.
Content: 1 In your introduction, repeat the statement in your own words and briefly say why you people might believe this. Your essay should answer the question 'Do you agree?', so make sure your opinion is clearly stated and give reasons for why you think this. You could also consider the other point of view.
   2 You could divide the main body of your essay into three separate paragraphs, focussing on the three points. Don't forget to include your own idea for the third point. In the second paragraph you should talk about how relationships can be affected by having or not having money, for example, if you have a lot of money, would people expect you to share it? Do people argue about money? What do they argue about? In the third paragraph, talk about how having or not having money can affect health, for example, if you have plenty of money, does this gain you access to better healthcare? In the fourth paragraph, discuss your own idea. Give reasons for your opinions in each paragraph and brief examples.
   3 In your conclusion summarise your opinion.

Question 2

Style: Neutral

Content: 1 Give the name of the programme you watched and briefly say what it was about.

2 In the second paragraph, write a description of the programme. Include more information about the subject of the programme, or the people who appeared in it.

3 In the third paragraph, write about what you found so interesting about the programme. For example, was an interesting discovery made? Did you hear about some interesting evidence? Did you learn some interesting facts about a new subject, or find out more about something you were already interested in?

4 In the final paragraph, say who else might have found the programme interesting, or if you'd like to find out more about the subject.

Question 3

Style: Neutral or informal.

Content: 1 Start your reply with an appropriate greeting, for example, *Hi Paula* or *Dear Paula*.

2 Tell Paula that you are happy to help her to think of some useful phrases to learn.

3 Explain to Paula what kind of phrases might be useful for her to learn before her trip. Think about which situations she might find herself in, for example: ordering food, buying tickets, using public transport, personal details, or asking for directions. Give a few examples of the kinds of phrases she might need, for example: 'How much is it?', 'Could I have a salad?' or 'Where is the museum?'. (Remember your answer must be in English, so don't use phrases from other languages!) You could tell Paula about any similar experiences you have had and what you found useful to know how to say.

4 Finish by saying you hope that the information you've provided is helpful. You could say that you hope Paula and her family have a good trip and ask her to tell you about it.

5 Use an appropriate closing formula such as *Bye for now* or *Write soon*.

Question 4

Report (*FIRST only*)

Style: Neutral or semi-formal.

Content: 1 Provide a title for your report. Decide how you will organise the information in your report.

2 In your first paragraph, explain what you are going to talk about in your report.

3 Give each paragraph its own heading, for example, 'How to become healthier', 'Services available', 'Places to go', 'Suggestions for a further service'. Under each heading, discuss these different points, for example, you could talk about places where people can eat healthily, or places where they can go to do exercise. You should also include a service or place which

you think should be available but isn't at the moment, for example, a free advice service.

4 In your final paragraph, you could say that you hope your suggestions are useful and that you hope to see the new service in your town soon.

Story (*FIRST FOR SCHOOLS only*)

Style: Neutral or semi-formal.

Content: 1 How could you tell that your brother was excited? What was he excited about?

2 You must include the two elements: What is the unusual gift? Why was there a trip to the city and what happened there? How were the two things connected? For example, was the trip to the city the unusual gift, or was the gift something else? Did you or your brother buy the gift for someone else? Did you have to go to the city to buy it? Why was this exciting?

3 Remember that your story must follow on from the prompt sentence. It should have a logical development and have a clear beginning, middle and end.

Question 5 (*FIRST FOR SCHOOLS only*)

Style: Neutral or semi-formal.

Content: 1 In your introduction, give the title of the set book and introduce the theme of your essay.

2 In the main body of the essay describe the ending of the story. Then write about the events that led to the ending, for example, was there an adventure or the development of a friendship? Was there a problem which was solved? Discuss whether you predicted the end of the story. Was it a surprise? Do you think it was a good ending for the story or was it disappointing? Do you think a different ending might have been better? You could finish your essay by saying why it is important to end a story in the right way.

PAPER 3 Listening

▶▶ **PART 1**

1 B   2 A   3 C   4 B   5 C   6 A   7 B   8 B

▶▶ **PART 2**

9 conservation
10 deer
11 gate
12 projects
13 map
14 river
15 chemistry
16 height
17 dairy
18 (local) honey

▶▶ **PART 3**

19 E   20 H   21 A   22 G   23 C

▶▶ **PART 4**

24 B   25 A   26 A   27 B   28 C   29 C   30 B

Audio

Click on the **Audio** button in order to listen to any of the audio files for the Listening paper. Each part of the Listening paper is labelled with a separate **Track** number.

Video

Click on the **Video** button, then choose **Model Speaking interview** to watch the interview or **Tips and advice** to listen to the examiner's tips.

Video Worksheet materials

Click on the **Video Worksheet materials** button, then follow the instructions to access the PDFs of the **worksheet, scripts** and **key.**

SPEAKING TEST WORKSHEET *Exam Essentials*

Watch the video of a model interview, based on Test 3 of the Cambridge English: First Speaking test, and do the activities, which relate to each part. You can check your answers and look at the full script on separate PDFs on this DVD-ROM.

Part 1 (00:04)

Watch Part 1 of the speaking test and answer the questions below.

1   **In this part of the speaking test the examiner will ask personal questions. Watch Part 1 and complete the questions.**

   a   Where .... from, (Angie)?

   b   (Raúl), ... in a city or a village?

   c   And .... living there?

   d   How can people .... free time in the place where you live?

   e   And what .... do people do in (Berlin)?

2   **In this part of the test, you talk about yourself. Match the model phrases below to their function.**

   ☐   ... but people call me (Angie).

   ☐   It's ... one of the (biggest) in the region.

   ☐   It's a brilliant place to ...

   ☐   ... because people from all over come to study there.

   ☐   What most people don't know is ...

   a   saying what is good about where you live

   b   comparing your city to other cities

   c   saying your nickname

   d   introducing a surprising fact

   e   giving reasons

3   **Raúl made a mistake while he was speaking, but he corrected himself. Write the mistake, together with its corrected form.**

   Mistake: ....

   Correction: ....

   Angie made and corrected two mistakes while she was speaking. Write each mistake, together with its corrected form.

   Mistake 1:   ....

   Correction: ....

   Mistake 2:   ....

   Correction: ....

4   **Prepare your own answers for the personal questions in exercise 1. Expand your replies by giving further information or reasons for your answer.**

   TIP: If you make a mistake while speaking, don't be afraid to correct it. You can introduce the correct version by saying *I mean* ... or *sorry* ...

© National Geographic Learning 2015 PHOTOCOPIABLE   Cambridge English: First **Speaking Test Worksheet**   1

For more information about the DVD-ROM please turn over to page 232 ▶

Introduction to the DVD-ROM

This edition of *Exam Essentials Practice Tests* for students of Cambridge English: First (FCE) includes a brand new DVD-ROM which focuses on the Speaking test component of the Cambridge English: First examination. The DVD-ROM includes two videos:

• a complete Cambridge English: First Speaking test based on Test 3 of the *Practice tests.*
• a short clip giving valuable advice about the Cambridge English: First Speaking test.

To maximise learning from the complete Speaking test, the following PDFs are also available on the DVD-ROM:

• a worksheet for individual or class use
• an answer key for the worksheet
• the complete script of the Speaking test.

A complete Speaking test

A full Cambridge English: First Speaking test interview is approximately 14 minutes in length. Please note that the interview shown on this DVD-ROM is a slightly extended version of the Speaking test. This allows for a wide range of language and types of response to be included. This interview also features high-level candidates whose performance would achieve a good pass in the exam. The video therefore provides a good model to follow. Don't worry if you feel you may not perform to this high standard in every area of the test. You will need to demonstrate a good level, but you will not need to use every structure or item of vocabulary perfectly in order to pass the test. Please see page 64 and pages 165–167 in the *Practice Tests* for the material used in this interview.

The video clearly details:

• the role of the examiners
• the timings of the test
• the four parts of the test and what is involved in each one.

Tips and advice

Following the Speaking test, there is a short clip to supplement the speaking tips given in the book. In this section, which is about five minutes long, an examiner gives some tips and advice about how to do well in the Cambridge English: First Speaking test.

The worksheet

This printable worksheet accompanies the complete Cambridge English: First Speaking test. Although primarily designed for self-study, the worksheet can also be used in the classroom. It provides in-depth information about the Speaking test and focuses on the language each candidate uses in the video.

The worksheet is divided into four sections, which relate to each part of the Speaking test. It includes activities which:

• draw students' attention to key features of the candidate's response
• relate these features to the marking criteria used by the examiners
• give the student practice in developing their own answers for similar questions.

A separate answer key and a full video script are also provided.